Business Process Improvement Workbook

Documentation, Analysis,
Design, and Management
of Business Process Improvement

H. James Harrington
Erik K. C. Esseling
Harm van Nimwegen

of

Ernst & Young LLP
and
Moret Ernst & Young

McGraw-Hill

New York   San Francisco   Washington, D.C.   Auckland   Bogotá
Caracas   Lisbon   London   Madrid   Mexico City   Milan
Montreal   New Delhi   San Juan   Singapore
Sydney   Tokyo   Toronto

McGraw-Hill

A Division of The McGraw·Hill Companies

6 7 8 9 0 DOC/DOC   0 2

ISBN: 0-07-026779-0

The sponsoring editor for this book was Philip Ruppel. Production was managed by John Woods, CWL Publishing Enterprises, Madison, WI. It was designed and composed at Impressions Book and Journal Services, Inc.

Printed and bound by R.R. Donnelley and Company.

Dedication

We dedicate this book to all the administrative people in Ernst & Young LLP who work so hard to make the managers and consultants look good in front of our clients. We seldom take the time to tell them how much we rely on them, and neither do we give them the proper amount of credit in front of our clients. Their dedication to perfection and excellence makes all the difference between the success and failure of our organization. Thanks for all the overtime and weekends spent by these dedicated professionals in Ernst & Young's pursuit of exceeding customers' expectations.

Contents

List of Illustrations

Preface

For more than 150 years, management and employees around the world have been enamored with improving organizational performance. Recently, the need for drastic improvement intensified when rapid advancements in technology, such as computers, satellite communications, and airplanes, opened the world market. Countries that previously relied on large bodies of water or large distances to protect them from foreign competition were prime targets for their share of the world market. Corporations, whose first loyalty was to their investors, abandoned their native countries and moved much of their internal activities to less costly and more cooperative locations. They took advantage of the reduced environmental controls, cheap labor, and a deprived labor force that was very willing to sacrifice their personal pleasures to dedicate themselves completely to their jobs.

A truly mobile world business environment drove such major shifts in organizational strategy. Designs that were completed in Mainz, Germany, at 5 P.M. could be transferred within minutes to Beijing, China, where a model would be built and tested within hours. The results of the tests would then be available in Germany at 9 A.M., when the designer arrived at work the next day.

With the world becoming increasingly mobile, organizations realized that the low-cost labor countries would capture the lion's share of the market if the people in the developed nations did not far outperform the workers in the developing nations. A greatly reduced standard of living threatened workers in the developed countries unless they increased productivity and produced higher quality output to the point where our output is an equal or better value than that of developing nations. This realization inspired the first wave of quality improvement programs in the 1970s and 1980s; these programs focused on defect elimination and continuous improvement, and they were directed at improving how employees performed their tasks, with the objective of producing "zero defects." Such efforts included

▲ Teams of individuals brainstorming to define problems
▲ Preparing pareto diagrams to prioritize problems
▲ Employee involvement
▲ Quality mission statements
▲ Fishbone diagrams to help define the root causes of problems
▲ Massive corrective action programs
▲ Statistical process control used to determine when an activity goes out of control
▲ Stock costs minimized through the use of just-in-time stocking methods and continuous-flow manufacturing

The continuous improvement approach was very effective. Japan is an excellent example of how it was used to position a country in the world market, but it had five major drawbacks:

1. Eighty percent of the problems could only be solved by management
2. It focused on individual tasks or activities, causing suboptimization to occur throughout the organization
3. It was a very costly program to maintain because it involved everyone in the organization
4. It worked best in the manufacturing environment
5. It did not require that a quality management system be in place before the improvement wave started

As a result of these drawbacks, the second wave of improvement efforts (currently being used) was born. It was a major breakthrough when management accepted the fact that production workers were able to produce output at the parts-per-million defect rate while the support personnel were working at the defects-per-item level. Management's first approach to solving this problem was through the use of information technology. This approach failed miserably, because automating or computerizing bad processes only allowed the organization to make more errors faster. Thus, a new methodology called Business Process Improvement was born.

Business Process Improvement (BPI) consists of four different approaches designed to improve the efficiency, effectiveness, and adaptability of administrative business processes. From this new concept, the organization achieves breakthrough performance improvement by analyzing hundreds of activities and tasks with the objective of optimizing total performance in a relatively short time period (see figure 0.A). This second wave of performance improvement was first addressed in the what-to-do book called *Business Process Improvement,* by H. James Harrington (McGraw-Hill, 1991), which defined the BPI methodology. Building on *Business Process Improvement,* this workbook provides the technical procedures for implementing BPI in the organization. It is designed for the BPI practitioner defining how to accomplish process redesign and reengineering activities. This book is a *how*-to-do it book rather than a *what*-to-do book.

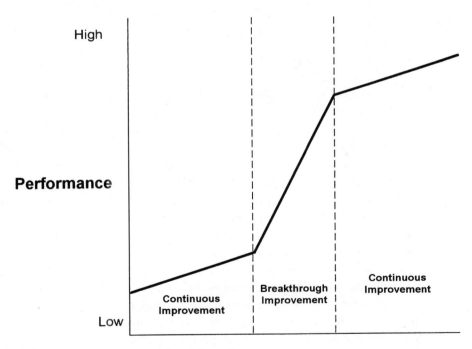

FIGURE 0.A   Continuous vs. breakthrough improvement

We will also address the third improvement wave that is beginning to swell in popularity. We will call it Business Systems Improvement. Just as Business Process Improvement was a major advance because it focused on processes that are large parts of the organization, Business Systems Improvement focuses on an even bigger part of the organization because it evaluates how processes integrate to support the key operating systems within the organization. This methodology is still evolving today. The two approaches that are already apparent are

1. Applying error prevention systems
2. Upgrading and refining the business systems

Typical business systems that are currently being redefined, refined, and upgraded are

- ▲ Quality management systems
- ▲ Environmental management systems
- ▲ Financial management systems
- ▲ Security management systems
- ▲ Software management systems
- ▲ Safety management systems
- ▲ Information management systems
- ▲ Project management systems

There are many organizations—governmental, private, and professional—that are setting the new standards for your business systems. For example, international standards are now available for publicly owned financial systems, quality management systems (ISO 9000 series), and environmental systems (ISO 14000). The International Organization for Standardization will soon start work on a standard for safety management systems. Most of these standards set the minimum requirements that should have been deployed around the world for years. Unfortunately, these standards have not been an executive management team priority because management has not understood the impact that these critical business systems have on the total organization's performance.

These standards have reset the bar for organizations that want to enter the international market. Today, most organizations around the world are struggling to meet these minimum requirements for their business systems. Only a few organizations are looking at how the processes that make up the critical business

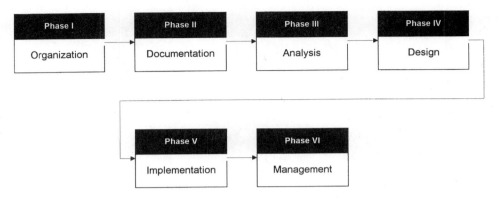

FIGURE 0.B The six phases of administrative business process improvement

systems interrelate with each other and how the organization is impacted by the information systems that provide the knowledge drivers. We believe this is the next horizon for the performance improvement movement.

This workbook has been prepared to provide the reader with a practical, proven approach to analyzing and improving an organization's critical administrative business processes and related systems. It will first provide the reader with an understanding of the four business process improvement approaches that have proven to be the most useful in bringing about radical process improvement (chapter 1). It will then take the reader through a six-phase process that leads to the implementation of the best-value future-state solution (see figure 0.B). The six phases are

Phase I—Organization: Organizing for process improvement
Phase II—Documentation: Selecting a documentation approach
Phase III—Analysis: Defining improvement opportunities
Phase IV—Design: Designing the new administrative business process
Phase V—Implementation: Installing the future-state solution
Phase VI—Management: Managing the administrative business process
      organization for continuous improvement

It is our hope that this workbook will provide deeper insight into the BPI process, preventing your organization from making the mistakes made by so many organizations that have been unsuccessful at implementing the BPI concept.

Acknowledgments

We want to acknowledge the many contributions made to this book by the team at Ernst & Young LLP. This book was originally written by Ernst & Young LLP consultants and published in Holland in the Dutch language. It was so popular in Holland that the decision was made to translate it into English.

We would particularly like to acknowledge Lee Sage and Terry Ozan for their support in this project and their leadership in the development of the "Performance Improvement" concepts. But most of all, we want to recognize and acknowledge the contribution of Cindy Yi, who worked with us at Ernst & Young LLP. She rewrote and proofread, corrected grammar, and standardized the format throughout the book.

It is important to note that this book is based on Ernst & Young's 1991 book, *Business Process Improvement.* This book reflects an additional six years of applying these basic concepts to many organizations, plus hundreds of employee-years of Ernst & Young's experience. This book therefore brings to light a new dimension that goes way beyond the original process reengineering concept.

1 Introduction to Administrative Business Process Improvement

In today's information age, our business processes can become more dependent on the information systems that support them than they are on the people who operate them.

H. James Harrington

1.1 Overview

During the first wave of performance-improvement activities in the 1970s and 1980s, a great deal of work was done to reduce error rates to the parts-per-million level and maximize productivity in the product processes. In the second wave of improvement, most of the methodologies have been directed at improving administrative processes. The Business Process Improvement (BPI) methodology focuses on improving administrative and support processes, not on manufacturing processes, although the concepts can be applied equally well to the product processes. This book will focus on the administrative and support processes. Figure 1.A shows the process hierarchy.

DEFINITION A **process** is a logical, related, sequential (connected) set of activities that takes an input from a supplier, adds value to it, and produces an output to a customer.

A **major process** is a process that usually involves more than one function within the organizational structure, and its operation has a significant impact on the way the organization functions. When a major process is too complex to be flowcharted at the activity level, it is often divided into subprocesses.

Major processes

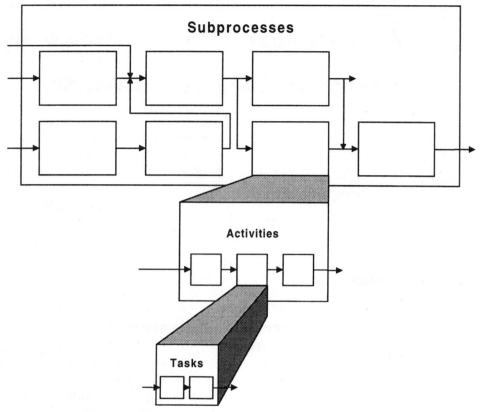

FIGURE 1.A   Process hierarchy

A **subprocess** is a portion of a major process that accomplishes a specific objective in support of the major process.

Activities are things that go on within a process or subprocess. They are usually performed by units of one (one person or one department). An activity is usually documented in an instruction. The instruction will document the tasks that make up the activity.

Tasks are individual elements and/or subsets of an activity. Normally, tasks relate to how an item performs a specific assignment.

1.1.1 Administrative Business Process

An *administrative business process* is defined as a series of successive activities by which administrative tasks are performed. These processes extend throughout the organizational framework in which they take place. They define the enablers and techniques employed, and the manner, the sequence, and the process in which the activities are executed. Administrative business processes unite the databases and the organization.

DEFINITION ‖ An **enabler** is a technical or organizational facility/resource that makes it possible to perform a task, activity, or process. Examples of technical enablers are personal computers, copying equipment, decentralized data processing, voice response, etc. Examples of organizational enablers are enhancement, self-management, communication, education, etc.

Since individual systems often impact many different processes, it was not long before we began to realize the need for process analysis as well as analysis of the systems that they are part of. In the 1990s, we have learned that the systems that tie processes together play a critical role in improving an organization's total performance because they define the organization and the operation of major processes.

DEFINITION ‖ A **system** is an assembly of components (hardware, software, procedures, human functions, and other resources) united by some form of regulated interaction to form an organized whole. It is a group of related processes that may or may not be connected (see figure 1.B).

The organization's business processes can be subdivided into two major classifications:

1. Product Business Process Improvement (PBPI)
2. Administrative Business Process Improvement (ABPI)

(At the end of this chapter there is a list of typical administrative business processes.)

Product Business Process Improvement is directed at improving the processes that are involved in producing the delivered products or services, such as manufacturing a boat or processing a check in a bank. Administrative

System

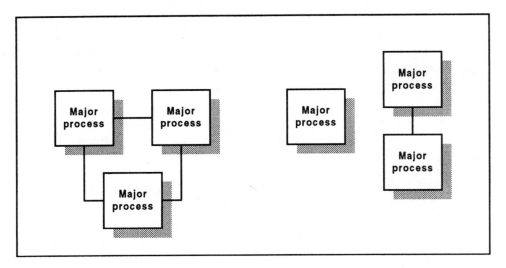

FIGURE 1.B   System grouping

Business Process Improvement is directed at all of the support processes, such as new product development, order processing, and accounts payable.

1.1.2 Business Process Improvement

DEFINITION ‖ An **organization** is any group, company, corporation, division, department, plant, or sales office.

The focus on BPI has penetrated into every dark corner of the entire organization. The concepts in the BPI methodology are directed at creating extremely rapid breakthrough improvement in a single administrative business process. The BPI efforts started by focusing on defining, understanding, and improving the activity flow within major processes. Business Process Improvement brings about major reductions in cost, cycle time, and error rates. The BPI concepts consist of four approaches:

1. Fast Analysis Solution Technique (FAST)
2. Process benchmarking
3. Process redesign
4. Process reengineering

DEFINITION || **Business Process Improvement (BPI)** is a methodology that is designed to bring about step-function improvements in administrative and support processes using approaches such as FAST, process benchmarking, process redesign, and process reengineering.

1.2 BPI Approaches

Three of the four BPI approaches (process benchmarking, process redesign, and process reengineering) are covered in the book *Business Process Improvement,* published by McGraw-Hill, 1991. Fast Analysis Solution Technique (FAST) is a more recent concept that is designed to identify and rapidly harvest the low-hanging fruit that has grown within our business processes. Because each of the BPI individual approaches (with the exception of FAST) are discussed elsewhere, they will only be summarized here.

1.2.1 FAST (Fast Analysis Solution Technique)

Fast Analysis Solution Technique is based on an improvement tool first used by International Business Machines in the mid 1980s. General Electric refined the approach in the 1990s. The Ford Motor Company further developed it under the title "RAPET." Today, Ernst & Young extensively uses this approach (which they call Express) with many clients around the world, and it is often used by other organizations throughout the Americas.

DEFINITION || **Fast Analysis Solution Technique (FAST)** is a breakthrough approach that focuses a group's attention on a single process for a one or two-day meeting to define how the group can improve the process over the next 90 days. Before the end of the meeting, management approves or rejects the proposed improvements.

FAST can be applied to any process level, from a major process down to and including the activity level. The FAST approach to BPI centers around a single one or two-day meeting that identifies root causes of problems and/or no-value-added activities designed into a present process. Typical improvements that result from the FAST approach are reduced cost, cycle time, and error rates between 5–15% in a three-month time period. The potential improvements are identified and approved for implementation in one or two days, hence the term FAST was given to this approach.

The FAST approach evolves through the following eight phases:

1. A problem or process is identified as a candidate for FAST.
2. A high-level sponsor agrees to support the FAST initiative related to the process that will be improved. (The process must be under the sponsor's span of control.)
3. The FAST team is assigned, and a set of objectives is prepared and approved by the sponsor.
4. The FAST team meets for one or two days to develop a high-level process flowchart and to define what actions could be taken to improve the process' performance. All recommendations must be within the span of control of the team members and able to be completely implemented within a three-month time period. All other items are submitted to the sponsor for further consideration at a later date.
5. A FAST team member must agree to be responsible for implementing each recommendation that will be submitted to the sponsor.
6. At the end of the one or two-day meeting, the sponsor attends the meeting at which the FAST team presents its findings.
7. Before the end of the meeting, the sponsor either approves or rejects the recommendations. It is very important that the sponsor not delay making decisions related to the suggestions, or the approach will soon become ineffective.
8. Approved solutions are implemented by the assigned FAST team members over the next three months.

1.2.2 Process Benchmarking

Process benchmarking is an old methodology that was given new life when Xerox gave it primary credit for their turnaround and their winning of the Malcolm Baldrige Award. This approach is very misunderstood today.

Most people think they are benchmarking when they compare their process-performance measurements to another organization's measurements. This is only an early step in the benchmarking process. This type of activity should correctly be called comparative analysis.

DEFINITION ‖ **Benchmarking** is a systematic way to identify, understand, and creatively evolve superior products, services, designs, equipment, processes, and practices to improve the organization's real performance by studying how other organizations are performing the same or similar operations.

Comparative analysis is the act of comparing a set of measurements to another set of measurements for similar items.

Typically, the benchmarking process will reduce cost, cycle time, and error rates between 20–50%. A typical benchmarking project takes four to six months to design a Best-Value Future-State Solution (BFSS). Based on our experience, this is the correct approach to use on 5–20% of an organization's major processes.

Of course, there are many different types of benchmarking approaches. Some of them include product, business process, production process, and equipment. Business process benchmarking is the approach that is relevant here.

In business process benchmarking, key processes are identified, understood, and compared to the best equivalent processes to define negative gaps. Typically, the analysis identifies a number of organizations that are performing better than the organization conducting the study, based on a comparative analysis. Then the benchmarking team evaluates the other organizations' processes to define why they are operating better than the study organization's processes. The benchmarking team uses this information to design and implement an improved process that combines the best features of the other organizations' processes, often creating a process that is better than any of the organizations' processes that were studied. This redesign process concept is often called the Best-Value Future-State Solution. Frequently, the BFSS will not represent the very best practices that are available. For example, it may be a better business decision to get a 30% improvement in 90 days than a 40% improvement in 18 months.

DEFINITION   **Future-State Solution (FSS)** is a combination of corrective actions and changes that can be applied to the item (process) under study to increase its value to its stakeholders.

Best-Value Future-State Solution (BFSS) is the solution that results in the most beneficial redesign item as viewed by the item's stakeholders. It is the best combination of desired cost, implementation cycle time, risk, and results (examples: return on investment, customer satisfaction, market share, risk, value-added per employee, time to implement, cost to implement, etc.)

1.2.3 Process Redesign (Focused Improvement)

The process redesign approach focuses the efforts of the Process Improvement Team (PIT) on refining the present process. Process redesign is normally applied to processes that are working fair to well today. Typically, process redesign projects will reduce cost, cycle time, and error rates between 30–60%. With process redesign, it takes between eighty and one hundred days to define the BFSS. This is the correct approach to use with approximately 70–90% of major business processes. This approach is used if improving the process' performance by 30% to 60% would give the organization a competitive advantage.

In redesigning processes, an as-is simulation model is constructed. Then, the following streamlining tools are applied:

▲ Bureaucracy elimination
▲ Value-added analysis
▲ Duplication elimination
▲ Simplification methods
▲ Cycle time reduction
▲ Error proofing (current problem analysis)
▲ Process upgrading (organizational restructuring)
▲ Simple language
▲ Standardization
▲ Supplier partnerships
▲ Automation, mechanization, and information technology

You will note that the information-technology enablers are applied after the present process' activities have been optimized. Once the process' activities have been optimized, information technology and computerization best practices are used to support the optimum process. This truly puts information technology in the role of being a process enabler rather than a process driver. With the redesign concept, the Process Improvement Team (PIT) does not create new Information Technology (IT) applications but takes advantage of the best practices that are already proven. Often, a process-comparative analysis is conducted in parallel to the redesign activities to ensure that the redesign process will be equivalent to or better than today's best practices.

1.2.4 Process Reengineering (New Process Design or Process Innovation)

Process reengineering is the most radical of the four BPI approaches. It is sometimes called Process Innovation because its success relies heavily on the PIT's innovation and creative abilities. Other organizations call it Big Picture Analysis or New Process Design. We like the term New Process Design best because the approach used is the same as if the organization were designing the process for the first time. This approach takes a fresh look at the objectives of the process and completely ignores the present process and organizational structure. It is starting with a blank sheet of paper as you would if you were engineering the process for the first time.

Process reengineering, when applied correctly, reduces cost and cycle time between 60–90% and error rates between 40–70%. It is a very useful tool when the current-state process is so out of date that it is not worth salvaging or even influencing the BFSS. Process reengineering is the correct answer for 5–20% of the major processes within an organization. If you find it advantageous to use process reengineering in more than 20% of your major processes, the organization should be very concerned, as it may be indicative of a major problem with the management of the organization. This management problem should be addressed first, before a great deal of effort is devoted to improving processes that will not be maintained.

The process reengineering approach to BPI allows the PIT to develop a process that is as close to ideal as possible. The PIT steps back and looks at the process with a fresh set of eyes, asking itself how it would design this process if it had no restrictions. The approach takes advantage of the available process enablers, including the latest mechanization, automation, and information techniques, and improves upon them. Often, this process stimulates the PIT to come up with a radical new process design that is truly a major breakthrough.

The process reengineering approach provides the biggest improvement but is the most costly and time-consuming BPI approach. It also has the highest degree of risk associated with it. Often, the process reengineering approach includes organizational restructuring and can be very disruptive to the organization. Most organizations can only effectively implement one change of this magnitude at a time.

The process reengineering approach to developing a BFSS consists of four tasks:

▲ Task 1: Big Picture Analysis
▲ Task 2: Theory of Ones
▲ Task 3: Process Simulation
▲ Task 4: Process Modeling

Task 1: Big Picture Analysis. With this task, the PIT is not constrained in its vision. The results of the process reengineering activities must be in line with the corporate mission and strategy. They should also reinforce the organization's core capabilities and competencies. All the other paradigms can and should be challenged. Before the PIT starts to design the new process, it needs to understand where the organization is going, how the process being evaluated supports the future business needs, and what changes would provide the organization with the most important competitive advantage.

Once this is understood, the PIT can develop a vision statement of what the best process would look like and how it would function. In developing the vision statement, the PIT needs to think outside the normal routine (think outside the box) and challenge all assumptions, challenge all constraints, question the obvious, identify the technologies and organizational structures that are limiting the process, and define how they need to be improved to create processes that are better than today's best. The vision statement defines only what must be done, not what is being done. Usually, the vision statement is between 10 and 30 pages and, in reality, is more like a new process specification. This will define all of the process, information technology, and organizational and people enablers that would be applied in designing the new process.

Task 2: Theory of Ones. Once the vision statement is complete, the PIT should define what must be done within the process from input to delivery to the customer. It needs to question why the process cannot be done in one activity by one person in one place, or, better still, at one time with no human intervention. The PIT should be a miser in adding activities and resources to the process (see figure 1.C).

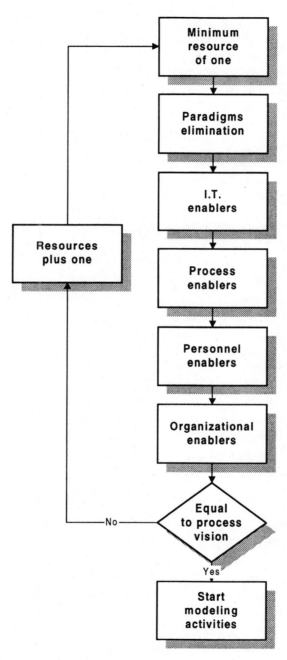

FIGURE 1.C   Theory of Ones

To use the Theory of Ones, the PIT sets the minimum quantity of units that you are trying to optimize. For example, if the PIT is interested in optimizing cycle time and the previous cycle time was five days, it might ask the questions, "What if I had to do it in one second? What enablers would have to be used, and what paradigms would have to be discarded to accomplish this?" Basically, four sets of enablers are addressed:

▲ Process enablers
▲ Information technology enablers
▲ Personnel enablers
▲ Organizational enablers

After the PIT has looked at each of the enablers and defined how the present state of the process could be upgraded to accomplish the desired function, the resulting process is compared to the vision statement from Task 1. If the PIT gets an acceptable answer, it goes forward. If not, it repeats the cycle with the objective of doing the total process in one minute. At some point in time, the process and vision statement will be in harmony. As you can see, reengineering is very much an iterative process.

Task 3: Process Simulation. When the new process design is theoretically in line with the objectives set forth in the vision statement, a simulation model is constructed. The simulation model is then exercised to evaluate how the new process design will function. If the simulation model proves to be unstable or produces unsatisfactory results compared to the requirements defined in the vision statement, the PIT should reinitiate the Theory of Ones activity. Then the PIT prepares and exercises a new simulation model. This cycle is repeated until an acceptable simulation model is constructed.

Task 4: Process Modeling. Once the simulation model indicates that the newly designed process will meet the vision statement, the theoretical model is physically modeled to prove the concepts. Typically, the new process design will be evaluated as follows:

▲ Conference room modeling (without computerization support) to verify the soundness of the new process design
▲ Pilot modeling in an individual location or small part of the total organization to prove the details of the concepts one at a time
▲ Pilot modeling of the entire process in a small part of the total organization

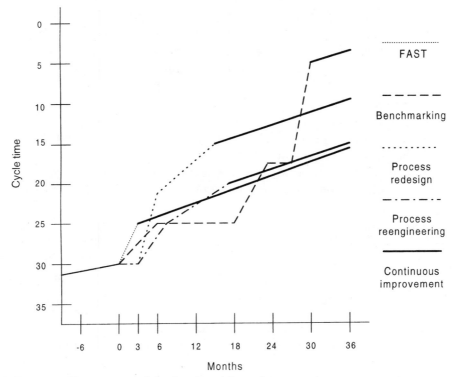

FIGURE 1.D   Comparison of the four breakthrough approaches on a typical process' cycle time

1.2.5 Impact of Different BPI Approaches

Figure 1.D compares how typical benchmarking, redesign, and reengineering methodologies improve cycle time in a process over time. It clearly shows the different levels of improvement that the four BPI approaches, combined with continuous improvement, have on a typical process over a 36-month period.

1.3 Continuous Improvement

In addition to the four BPI approaches to drastically improving business processes, a great deal of effort is being focused on continuous improvement of subprocesses, activities, and tasks. Although approaches to continuous improvement will not be discussed extensively in this book, it is very important that the processes that are subject to BPI have a continuous improvement plan prepared for them as soon as the BPI project nears completion.

Too often, after a BPI solution is implemented, management turns their back on the process, thinking it is performing well, which it probably is. The problem is that when you are standing still, you are not actually standing still. You are really slipping backward, because your competition is continuously improving. A process that was great yesterday is just adequate today and will be substandard tomorrow. As a result, a continuous improvement effort driven by the natural work teams and the individuals involved in the process must be undertaken. The continuous improvement process should result in a 10–15% yearly ongoing improvement in the process. This is necessary if the organization is going to maintain the strategic gains made as a result of the BPI methodology. We recommend reading the book entitled *Total Improvement Management,* by H. James Harrington (McGraw-Hill, 1995), to get a more detailed understanding of how BPI relates to a continuous improvement process.

A desire is often expressed to use the results of documentation, analysis, and/or a design project for administrative processes on a continuing basis after the project is completed, and this is a good business practice. The need for this is clear, since the documentation can be used for the instruction and training of staff. Results also provide an effective tool for evaluating the impact of future potential improvement on the process.

1.4 Documenting, Analyzing, and Designing Improved Administrative Business Processes

Throughout this book, ways to define, understand, and improve your processes are discussed, but the job is not done until the processes are well documented, so that their content can be easily communicated to everyone who needs to use or understand them. In addition, the documentation trail should provide direct traceability from each task to the organization's business plan and the organization's critical success factors. This can only be accomplished when an effective hierarchical documentation structure is used. Figure 1.E shows the five tiers that make up a typical documentation system. This is the documentation structure that will be used throughout this book.

Tier	Level	Description				Breakdown	Standard
1	---	Organization's mission, visions, beliefs, etc.					
2	A	Manuals— defines concepts	Quality	Personnel			95%
3	B	Procedures— provides the 4 Ws: What, When, Who, and Where				Process to activities	50%
4	C	Instructions— tells how to do it				Activity to tasks	40%
5	C	Record— proves it was done				Database	40%

FIGURE 1.E   Documentation breakdown

A number of factors drive the need to understand, document, and improve all of the processes used throughout the organization. Typical factors that inspire an organization to focus on process and/or system improvement are

▲ Installing a new computer system
▲ Merger of two or more organizations
▲ Need to be registered to ISO 9000 quality system standards
▲ Need to be registered to ISO 14000 environmental system standards
▲ Implementation of a Total Quality Management (TQM) program
▲ Need to reduce cost or cycle time
▲ Need to prepare for a financial audit
▲ Need to react to a customer- or government-imposed requirement

When making changes to existing processes, documentation is also useful for comparing the existing and proposed methods. Another reason for documenting administrative processes is to facilitate the transfer of knowledge from one person to another within the framework of a project or after a project has been completed. Even though a project is not being executed for the purpose of analyzing or changing current procedures, the existence of documentation is useful, particularly for instruction and process quality control. This concept has been reinforced with the worldwide acceptance of the ISO 9000 series of specifications.

1.4.1 New International Standards Focus on Processes

Government and customer requirements have driven many organizations to analyze their processes and systems more than ever before. The International Organization for Standardization has released the ISO 9000 series of quality system standards, which have been embraced by more than 95 different nations around the world. The primary focus of ISO 9000 is defining the quality system, understanding it, and documenting its processes down to the task level. This international standard makes effective use of third-party registrars who evaluate and register the quality systems for both service and manufacturing industries. Customers around the world are now including in many of their requests for quotes a requirement that the organization be registered to the related ISO 9000 standard.

Some individuals feel that this quality standard does not apply to their activity, but in truth, when you look at the quality system, it penetrates everyone's job within an organization. As such, the processes involved include most of the processes within the organization and all of the processes related to the entire product cycle. Organizations that do not have a quality system that is understood, documented, and followed are being barred from the starting gate, let alone having a chance of winning the race for a customer's order.

Following on the heels of ISO 9000 is another process-focused international standard entitled ISO 14000, which defines the environmental management system requirements. It has been estimated that its impact will be ten times greater than the impact ISO 9000 has had on international business. It also makes use of third-party registration. The ISO 14000 standards were formally released in mid 1996.

1.4.2 Selecting Appropriate Techniques

A description of the administrative business processes and their interrelationships is usually insufficient for obtaining a proper understanding of the manner in which the processes are organized. For this reason, documentation techniques are frequently used. The number of techniques one can choose from is large. Diagramming is one popular technique. The purpose of diagrams is to give the user a clear and concise schematic picture of a (limited) number of factors of the administrative business processes with or without a short prose explanation. In diagrams, symbols are repeatedly used to represent activities, departments, persons, and objects.

The choice of technique or combination of techniques must be determined by one's goals in documenting the processes. Sufficient thought should be given to objectives so that the correct choice of technique is made. It is important to mention that in addition to the objectives one wants to achieve with a particular technique, other criteria (such as simplicity, user-friendliness, the existence of other documentation, maintenance, the availability of technological enablers, etc.) may also help determine the choice of technique. Even though the objective of the documentation has been determined in advance, the optimal technique is often not chosen.

In addition to choosing an optimal technique, the correct approach to such a project is of great importance. Many projects fail because they do not match the needs of an organization. They are poorly accepted and supported by that organization. Consequently, the projects do not produce the desired result and are often abandoned.

In practice, many improved administrative business processes can be designed (as well as documented and analyzed), and they can often be contradictory. In setting one's priorities, the art is to define which one or which combination of approaches represents the best-value solution for the particular organization.

1.4.3 Implementing a Documentation, Analysis, and Design Project for Administrative Business Processes

Preferably, the documentation, analysis, and design of administrative processes should be carried out on a project basis. A project basis is preferable because it consists of nonrecurring activities that include various departments that, in general, have little contact with each other on a daily basis and that often have no existing structured channels of communication.

Ideally, a project is so firmly rooted in an organization's structure that the managers of subdivisions of the administrative organization (administrative information management system) are already playing their roles while the project is being implemented. The project organization is then consistent with the management situation. Thus, the results can be supported and managed immediately (see chapters 6 and 7). Embedding the project into the organization is discussed in detail in chapter 2.

1.5 Organizational Change Management

Applying the four BPI approaches to your processes can cause more trouble than it is worth if your organization does not manage the change process that results from the BPI activities. Approaches like reengineering only succeed if we challenge and change our paradigms and our organization's culture. It is a fallacy to think that you can change the processes without changing the behavior patterns or the people who are responsible for operating these processes. This means that the organization has to manage the change process, identifying new desired behaviors and not rewarding old behaviors that are undesirable in support of the new process. It often means that performance standards will have to change. Performance that was outstanding using the old process often becomes unacceptable in the new process. Not only does the level of performance need to change, but also the variation in performance must lessen.

We now know that change is a process that can and must be managed if major projects are going to be successfully completed on time, within the approved budget, and produce the desired results. It is the process of moving from a current-state condition to a future-state condition, separated by a transitional phase. In the present state, the people who will be required to change are very comfortable. No one knows their assignment better than they do. Although things may not always go just right, they know what to expect and feel comfortable that they can take care of the problems as they arise. They are truly in control and feel confident they can perform at an acceptable level. But change is designed to shatter all of that. Change occurs when your expectations are not met. What happens when your expectations are not met? What would happen to you personally if you came into work tomorrow and someone had taken away your desk? Well, you would probably be

- ▲ Shocked
- ▲ Bewildered
- ▲ Unhappy
- ▲ Unproductive
- ▲ Mad

As the people who work within the process that is being improved enter the transitional phase of the change process, they have a tendency to lose their cool. All of a sudden they are not in control; they are not the authority at their own job. They don't even know if they will be successful in the new process. They have a tendency to try to pull back, try to stop the change. If they can't do that, they will try to shield themselves from the change.

Everybody is for change: "I think that you should change, that she should change, that they should change, but should I change? NO WAY. I have everything under control already. If the other people who are causing all the errors and wasting all the money will change, that's all that is necessary." The truth of the matter is that we all must change and change fast if our organizations are going to survive. In fact, we need to feel uncomfortable if we are not changing and learning a new way of getting our job done.

There are a number of tools and techniques that are effective in managing the change process, such as pain management, change mapping, and synergy. The important thing is that every BPI program must have a very comprehensive change management plan built into it, and this plan must be effectively implemented. The Organizational Change Management process should be implemented well in advance of the change to the process. In fact, it should start as soon as possible after the decision is made to work on a specific process and always before the PIT starts to flowchart the process. The Organizational Change Management methodology will be discussed in further detail in section 2.7.4.

1.6   The Role of Information Technology in Administrative Business Process Improvement

In the 1970s and 1980s, information technology was used as a process driver that reshaped our business processes around the information technology programs and the available equipment. This led to the implementation of many new systems driven by information technology that never delivered the promised results. In the 1990s, information technology is being used as a process enabler rather than a process driver. Organizations define and improve their processes before they apply information technology to optimize the processes' total performance. This approach takes the responsibility for processes and systems out of the information technology manager's hands and places it in the line manager's hands, where it should have been all the time.

Using information technology as an enabler and not as a process driver greatly improves return on investment, often by as much as 1,000%.

An Administrative Information Management System (also referred to as Administrative Organization or Information Management Systems) is based on the following:

▲ The information required for various functions at strategic, tactical, and operational levels
▲ The information quality requirements in terms of relevance, reliability, presentation, and efficiency: the information quality range
▲ The internal control requirements and specific procedures necessary to generate reliable information

These requirements form the basis for developing an information system. This system will, by necessity, consist of a data architectural environment and an organizational process environment, which jointly constitute an information system. For the purposes of this book, a distinction is drawn between the data and process architecture knowing, though, that in practice, they are inseparable and should be developed jointly and simultaneously.

The information systems department is, or at least should be, a support department. Its output, in many cases, is not considered real-value-added. Rather, the information systems department's output is business-value-added, and sometimes it is no-value-added. That does not mean it is not important. In fact, it is an essential part of the organization that helps transform data into information.

DEFINITION || **Information** is data that has been analyzed, shared, and understood.

1.6.1 Relationship Between Electronic Data Processing Systems and This Book

In this book, the view of administrative business processes is limited to a series of activities involving each successive step that takes inputs, processes them, and produces outputs, data (information), and other deliverables. Thus, Electronic Data Processing (EDP) is also a factor in administrative business processes and will be discussed as such. The techniques discussed are of particular importance for documenting existing EDP systems, analyzing the strengths and weaknesses of the present systems, and developing and managing new working methods and processes. This book is in no way intended, however, to address the specific problems of designing and evaluating EDP systems, as there is sufficient literature of good quality available on this subject.

1.7 Organization of This Book

Chapter 2 discusses how to identify processes that can be improved and how to organize a project team to improve the selected processes. This approach may have to be adapted to the particular organization using it. The reader will find that the book's description is complete enough to serve as a checklist for assessing the project approach.

Chapter 3 addresses a number of specific factors in documenting (describing) administrative business processes. The chapter explains the objectives for documenting the process, the factors described for each process, and the desired level of detail of the description. Only a few of the many available techniques were selected, but they should give the reader a good understanding of the different types of techniques that are available. It also deals with a number of documentation techniques as well as with how different objectives dictate the choice of one or more documentation techniques (documentation sets). For each objective, one or more techniques are discussed. This explains one of the purposes of this book; namely, to serve as an aid in choosing documentation techniques. Throughout this chapter, references are made to the appendices, which give a detailed account of the various documentation techniques as well as guidelines for designing documents/forms and for holding interviews.

Chapter 4 is dedicated to the discussion of methods and angles of approach for the purpose of analyzing administrative business processes. Apart from the documentation techniques, there are a number of techniques used specifically for analyzing administrative business processes. These include techniques for analyzing the efficiency of information management, the suitability of potential enablers, the routing of processes, identifying duplicate and unnecessary activities, reducing cycle time, and applying internal control.

The design of new processes and adaptation of existing ones are discussed in chapter 5. Techniques used in designing administrative business processes are also discussed. Chapter 6 provides the reader with guidance on how to implement future-state solutions.

Chapter 7 discusses documenting all the administrative business processes in a manual and managing the completed documentation manual so that it remains current. In addition to procedures for updating the documentation, the discussion includes procedures for making changes to the administrative organization and incorporating these changes into the process documentation. The question of which elements should form part of the documentation system is addressed as well as the duties and tasks of the various staff members involved in managing the documentation.

1.8 Intended Audience

This book is intended for those who, because of their work or field of study, are involved or interested in the problems of managing and the quality of administrative business processes. These include the administrative and accounting staff of an organization, system developers, information managers, controllers, accountants, and management consultants, but the book is written especially for the users of administrative business processes:

- ▲ Marketing
- ▲ Research and development
- ▲ Materials control
- ▲ Information systems
- ▲ Product engineering
- ▲ Process engineering
- ▲ Distribution
- ▲ Human relations
- ▲ Maintenance
- ▲ Sales
- ▲ After-sales support

In fact, this book should be of interest to all areas relying on large quantities of information to perform their assigned tasks and to measure the effectiveness of their activities.

1.9 Typical Business Processes

The following is a list of typical business processes that are used to classify business process benchmarking activities by the International Benchmarking Clearinghouse, located in Houston, Texas. The processes that are considered administrative business processes are as follows:

1. Understand Markets and Customers
  1.1 Determine customer needs and wants
      1.1.1 Conduct qualitative assessments
          1.1.1.1 Conduct customer interviews
          1.1.1.2 Conduct focus groups
      1.1.2 Conduct quantitative assessments
          1.1.2.1 Develop and implement surveys
      1.1.3 Predict customer purchasing behavior
  1.2 Measure customer satisfaction
      1.2.1 Monitor satisfaction with products and services
      1.2.2 Monitor satisfaction with complaint resolution
      1.2.3 Monitor satisfaction with communication
  1.3 Monitor changes in market or customer expectations
      1.3.1 Determine weaknesses of product/service offerings
      1.3.2 Identify new innovations that are meeting customers' needs
      1.3.3 Determine customer reactions to competitive offerings

2. Develop Vision and Strategy
  2.1 Monitor the external environment
      2.1.1 Analyze and understand competition
      2.1.2 Identify economic trends
      2.1.3 Identify political and regulatory issues
      2.1.4 Assess new technology innovations
      2.1.5 Understand demographics
      2.1.6 Identify social and cultural changes
      2.1.7 Understand ecological concerns
  2.2 Define business concept and organizational strategy
      2.2.1 Select relevant markets
      2.2.2 Develop long-term vision
      2.2.3 Formulate business unit strategy
      2.2.4 Develop overall mission statement

2.3　Design organizational structure and relationships between organizational units

2.4　Develop and set organizational goals

3. Design Products and Services

3.1　Develop new product/service concept and plans

　　3.1.1　Translate customer wants and needs into product and/or
service requirements

　　3.1.2　Plan and deploy quality targets

　　3.1.3　Plan and deploy cost targets

　　3.1.4　Develop product life cycle and development timing targets

　　3.1.5　Develop and integrate leading technology in product/ser-
vice concept

3.2　Design, build, and evaluate prototype products and services

　　3.2.1　Develop product/service specifications

　　3.2.2　Conduct concurrent engineering

　　3.2.3　Implement value engineering

　　3.2.4　Document design specifications

　　3.2.5　Develop prototypes

　　3.2.6　Apply for patents

3.3　Refine existing products/services

　　3.3.1　Develop product/service enhancements

　　3.3.2　Eliminate quality/reliability problems

　　3.3.3　Eliminate outdated products/services

3.4　Test effectiveness of new or revised products or services

3.5　Prepare for production

　　3.5.1　Develop and test prototype production process

　　3.5.2　Design and obtain necessary materials and equipment

　　3.5.3　Install and verify process or methodology

3.6　Manage the product/service development process

4. Market and Sell

4.1　Market products or services to relevant customer segments

　　4.1.1　Develop pricing strategy

　　4.1.2　Develop advertising strategy

　　4.1.3　Develop marketing messages to communicate benefits

　　4.1.4　Estimate advertising resource and capital requirements

　　4.1.5　Identify specific target customers and their needs

6. Produce and Deliver for Service Oriented Organizations

6.1 Plan for and acquire necessary resources
    6.1.1 Select and certify suppliers
    6.1.2 Purchase materials and supplies
    6.1.3 Acquire appropriate technology
6.2 Develop human resource skills
    6.2.1 Define skill requirements
    6.2.2 Identify and implement training
    6.2.3 Monitor and manage skill development
6.3 Deliver service to the customer
    6.3.1 Confirm specific service requirements for individual customers
    6.3.2 Identify and schedule resources to meet service requirements
    6.3.3 Provide the service to specific customers
6.4 Ensure quality of service

7. Invoice and Service Customers

7.1 Bill the customer
    7.1.1 Develop, deliver, and maintain customer billing
    7.1.2 Invoice the customer
    7.1.3 Respond to billing inquiries
7.2 Provide after-sales service
    7.2.1 Provide post-sales service
    7.2.2 Handle warranties and claims
7.3 Respond to customer inquiries
    7.3.1 Respond to information requests
    7.3.2 Manage customer complaints

8. Develop and Manage Human Resources

8.1 Create and manage human resource strategies
    8.1.1 Identify organizational strategic demands
    8.1.2 Determine human resource costs
    8.1.3 Define human resource requirements
    8.1.4 Define human resource's organizational role
8.2 Work level analysis and planning
    8.2.1 Analyze, design, or redesign work
    8.2.2 Define and align work outputs and measurements

8.2.3 Define work competencies
8.3 Manage deployment of personnel
    8.3.1 Plan and forecast workforce requirements
    8.3.2 Develop succession and career plans
    8.3.3 Recruit, select, and hire employees
    8.3.4 Create and deploy teams
    8.3.5 Relocate employees
    8.3.6 Restructure and rightsize workforce
    8.3.7 Manage employee retirement
    8.3.8 Provide outplacement support
8.4 Develop and train employees
    8.4.1 Align employee and organization development needs
    8.4.2 Develop and manage training programs
    8.4.3 Develop and manage employee orientation programs
    8.4.4 Develop functional/process competencies
    8.4.5 Develop management/leadership competencies
    8.4.6 Develop team competencies
8.5 Manage employee performance, reward, and recognition
    8.5.1 Develop performance measures
    8.5.2 Develop performance management approaches and feedback
    8.5.3 Manage team performance
    8.5.4 Evaluate work for market value and internal equity
    8.5.5 Develop and manage base and variable compensation
    8.5.6 Manage reward and recognition programs
8.6 Ensure employee well-being and satisfaction
    8.6.1 Manage employee satisfaction
    8.6.2 Develop work and family support systems
    8.6.3 Manage and administer employee benefits
    8.6.4 Manage workplace health and safety
    8.6.5 Manage internal communications
    8.6.6 Manage and support workforce diversity
8.7 Ensure employee involvement
8.8 Manage labor/management relationships
    8.8.1 Manage collective bargaining process
    8.8.2 Manage labor/management partnerships
8.9 Develop Human Resource Information Systems (HRIS)

9. Manage Information Resources

9.1 Plan for information resource management
- 9.1.1 Derive requirements from business strategies
- 9.1.2 Define enterprise system architectures
- 9.1.3 Plan and forecast information technologies and methodologies
- 9.1.4 Establish enterprise data standards
- 9.1.5 Establish quality standards and controls

9.2 Develop and deploy enterprise support systems
- 9.2.1 Conduct specific needs assessments
- 9.2.2 Select information technologies
- 9.2.3 Define data life cycles
- 9.2.4 Develop enterprise support systems
- 9.2.5 Test, evaluate, and deploy enterprise support systems

9.3 Implement systems security and controls
- 9.3.1 Establish systems security strategies and levels
- 9.3.2 Test, evaluate, and deploy systems security and controls

9.4 Manage information storage and retrieval
- 9.4.1 Establish information repositories (databases)
- 9.4.2 Acquire and collect information
- 9.4.3 Store information
- 9.4.4 Modify and update information
- 9.4.5 Enable retrieval of information
- 9.4.6 Delete information

9.5 Manage facilities and network operations
- 9.5.1 Manage centralized facilities
- 9.5.2 Manage distributed facilities
- 9.5.3 Manage network operations

9.6 Manage information services
- 9.6.1 Manage libraries and information centers
- 9.6.2 Manage business records and documents

9.7 Facilitate information sharing and communication
- 9.7.1 Manage external communications systems
- 9.7.2 Manage internal communications systems
- 9.7.3 Prepare and distribute publications

9.8 Evaluate and audit information quality

10. Manage Financial and Physical Resources

10.1   Manage financial resources
    10.1.1   Develop budgets
    10.1.2   Manage resource allocation
    10.1.3   Design capital venture
    10.1.4   Manage cash flow
    10.1.5   Manage financial risk

10.2   Process finance and accounting transactions
    10.2.1   Process accounts payable
    10.2.2   Process payroll
    10.2.3   Process accounts receivable, credit, and collections
    10.2.4   Close the books
    10.2.5   Process benefits and retiree information

10.3   Report information
    10.3.1   Provide external financial information
    10.3.2   Provide internal financial information

10.4   Conduct internal audits

10.5   Manage the tax function
    10.5.1   Ensure tax compliance
    10.5.2   Plan tax strategy
    10.5.3   Employ effective technology
    10.5.4   Manage tax controversies
    10.5.5   Communicate tax issues to management
    10.5.6   Manage tax administration

10.6   Manage physical resources
    10.6.1   Manage capital planning
    10.6.2   Acquire and redeploy fixed assets
    10.6.3   Manage facilities
    10.6.4   Manage physical risk

11. Execute Environmental Management Program

11.1   Formulate environmental management strategy
11.2   Ensure compliance with regulations
11.3   Train and educate employees
11.4   Implement pollution prevention program
11.5   Manage remediation efforts

11.6 Implement emergency response program

11.7 Manage government agency and public relations

11.8 Manage acquisition/divestiture environmental issues

11.9 Develop and manage environmental information system

11.10 Monitor environmental management program

12. Manage External Relationships

12.1 Communicate with shareholders

12.2 Manage government relationships

12.3 Build lender relationships

12.4 Develop public relations program

12.5 Interface with board of directors

12.6 Develop community relations

12.7 Manage legal and ethical issues

13. Manage Improvement and Change

13.1 Measure organizational performance

13.1.1 Create measurement systems

13.1.2 Measure product and service quality

13.1.3 Measure cost of quality

13.1.4 Measure all costs

13.1.5 Measure cycle time

13.1.6 Measure productivity

13.2 Conduct quality assessments

13.2.1 Conduct quality assessments based on external criteria

13.2.2 Conduct quality assessments based on internal criteria

13.3 Benchmark performance

13.3.1 Develop benchmarking capabilities

13.3.2 Conduct process benchmarking

13.3.3 Conduct competitive benchmarking

13.4 Improve processes and systems

13.4.1 Create commitment for improvement

13.4.2 Implement continuous process improvement

13.4.3 Reengineer business processes and systems

13.4.4 Manage transition to change

13.5 Implement TQM

13.5.1 Create commitment to TQM

13.5.2 Design and implement TQM systems

13.5.3 Manage TQM life cycle

2 | Phase I—Organization: Organizing for Process Improvement

2.1 Introduction

The BPI project should be designed to complement the organization. A large number of departments and disciplines (line management, administrative staff members, administrative organization experts) will be involved in the project. The desired full-time commitment of staff members who are involved with the project as well as the random nature of activities make the setup of a temporary separate project structure an effective approach.

DEFINITION The **BPI Project Management Team (PMT)** is established to coordinate and manage the administrative business process improvement activities that take place within the organization.

The **Process Improvement Team (PIT)** is a project team assigned to improve a specific process. These teams are normally made up of people who represent a number of different departments. The PIT reports to the PMT for direction and support.

Contact Groups are not part of the BPI project organization but serve as sounding boards for the PITs. A contact group will review the best-value future-state solution developed by a PIT as well as the supporting

31

documentation, analysis, projected improvement, and related return on investment to validate the PIT's work. They may also be used to give technical advice related to a specific enabler.

Organization of the project occurs during the course of the project and is discontinued once the project has ended. During the project organization, a team is created for controlling and monitoring the entire BPI project. This team is called the BPI Project Management Team (PMT). In addition, a new project team called the Process Improvement Team (PIT) is created each time a new administrative business process is studied (see figure 2.A).

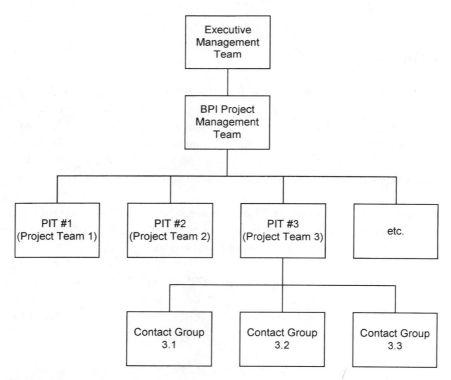

FIGURE 2.A Administrative business process improvement organization structure

2.2 Business Process Improvement Project Management Team

The *BPI Project Management Team* (PMT) is the highest unit in the project organization. Executive management delegates the responsibility of managing the BPI project to a PMT. Sometimes, the executive team will fill the PMT role. The PMT is responsible for the quality of the results of the entire project, but in the end, the project leader of the PMT is the responsible staff member.

PMT members should have the authority to make management decisions. A PMT should have enough authority to complete the tasks listed in this section. The organization should only consider a BPI project if it knows that the project has the full support of executive management.

The PMT leader will usually be a member of management. The key functional managers should also be members of the PMT. If less than four or five departments are involved in the project, departmental managers can be included as well. A personnel department manager may also be included. It is desirable for the information management and the systems development departments to be represented if computerized data processing is or will be used with the administrative business processes. If an administrative organization department exists, it should also be represented on the PMT. Sometimes, it can be effective to have one or several of the individual PIT members on the PMT (see section 2.4). Figure 2.B presents an example of the composition of a PMT and contact groups.

The PMT's responsibilities involve choosing the project's objectives and supervising the realization of these objectives. The PMT is also responsible for managing the cost and time of the project. In addition, the PMT concerns itself with the incorporation of the project into the organization and the associated consequences, which involves both the project execution (such as managing employee time) and the introduction of the results (such as managing how the operational organization incorporates the revised procedures). Another important aspect of project management is creating the conditions in which the project organization can optimally function.

The most important tasks of a PMT are

▲ Organizing the project
▲ Planning the phases of the project

▲ Making the final decisions on the proposals produced by the PITs during the different project phases (included in the decision-making process are identifying the administrative business processes to be improved, selecting the methods and techniques to be applied, setting priorities, etc.)

Date:	11 - 30 - 1992	Document code:	
Project:	Adm. organization	Project phase:	Project proposal
Project team:	Personnel	Subject area:	Staffing the various teams
Documentarian:		Subject:	Compiling the management and contact teams

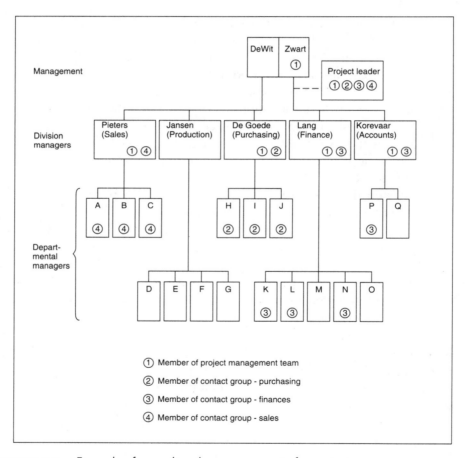

FIGURE 2.B   Example of compiling the management of a project

▲ Approving the final project proposal
▲ Distributing information about the project to the organization
▲ Installing and managing the PIT(s) and the contact group(s) (the PMT determines the functions and tasks of these groups)
▲ Monitoring progress
▲ Managing staff member availability for the project
▲ Determining the budgets and performing budget audits
▲ Approving the recommended best-value future-state solution
▲ Tuning the project to the daily operational activities and other projects in the organization (such as computerization projects)

2.3 Project Leader

The main role of the project leader, sometimes called the process owner, is to manage the PIT. The project leader delegates responsibilities to the PIT members at the times designated by the PMT. She is usually the author of the project proposal (see section 2.6.1). In every case, the responsibilities are also delegated at the end of each phase of the project.

The leadership position does not have to be full-time. The time commitment of the project leader is dependent on the number of PIT members, their qualifications, the scope of the process being improved, and how soon the best-value future-state solution is scheduled to be completed.

The project leader is responsible for carrying out the project in accordance with the guidelines set by the PMT. He has the following tasks:

▲ Providing the daily direction to the project
▲ Monitoring the progress of the project
▲ Controlling the project budget
▲ Monitoring the use of the applied methods, techniques, and enablers
▲ Coordinating the different PITs
▲ Instructing, training, and guiding the members of the PITs
▲ Informing and advising the contact groups
▲ Reporting to the PMT and making decisions on behalf of the PMT

The choice of a good project leader is critical to the success of the project. The project leader should contribute expertise regarding both the project and the general administrative organization. This expertise should be based on theoretical knowledge and practical experience. The practical experience is particularly helpful for choosing and implementing the applied methods and techniques not only in the administrative/organizational area but also in obtaining information (interviews, etc.).

Because expertise and management skills are so important in choosing a good project leader, it is not necessary for the project leader to be an employee of the organization. The required knowledge of the organization can be acquired at the beginning or during the course of the project. The project leader is sometimes recruited from outside the process being improved. Choosing an objective leader can be advantageous in evaluating administrative business processes. Finally, an external project leader is appropriate for the temporary nature of the project.

Another important qualification for a project leader is the ability to lead the PIT and motivate the staff members who are connected to the project in other ways (contact groups). She will need to have experience in providing leadership in similar projects, leading meetings, resolving conflicts, facilitation, etc. In addition, he must be able to use the planning and budgeting techniques applied in the project.

2.4 Process Improvement Team (PIT)—Project Team

The actual execution of the project is done by the project teams, often called the Process Improvement Team (PIT). The number of PITs depends on the size of the organization and the time limits for the project. Usually, one or a few teams will suffice, especially for projects in which less than five or six staff members are involved with the documentation and analysis of the processes. If a very large process is being analyzed in a large, multisite organization, the number of people who need to be involved in the evaluation is so great that the PIT will need to be divided into sub-PITs that work on specific sub-processes. The leader of the sub-PIT will represent the sub-PIT members and serve as a member of the PIT. Sub-PITs are normally formed when the PIT membership is more than 15 people or when the process being analyzed is located at many different locations. In smaller organizations and with less extensive projects, it may be advisable to make the PIT a subgroup of the PMT. In such a situation, all the PIT members are also on the PMT. With larger projects, this is no longer possible because of the larger number of individuals who are involved with the project.

If the project leader provides expertise in project organization and the applied methods, techniques, and enablers, other members of the PIT should provide the knowledge concerning the organization (its functions, the formal structure, work methods, etc.). They are the staff members from the administrative organization department or staff members who are involved with administrative business processes. With larger projects, these staff members could come from a number of different departments. Thus, attention should be paid to training regarding the documentation and analysis techniques that are to be applied. Some of this training will take place prior to the project and part of it will be just-in-time training during the project while working under the direction of the project leader. If the PIT is redesigning or reengineering the process, the PIT should include some people who are not involved in the process. These outside PIT members often provide a fresh view that brings about major breakthrough improvements.

The duties of the PIT can be divided as follows:

▲ Charting the administrative business processes and the associated documentation according to the selected documentation techniques and the documentation standard

▲ Performing the analysis, doing further research, and reporting about both

▲ Drafting proposals that define the best-value future-state solution and implementing approved process proposals. The level of detail of these proposals depends on the extent to which computerization can play a role in completing the proposal. Assuming that a great deal of emphasis is placed on computerization, the PIT will be limited to the performance of a definitive suitability study. In addition, the PIT can be involved in specifying the user requirements. Both are still heavily dependent on the project structure that is followed during the performance of computerization projects in the organization. The design of projects is discussed in chapter 5.

The PIT members should be available to work full time on the project if the project is to progress well. If the members of the PIT only have part of their time available, then the PMT and the departmental managers should prepare clear, formal agreements on the maximum and minimum time commitment.

The full-time participation of those involved in the project is still not guaranteed. It is possible that a participant will be alienated from his department after time. To prevent this, it is advisable that during the execution of the project, contacts with the department are maintained, such as attending periodic departmental meetings. In addition, the term of the full-time availability should be limited to a few weeks and no more than a few months.

2.5 Contact Groups

Sometimes, it is desirable to establish special contact groups, in situations in which too many departments and managers are involved with the process to be included in the PMT. A contact group is composed of staff members from departments that are involved with the process to be defined and analyzed. Usually, they are the managers of these departments. The contact groups should be organized by division (see figure 2.B). The division manager will be the leader of the contact group. In addition, the PIT members who have specifically been involved with analyzing the part of the process related to the department(s) will participate in the meetings. Depending on the situation, the meetings can be attended by the project leader, the (external) accountant, and staff members. The PMT makes the final decision about the differences between the contact groups and the PITs.

The contact groups have the following tasks:

▲ Supplying information to the PIT members as part of the identification procedure (this is done, in addition to the gathering of information by the PIT members, by means of interviews, document analysis, etc.)
▲ Approving the documentation of the administrative business processes drawn up by the PIT members
▲ Discussing and commenting on the analysis of the processes drafted by the PIT
▲ Discussing and commenting on the proposals that are drafted by the PIT members for the purpose of modifying or setting up new processes
▲ Regulating the modification of the existing process or the introduction of a newly developed process

2.6 Project Plan

The objective of the planning activity is to make the project more manageable. The number of activities that make up the project is dependent on the project's objectives.

With regularly scheduled project reviews, progress can be tracked by reviewing whether the project is still producing the desired results and whether the results are developing according to expectations. If necessary, the project can also be modified. These modifications can be related to the width of the study (the number of processes and departments to be reviewed) and the depth of the project (the degree of detail). In addition, modifications of the plans or the budgets may be desired. A project plan should be prepared by the PMT for the total BPI activities for the organization. Individual project plans should be prepared by the assigned PIT for each process.

The project plan prepared by a typical PIT should include the following:

- Designing the project proposal
- Defining the details of the project
- Drawing up a project proposal
- Documenting the processes
- Designing the project Organizational Change Management plan
- Analyzing the processes
- Modifying the existing processes as well as setting up new processes (formulating, proposing)
- Integrating and evaluating modified or newly setup processes.

In principle, each activity begins when the PMT defines/approves a project to evaluate an individual process. This project approval should include a list of the activities to be performed, the time limits, and the budgets. During the implementation activity, the project can be split up into subprojects that are conducted in parallel to each other. This can be accomplished if different subprojects are somewhat independent. Finally, each phase of the project is closed with a report to the PMT prepared by the PIT. On the basis of these reports, the PMT makes decisions about the progress of the project and makes adjustments if necessary. The next phase should not be started until the PMT approves the final report of the preceding phase. The flow of the activities is defined in figure 2.C.

2.6.1 The Project Proposal

In the project proposal, the reasons for initiating the project and its objectives are described. The proposal also includes the outline of the structure of the project, which is submitted to the PMT. In the proposal, the makeup of the PIT and the project leader should be recommended.

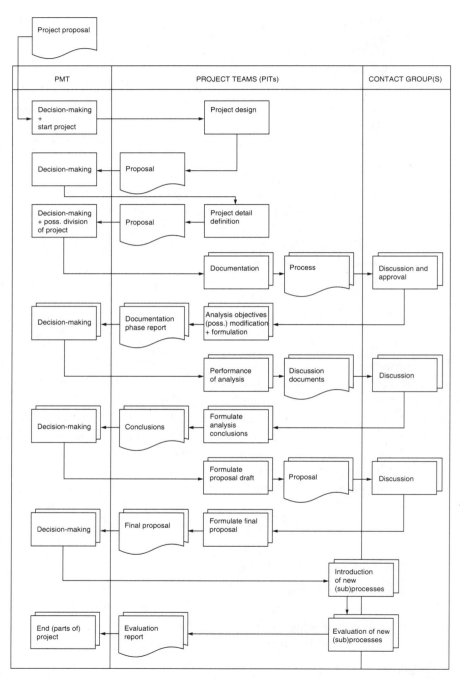

FIGURE 2.C Project overview

Usually, one or more of the staff members initiates the planning of the project proposal. The reason for this could be any of the following:

▲ Changes in the internal organization and/or the method of management of the business processes that result in the information management system no longer satisfying current requirements

▲ Requirements that, as a result of changing market/competition relations, must be respecified

▲ Questions from the external accountant regarding the internal control of the administrative business processes (These questions can result from the need to diagram the internal control system. On the other hand, they can result from the desire to improve the internal control within the administrative business processes.)

▲ Requirements that are placed on the administrative organization by external authorities (such as the government) or the final results of the administrative business process

▲ Complaints concerning the completion of the processes because of backlogs, cancellations, long delivery times, etc.

▲ The need to improve the work methods (the reason for this can be the increase in the scope of the activities, the need to improve efficiency, or the possible application of information technology)

▲ The desired inventorying of administrative business processes as part of computerization projects

The project proposal is written before the decisions about the project structure and phase objectives have been approved. This means that the proposal is often written by the future project leader or other staff members that would like to be involved with the project. Based on the proposal, management determines whether a PIT will be established and included in the budget.

An external expert is often used to act as the project advisor or as the project leader. By involving the expert early on in the project, he can contribute to the design of the project and the choice of applicable methods, techniques, and enablers. A process expert is often assigned during this activity.

2.6.2 Designing the Project

In designing the project, the structure of the project and the methods, techniques, and enablers that are to be used in the project are further defined.

Defining the structure of the project is related to the creation and the composition of the PIT and any contact groups. A discussion of the time that the various staff members can spend on the project, conditions for bringing in each of the staff members, and further development of the meeting structure in terms of frequency, subjects to be discussed, etc., can have a significant impact on the way the PIT is organized. A change to a process can also result in the formation of a PIT.

The relationship between the different techniques and the importance of the techniques to the project objectives are of great concern. At the same time, all of the processes that are to be described, analyzed, and/or developed are determined. Finally, for each administrative business process, the departments and the individuals involved with the process will be specified. This can be done in a practical fashion by placing Xs at the intersection of the departments and processes in the matrix (see appendix IV).

One element in the design of a project is the clarification of the relationships between the BPI project and any related projects in the organization. In these cases, a global process plan is prepared and presented to the PMT.

2.6.3 Defining the Details of the Project

In defining the details of the project, the project proposal is further elaborated and a definitive project plan is drawn up in eight concrete steps:

1. Determine the documentation standards (see chapter 3)
2. Determine the order of the approach and set priorities for the documentation and analysis of the processes
3. Determine who should perform the various activities
4. Manage training and education
5. Keep the involved departments and staff members informed
6. Introduce the project into the organization
7. Draw up a detailed plan for the project
8. Develop a project Organizational Change Management plan

During Phase I, the detailed project plan will not be complete. The project plan will define what needs to be done, when it should be done, and who will do it. As the project progresses through the remaining phases, the project plan will be updated until it represents a complete history file.

Determine the Documentation Standards

First, this involves the accepted norms regarding the documentation and analysis techniques that will be used. For each technique, the following should be recorded in the standards:

▲ A description of the technique
▲ An explanation of the symbols that will be employed and a description of how these symbols should be applied
▲ An example of the form (as seen on the computer screen display) that will be used with each technique
▲ A description of the depth of detail that should be maintained during the implementation of the technique (whether details should be defined at the subprocess, activity, or task level; see section 3.4)
▲ An indication of the amount of information that should be recorded for each form (should the entire process be recorded on one form or should several forms be used for one process for each department)
▲ Instructions for completing the form
▲ An example of a completed form

Second, the documentation standards should indicate how the different descriptions in the project are recorded. Each form is provided with a five-number code that represents

▲ The name of the project
▲ The phase in which the document originates
▲ The subject-matter number
▲ The number of the order of the document within the subject matter
▲ The version number

Each document should also contain the date as well as the name of the documenter.

Documents that originate during the course of the project are recorded in a project file. This project file is maintained for each subject-matter number in and during each phase. In each subject-matter number, the documents with that number are filed according to the series number.

Third, the documentation standards contain a description of the method by which all the documentation of the administrative business processes (both the documentation of the existing situation and the documentation of the modification proposals) are recorded in an *Administrative Organization Manual* (or *Administrative Information Management System Manual*). As part of this method, all the administrative business processes, departments, subdepartments, and forms are coded. In addition to the five-number code previously mentioned, the documents that originate during the project and that are recorded in the manual are provided with the manual codes. The *Administrative Organization Manual* is further described in chapter 7.

Coding all of the documents in the project as well as all of the departments, subdepartments, processes, and forms appears to be overwhelming. Still, the application of this coding system is essential for

▲ Systematically grouping all the documents so that a logical relationship exists between them and they can easily be stored in and recovered from the project file and the *Administrative Organization Manual*

▲ Achieving clear and precise communication among the individuals involved in the project

▲ Having concise and simple references on the various documents

Determine the Order of the Approach and Set Priorities for the Documentation and Analysis of the Processes

Setting priorities and determining the order of the approach are usually specified by

▲ The extent to which problems arise in the various processes
▲ The seasonal factors relating to the scope of work for each process
▲ The expected scope of the documentation activities of the various processes
▲ The complexity of the processes and their interrelationships

Determine Who Should Perform the Various Activities

The time required for describing, analyzing, modifying, and setting up processes is estimated for each process. On the basis of this estimate and the time that various staff members have available for the project, different sub-PITs are formed to deal with the various components of the study. In one PIT, a number of sub-PITs dealing with the different subdivisions can be effective. As soon as a PIT includes more than 12 to 15 people (including the project leader), it is more effective to divide the PIT members up into two or more sub-PITs.

Manage Training and Education

It is important that all of the staff members involved with the project speak the same language with respect to the applied techniques. In addition, the proficiency of the different staff members regarding information collection (interviewing techniques, etc.) often needs to be improved. The staff members should also become proficient in documenting the administrative business processes with the chosen techniques and with the associated computerized documentation techniques. In addition, all of the PIT members should have a good understanding of the Organizational Change Management methodology.

Keep the Involved Departments and Staff Members Informed

It is clearly important that all of the individuals involved with the project get information about

- The structure of the project
- The qualifications of the other individuals involved with the project
- The time frame of the project
- The consequences of that time frame for the business, the structure of the organization, and their different tasks
- The manner by which communication in the project takes place
- The reasons behind why they were selected to take part in the project
- The extent to which others are involved in the decision-making process

It is essential that all those involved with the project have a good understanding of how the results of their work will impact the organization's performance. This is done in the form of one or more meetings between the PMT, the participants in the contact groups, and the PIT.

Introduce the Project into the Organization

Distributing information to individuals other than those involved with the project is of great importance. Information on the objective of the project, the structure, the qualifications of the different teams, the consequences of the project for the various organizational subdivisions, and the extent to which others are involved in the decision-making process should be distributed.

Secrecy concerning the project must be minimized. The omission of a suitable introduction will result in resistance, disrupting the collection of information during the course of the project and causing unnecessary unrest.

Don't think you can keep the employees from knowing that management is redesigning or reengineering the processes that involve them. Once the word gets out, the first-line managers and employees always paint a worst-case scenario. There is always someone who knows or has read about a case where process reengineering reduced the workforce by 90%. The word soon gets around that, "If you cooperate, only one out of every 10 of us will have a job when the new process is implemented." This attitude prevents any chance of cooperation between the employees and the PIT. As a result, the PIT is viewed as the enemy by the first-line managers and the employees, and a strong underground movement grows with the single objective of proving that the newly designed process will not work.

In European organizations, the works council (organized labor) will be involved with the distribution of information to the organization. With structural changes, advice should be asked for from these representatives in accordance with the respective legal requirements.

Draw Up a Detailed Plan for the Project

A detailed plan of the project can be drawn up on the basis of the preceding data. It is recommended that standard forms be used for this purpose. The plan should relate to the efforts of the different staff members and the possible enablers over the course of the project as a whole as well as at the time different parts are addressed. Deadlines are indicated for the various parts. The activity is closed with a report to the PMT. The PMT should approve the report before the next phase is begun.

Develop a Project Organizational Change Management Plan

During Phase I, an oOrganizational Change Management plan should be prepared that will define the change-management-related activities that should take place during Phases II through IV. As the project progresses, the details related to the change management will be added to the plan.

2.7   Planning and Monitoring Techniques

The project is composed of a number of activities that must be completed sequentially or performed simultaneously before a certain date and within a specified budget. In order to achieve this, management of the following four elements is necessary:

▲ The available time for the project (in man-hours)
▲ The time factor (the progress of the project)
▲ The costs of the project
▲ The Organizational Change Management plan

These four elements are included in the project plan, and the plan is compared to the results during the course of the project. The four plans for these elements are the *detailed time plan*, the *work plan*, the *financial plan*, and the *Organizational Change Management plan*.

2.7.1 Detailed Time Plan

The detailed time plan is drafted according to figure 2.D. The processes that are to be analyzed are recorded in the columns. The different activities in the various project phases are marked in the rows. With regard to the phase in which the project is recorded, the processes that should be described, the number of involved departments (per process), and the documentation techniques that are going to be applied are all known facts. For each process, the activities that should be further developed are known, such as

▲ Gathering the basic materials
▲ Examining the current procedures
▲ Documenting according to the selected techniques
▲ Giving feedback to and receiving approval from the involved individuals
▲ Drawing up the definitive documentation and entering it into the documentation set

For each of these activities, an estimate of the time needed to complete the activity can be made. Percentages should be calculated for the time spent in consultation by the PMT and the PIT and the time spent by the project leader in giving direction, drawing up plans, etc. On the basis of the diagram (see figure 2.E), the different degrees of difficulty of the processes can be considered. This required number of hours is noted in figure 2.D.

Filling in the times needed to complete the process-analysis phase can be a problem. After all, it is not always known which techniques will be used for this analysis. Those that are already known during the project-design phase can be considered. For planning this phase, use will be made of a percentage

Date:	02 - 15 - 1992	Document code:	
Project:	Adm. organization	Project phase:	Defining project details
Project team:	Human Res. proc.	Subject area:	Planning labor capacity
Documentarian: Project leader		Subject:	Plan of hours for each group of processes

No.	Activity	Total	General.	Processes to be analyzed								
				41	42	43	44	45	46	47	48	49
V.	Documenting											
V.1	basic material	82	40	4	4	6	4	8	4	4	4	4
V.2	inventory	160	20	12	12	20	16	24	12	16	16	12
V.3	registration	164	20	12	12	20	16	28	12	16	16	12
V.4	give feedback	76	8	6	6	8	8	12	6	8	8	6
V.5	final version	76	8	6	6	8	8	12	6	8	8	6
	subtotal	558	96	40	40	62	52	84	40	52	52	40
V.6	consulting file, etc.	88	40	4	4	6	6	8	4	6	6	4
V.7	project leader file	128	128									
	Documentation total	774	264	44	44	68	58	92	44	58	58	44
A.	Analysis											
A.1	project team members	420	50	30	30	44	44	60	30	44	44	44
A.2	project leader	120	120									
	Analysis total	540	170	30	30	44	44	60	30	44	44	44
						(direct 880 hours)						
	Total of documenting and analysis	1314	434	74	74	112	102	152	74	102	102	88

FIGURE 2.D An example of a detailed time plan

of the time that is required to describe the processes. Depending on the selected consultation model (whether or not contact groups are used) and the objectives of the project (an analysis of the procedures in the form of quantitative optimization takes considerably more time than an internal control analysis), a percentage will be chosen that lies somewhere between 50% and 100%, based on experience.

Process	Number of involved (sub)departments	Number of steps (activities) (sub)department	Number of transfers from one to another
New hires	7	140	35
Dismissals	7	60	15
Extensions	7	40	12
Promotions	7	40	20
Educ. reimbursement	7	20	10

FIGURE 2.E   Example of a routing overview

In the project-design phase, planning the time that is necessary for formulating the process-modification proposals, the new design of processes, and integrating these processes is not an easy task. It will also occur that a certain impression already exists of whether the project should first be modified in parts for the existing processes or whether an entirely new system of the administrative organization should be developed. Depending on this, a percentage will also be used in this phase for the planning of time.

An idea for the overall time needed for the project can be estimated. Naturally, the detailed time plan will need to be adjusted and refined during the course of the different project phases (as the project progresses, the PIT will be in a better position to plan the next phases). The detailed time plan will first be refined at the end of the phase in which the project details are defined.

The availability of labor should be planned next. This can be done on the basis of figure 2.F. For each of the months over which the project is expected to extend (these will be weeks for small projects), the staff members who are available and the amount of time that they have for the project will be indicated in this figure. Filling out the overview for the staff members who are going to take part in the PIT is sufficient. The members of the PMT or the contact groups account for a relatively small amount of the total effort.

2.7.2 Work Plan

In the work plan, the activities that will be developed in the project are scheduled over the time frame of the project. This is done by determining the

Date:	02 - 15 - 1992	Document code:	
Project:	*Adm. organization*	Project phase:	*Defining project details*
Project team:	*Human Res. proc.*	Subject area:	*Planning labor capacity*
Documentarian:	*Project leader*	Subject:	*Planning of labor hours per week*

Staff member	Total	Week number											
		1	2	3	4	5	6	7	8	9	10	11	12
Project leader	280	32	24	24	24	24	24	24	24	24	24	16	16
Project team members													
C. Jansen	192	32	32	32	32	–	–	–	32	26	–	–	6
R. de Wit	320	32	32	16	16	32	32	32	32	32	32	16	16
J. Pieters	180	20	20	20	20	20	20	–	–	–	20	20	20
R. de Korte	416	16	16	32	40	40	40	40	40	40	40	40	32
Project team total	1108	100	100	100	108	92	92	72	104	98	92	76	74
General total	1388	132	124	124	132	116	116	96	128	122	116	92	90

FIGURE 2.F Example of a personnel availability plan

personnel involved during the course of the project. Figure 2.G can be of assistance in doing this. This form is filled in for each PIT member for smaller projects or for each category of staff member for larger projects. The activities in figure 2.D are now assigned to the different PIT members. The PIT should always take waiting time into account in light of the fact that a number of activities can only be done serially or periodically (for example, approval in PMT and contact group meetings). These factors can be accounted for by assigning a number of activities to each staff member at the same time and indicating how much time she should actually spend on the activity during the period in question.

In filling out figure 2.G, two variables need to be taken into account: the number of available PIT members and the final form of the project. Weighing both of these variables is called *balancing*. If the project cannot be completed by the selected final date, a choice must be made between increasing the time commitments of the PIT members already involved with the project, putting more people on the PIT, or extending the final date.

Date:	02 - 15 - 1992	Document code:	
Project:	Adm.organization	Project phase:	Defining project details
Project team:	Human Res. proc.	Subject area:	Personnel schedule
Documentarian:	Project leader	Subject:	Schedule for R. de Wit

Staff member	Week number												
	Total	1	2	3	4	5	6	7	8	9	10	11	12
R. de Wit available	320	32	32	16	16	32	32	32	32	32	32	16	16
General	26	4	4	2	2	2	2	2	2	2	2	2	
Document 41	44	28	12	2	2								
Document 42	44		16	12	5	5	6						
Document 43	68				7	25	24	12					
analysis 41	30							18	5	4	3		
analysis 42	30								25	1	4		
analysis 43	44									25	14	5	
Total	286	32	32	16	16	32	32	32	32	32	23	7	0
Remaining	34	–	–	–	–	–	–	–	–	–	9	9	16

FIGURE 2.G   Example of a personnel schedule

The results of the plans can be visually presented (see figure 2.H). The arrows represent the duration of the respective activities and indicate which (groups of) staff members look after the execution of the activities. Codes can be used to indicate the number of planned meetings of the PIT, PMT, and contact groups.

As the project progresses, the plans will need to be refined. This is particularly true in support of the analysis phase (Phase III) and the design phase (Phase IV).

Making plans according to the system presented is very simple. The planning process should be modified to meet the particular need of the individual project. System planning such as Program Evaluation and Review Technique (PERT) and Critical Path Method (CPM) can be used for large projects. However, a discussion about these techniques falls outside the scope of this book.

Date:	02 - 15 - 1992	Document code:	
Project:	Adm.organization	Project phase:	Defining project details
Project team:	Human Res. proc.	Subject area:	Personnel schedule
Documentarian: Project leader		Subject:	

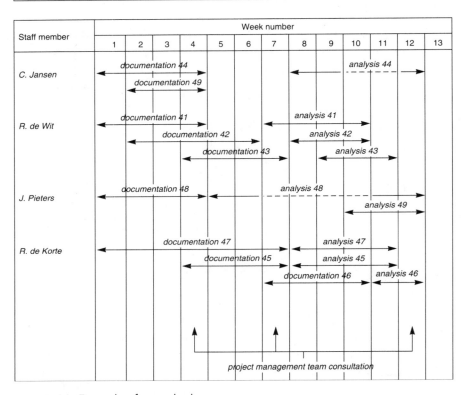

FIGURE 2.H   Example of a work plan

2.7.3 Financial Plan

Personnel plans make known how much time the different staff members (as well as categories of staff members) spend on the project in each period. Multiplying the number of workdays by a specified rate per workday provides an estimated labor cost for the different periods. In addition, the cost of any software, hardware, or other resources will also be included in the financial plan. During the course of the project, these other costs can also be divided between the different periods.

2.7.4 Organizational Change Management Plan

An Organizational Change Management (OCM) plan should ultimately be prepared in three parts that cover the periods when

▲ The process is being redesigned (preparation)
▲ The Best-Value Future-State Solution (BFSS) is being implemented (transition)
▲ After the BFSS has been implemented (stabilization)

DEFINITION | **Organizational Change Management** is a methodology developed to minimize the organization's inherent resistance to a change in the status quo, thereby facilitating the assimilation of the change into the organization at the minimum cost and cycle time. Organizational Change Management (OCM) is a methodology unto itself and as such the PIT needs to understand what it is and how it is applied.

The central purposes of OCM activities are to

▲ Gain an in-depth understanding of the potential enablers and barriers for the successful implementation of the BFSS
▲ Incorporate this knowledge into a participative implementation planning process
▲ Involve people at all levels of the organization in the assessing and planning process in order to build the necessary level of commitment

Without an adequate understanding of enablers and barriers (people, process, or technology-related) likely to change, transition plans will be less realistic and usable. In addition, people will be less willing to move to the future state. Effective transition management plans are developed with participation from all groups affected by the change, leading to a considerable reduction in the risks.

The key to change assessment and planning activities is to involve the maximum number of people who are impacted by the change in the process of defining the change. The assessment and planning activities consist of evaluating the readiness of the organization for the change and defining the change enablers and how to minimize the barriers to change. A major part of this component is designing and implementing a data-gathering process to identify reactions to the upcoming change. These reactions from changees (the individuals affected by the change) are then characterized as enablers or barriers to the change.

As a result of change assessment and planning activities, the organization should have the ability to anticipate and manage implementation risks and to validate and generate the appropriate level of commitment needed to ensure business results. The results of this activity are then incorporated into a comprehensive transition management plan that guides the change process as it unfolds. The transition management plan should provide strategies and tactics for managing the implementation risks.

The entire OCM plan should be prepared during this activity, but it is often necessary to conduct additional assessments at different times throughout the BPI process in order to complete the OCM plan. The individual plans to support implementation and the period after implementation should be detailed along with the plan to implement the BFSS. The reason for this distinction is that project-specific change plans must be based on an assessment of the risk factors implicit in the specific change. Execution of the principles of managing change tends to be theoretical at best until a concrete and specific change is undertaken. It is at that time that the specific risks cease being theoretical and become readily apparent. For process benchmarking, process redesign, and process reengineering, an assessment of the risk factors associated with the change should be made. The most common implementation risks are described below.

- ▲ Cost of the status quo
- ▲ Vision clarity
- ▲ Sponsor commitment
- ▲ Change agent skills
- ▲ Change advocate identification and skills
- ▲ Changee (target) response
- ▲ Culture/organizational alignment
- ▲ Internal/external organizational events
- ▲ Implementation architecture
- ▲ Improved performance

Cost of the Status Quo

This is the cost related to today's process because it is not perfect. Plus the additional cost of the process does not change because the organization will have lost opportunities (for example, if an organization does not get certified to ISO 9000, it will not be able to bid on many contracts in the future).

Vision Clarity

How clear is the definition of the best-value future state at a strategic and tactical level? Are people, process, and technology requirements of the future state defined?

Sponsor Commitment

How strong is the commitment of those individuals with the power to legitimize the change?

Change Agent Skills

How skilled are the change agents in developing transition management plans? Are they knowledgeable and experienced enough to address the human aspects of change management?

Change Advocate Identification and Skills

Have the change advocates required to support the change been identified and trained?

Changee (Target) Response

How resistant to the change are those individuals who must change the way they work? How successful has the organization been in the past at implementing change? If past change efforts have failed, there may be strong resistance to this change activity.

Culture/Organizational Alignment

How consistent or inconsistent is the change with the existing culture? How consistent or inconsistent are the current reward, recognition, performance management, compensation, employment, and communication mechanisms with the objectives of the change?

Internal/External Organizational Events

How prepared is the organization to deal with economic turns, market shifts, regulatory changes, changes in leadership, merger/acquisitions, and downsizing that occur in their industry? What events may occur in the near future and how might they affect the implementation of the change?

Implementation Architecture

How comprehensive are the plans and support structures in managing the people, process, and technological objectives?

Improved Performance

How will the organization handle the surpluses (people, space, time, etc.) that are created when the BFSS is implemented, and how will the employees react to the way with which the surpluses are disposed of? You cannot expect the managers and employees to contribute creative ideas if their contributions are rewarded by them or their friends being laid off.

One of the key decisions of the PIT at this juncture is the level of detail (the investment to be made) appropriate in assessing the answer to the preceding questions. Possibilities range from a minimal assessment (such as having the team members themselves provide subjective answers to these questions) to extensive interviewing, use of focus groups, evaluation of strengths and weaknesses of past implementations, and the like. The extent of change to be undertaken (the amount of disruption of expectations and status quo) should guide the decision regarding the investment to be made in the assessment. Competent consultants, internal and external, should have access to and experience with the variety of instruments available to conduct a thorough assessment when indicated. Possibilities include

▲ Change readiness assessment
▲ Organizational alignment assessment

CHANGE READINESS ASSESSMENT. This executive perspective of the organization's fitness for the change is created by

▲ Looking at the organization's history of implementing change
▲ Projecting the impact of the change
▲ Looking at resistance, culture, synergy, sponsors, the change inventory, and priority assessment of the organization

ORGANIZATIONAL ALIGNMENT ASSESSMENT. This assessment details the current state in light of the future-state context in the areas of organizational structure, compensation, benefits and rewards, performance management, leadership, management development, communications, human resource utilization, and education and training. The PIT should prepare an OCM plan that supports all of the phases of the BPI process. The plan should respond to the information obtained in the assessment and at a minimum include

▲ Role maps
▲ Enablers and barriers analysis report
▲ Change announcement plan
▲ Change communications plan
▲ Communications analysis

ROLE MAPS.   The role map identifies and depicts the relationships between the major constituency groups (sponsors, advocates, agents, changees) affected by the change. The role map also identifies supporting and nonsupporting managers at all levels and the individuals to fill the following key roles:

▲ Initiating sponsor
▲ Sustaining sponsor
▲ Change agent
▲ Changee (change target)
▲ Change advocate

DEFINITION   An **initiating sponsor** is the individual or group with the power to initiate or legitimize the change for all the people affected in the organization.

A **sustaining sponsor** is the individual or group with the political, logistic, and economic proximity to the people who actually have to change. We often talk about initiating sponsors as senior management and sustaining sponsors as middle management, but that is not necessarily the case all the time. Often sponsors can be someone in the organization who has no real line power but has significant influence as a result of relationships with the people affected by the change and past successes of the individual, knowledge, or power.

A **change agent** is the individual or group responsible for implementing the change. They are given this responsibility by a sustaining sponsor or a change advocate. Although agents may not have the power to legitimize change or to motivate the members of the organization to change, they certainly have the responsibility for making it happen.

A **changee (change target)** is the individual or group who must actually change. There really is nothing derogative associated with the word *target*. In fact, it is really more of an indication of where the resources that are allocated to any specific project must be focused in order to achieve successful change.

A **change advocate** is an individual or group who wants to have an item changed, but who lacks sponsorship. Their role is to advise, influence, and lobby in support of the change and help the sustaining sponsors focus on the change.

The PIT needs to identify the role of every individual who is impacted by the future-state solution. The formal organizational structure can be used to help develop a role map. The role map provides a picture of the organization that defines weaknesses in the change process. It also defines the change training and the performance required for each member of the organization.

People involved in the change process often fill more than one role, and their role often changes during different phases of the BPI process. For example, a middle manager may be a changee until he embraces the portion of the BFSS that relates to his organization. Once middle management understands and agrees with the need to implement the change, they can become sustaining sponsors. That same middle manager can, at the same time, become a change advocate for another middle manager in another function.

When the role map is completed, it should be reviewed by the individuals who perform roles as initiating or sustaining sponsors, change advocates, or change agents to obtain their approval. Appropriate training should also be provided to each of these individuals so that they clearly understand their roles. (Note: This approach is based on Organizational Development Resources and Ernst & Young LLP's change processes.)

In figure 2.I, Ms. A is known as the initiating sponsor. She approves and funds the project and legitimizes the process. As the initiating sponsor, she is responsible for converting Ms. B, Mr. C, and Mr. D from changees to sustaining sponsors and for ensuring that the three sustaining sponsors do not become black holes. *Black holes* are individuals who take information in but do

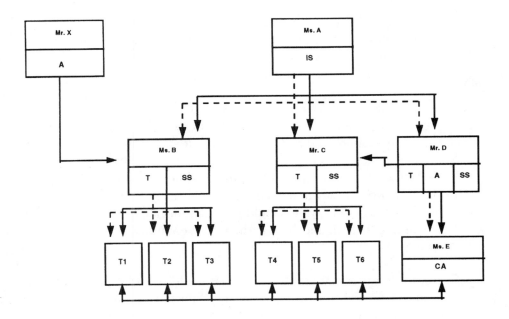

IS = Initiating Sponsor
SS = Sustaining Sponsor
CA = Change Agent
T = Change Target (Changees)
A = Change Advocate

——— Change structure
- - - Reporting structure

FIGURE 2.1 Organizational Change Management role map

not react to or disseminate the information. We have all seen managers who act as black holes. They receive a lot of information, but they do not make effective use of it to ensure that the project is completed on time, on schedule, and that it is embraced by the part of the organization they are responsible for.

Ms. A must convince Mr. D to serve as a change advocate to Mr. C. In this role, Mr. D encourages Mr. C to continuously support the change and to prepare changees 4, 5, and 6 to accept and embrace the change. Mr. X provides the same services to Ms. B. You will note that Ms. E, who is the change agent, has no organizational power that can impact the changees and is very ineffective in getting the changees to accept the change. Without Ms. B and Mr. C legitimizing Ms. E's activities, the change will probably fail. As you can see, figure 2.I presents a very simple change structure. In most BPI processes, much more complex role mapping is required.

ENABLERS AND BARRIERS ANALYSIS REPORT.   The *deliverable* is a document that presents the results of each of the assessment and feedback sessions and highlights the enablers and barriers that were identified.

CHANGE ANNOUNCEMENT PLAN.   This combines communication messages and channels evaluations and recommendations into a single, integrated document that describes what should be communicated to whom, when it should be communicated, and how it should be communicated to successfully announce the change.

CHANGE COMMUNICATIONS PLAN.   This should provide a comprehensive communications plan for managing change-specific communications throughout the change process, from the communications announcement through the celebration of successful attainment of the change project objectives.

COMMUNICATIONS ANALYSIS.   This combines communication effectiveness evaluations and recommendations into a single, integrated document. The results of these evaluations are used to update the change communications plan.

The entire OCM plan should be developed and begun to be applied during Phase I, because it will help offset some of the concerns that both management and the employees have. Figure 2.J is a typical OCM Gantt chart highlighting the OCM activities that take place during each of the phases in the BPI methodology.

The chairperson assigned to each document, process, or subprocess should prepare an individual OCM plan that supports her team's activities whenever the nature and extent of the planned changes are sufficiently clear to allow thoughtful assessment of risks and the planning necessary to mitigate them.

The OCM methodology is complex, but once understood, it can effectively aid you in managing the change process. When the PIT realizes that change truly is a process, the change activity takes on a set of new dimensions. The team begins to manage the change rather than the change managing the organization.

Change Management Activities	Phase I Assess	Phase II Plan	Phase III Redesign	Phase IV Implement	Phase V Audit	Phase VI Improve
Identify, document & communicate cost of the status quo (business imperative)	▬					
Create & communicate future state vision (people, process and technology)	▬					
Clarify change & obtain initiating sponsor understanding and commitment	▬					
Create infrastructure and implementation architecture	▬▬					
Conduct high level QMS-wide change risk assessment (8 risk factors)		▬				
Create high level organization change plan		▬				
Create role maps to identify all key roles in the change process		▬▬				
Conduct tier level change risk assessments (8 factors)		▬				
Change readiness assessment		▬				
Organizational alignment assessment (structure, compensation, rewards, etc.)		▬				
Assess enablers and barriers		▬				
Develop tier level transition management plans		▬				
Develop a communication plan		▬				
Cascade sponsorship (training and performance management techniques)			▬▬			
Implement the communication plan			▬▬▬▬			
Provide change management training for sponsors, change agents and others			▬			
Form change agent, sponsor and advocate teams			▬			
Provide training for targets (those affected by the change)				▬▬▬		
Implement organizational alignment enablers				▬▬▬		
Analyze effectiveness of communications and training strategies				▬▬▬		
Monitor commitment levels of sponsors, change agents, advocates & targets				▬▬▬		
Monitor and measure implementation effectiveness and schedule adherence					▬▬	
Modify transition management plans as needed					▬▬	
Track and report planned versus actual activities and results					▬▬	
Identify opportunities for continuous improvement to the change process						▬

FIGURE 2.J   OCM Gantt chart

2.7.5 **Monitoring Progress and Costs**

The progress and the cost of the project are monitored by a series of measures. First, the PIT members will account for time spent on the project according to the type of work they are performing and the process they are working on. From this data, the amount of time spent on a completed activity can be determined. Reports on progress and time spent will be prepared similar to those in figure 2.K.

Each week, all activities should be evaluated to define their status (percent complete). This estimate will be made by the PIT members in cooperation with the project leader. In figure 2.K, it is estimated that the activities "document 43" are 50% complete at the end of the fifth week. These activi-

Date:	04 - 09 - 1992	Document code:	
Project:	Adm. organization	Project phase:	Documenting
Project team:	Human Res. proc.	Subject area:	Progress report at end of week 5
Documentarian: Project leader		Subject:	R. de Wit, etc.

Activities	planned comple-tion date	Planned hours total	Planned hours to/incl. period	hours spent	% com-plete	Progress ahead	Progress behind	Efficiency advan-tage	Efficiency disad-vantage	Remarks
R. de Wit										
documentation 41	wk 4	44	44	46	100%	–	–	–	2	
documentation 42	wk 6	44	38	30	80%	–	3	5	–	
documentation 43	wk 7	68	32	41	50%	2	–	–	7	
analysis 41	wk 10	30	–	–	–	–	–	–	–	
analysis 42	wk 10	30	–	–	–	–	–	–	–	
analysis 43	wk 11	44	–	–	–	–	–	–	–	
C. Jansen										
documentation 44	wk 4	58	58	50	100%	–	–	8	–	
documentation 49	wk 4	44	44	42	100%	–	–	2	–	
analysis 44	wk 12	44	–	10	25%	11	–	1	–	
J. Pieters										
documentation 48	wk 4	58	58	70	100%	–	–	–	12	
analysis 48	wk 12	44	16	–	0%	–	16	–	–	
analysis 49	wk 12	44	–	–	–	–	–	–	–	
R. de Korte										
documentation 47	wk 7	58	50	50	90%	2	–	2	–	
documentation 45	wk 7	92	92	90	100%	–	–	2	–	
documentation 46	wk 10	44	–	–	–	–	–	–	–	
analysis 45	wk 11	60	–	–	–	–	–	–	–	
analysis 47	wk 11	44	–	–	–	–	–	–	–	
analysis 46	wk 12	30	–	–	–	–	–	–	–	
Subtotal		880	432	429	49%	15	19	20	21	
General		434	200	190	–	–	–	10	–	
Total		1314	632	619	49%		4	9		

FIGURE 2.K   Example of a progress report

ties should have been 47% complete ($^{32}/_{68}$ × 100%). This is called the *standard percent complete.* The processing of the activities is thus 3%, or two hours ahead of schedule.

The efficiency of the operations is measured by calculating the *percent of time spent.* With the same example, R. de Wit has spent 41 hours by the end of the fifth week on "document 43." The percent of time spent shows that an additional 10% (or seven hours) of the total planned hours was spent on these activities. The nine hours difference between the actual hours spent and the planned hours results in a loss of seven working hours and two lead-time hours. The causes of the discrepancy should be indicated. The project leader should determine whether this lost work effort will impact the project's schedule and budget.

2.8   Conditions for the Successful Completion of the Project (Summary)

The most common organizational structures in business, government, and nonprofit organizations are aimed at maintaining and managing existing work methods and procedures. The structure of these organizations has been fixed for some time. Routine and experience form the power of the organization to manage repetitive activities and assignments. The onetime nature of the BPI project places special requirements on the organization. Some of the things that should be considered follow.

First, a commitment from the highest levels of management of the organization is of great significance.

▲ The project will place demands on the organization's resources (man-power and money) that must be considered and addressed. Because of the onetime nature of the BPI project, special requirements are placed on the management of these factors.

▲ It should be clear within the organization that the project is being supported by top management. Otherwise, the danger exists that the project will not be taken seriously.

▲ The activities associated with the project will need to be based on the organization's general policies. This is particularly true for the conclusion and recommendations made during the analysis phase.

▲ The project should be embedded in all the levels of the organization to create optimal conditions for the actual modification of administrative business processes or the implementation of new processes.

Top management commitment is realized by its representation on the PMT. The need for the project should be felt within the organization, both by the involved departmental managers and the members of the PIT. This means that both of these groups should be motivated to complete the project. This motivation should be maintained for the duration of the project. The lasting motivation of the participating departmental managers involves special requirements.

▲ Staff members should be involved from the beginning. This means that they should contribute to the formulation of the objectives and the design of the project.
▲ The decision-making process during the course of the project should be made perfectly clear. Concerned staff members' input should be encouraged, especially during the analysis phase and the organization of new processes. The ways in which staff members are involved with the PIT should have their approval.
▲ The uncertainty that always arises over the future of the involved departments, the work, the organization, the status of the involved manager, etc., should be dispelled.
▲ There should be a balance between what the involved staff members give and what they receive. They should continually consider what impact the successful completion of the project will have on the organization so that a positive attitude is maintained.

For the continued motivation of the PIT members, open and effective communication within the project is important. The PIT members should understand the objective of the project and accept it. In addition, each member should see his contribution to the project as significant. It is also important that every member understands and sees the need for the potential contributions from others. Sufficient attention should be paid to providing the PIT members with an understanding of the impact that the successful completion of the project could have on their own futures. These issues will be important if the PIT members are involved in a process that may affect their futures.

This will play a lesser role if the project is executed by the permanent staff members; for example, an administrative organization department.

Sufficient time must be available for the project. To maintain the momentum of the project, it is necessary that a number of individuals are dedicated full time to the project. If part-time staff members are involved with the project, thought should be given to planning and progress control so that their other assignments do not conflict with the project's priorities. The time available for the project should be monitored frequently.

Choosing a good project leader is of vital importance. This individual must have the trust of all of the individuals who are involved with the project. A lot of thought should be given to the training and education of the PIT members with respect to applicable techniques. Good guidance from an expert is essential, particularly in the beginning.

PIT members must be trained to work as a team, understand the process, collect and analyze data, and improve the process. As a prerequisite to becoming a PIT member, each individual should have been trained in and should have used basic team and problem-solving tools such as:

- ▲ Team process
- ▲ Brainstorming
- ▲ Check sheets
- ▲ Graphs
- ▲ Histograms (frequency distributions)
- ▲ Pareto diagrams
- ▲ Scatter diagrams
- ▲ Nominal group techniques
- ▲ Delphi narrowing technique
- ▲ Force-field analysis
- ▲ Cause-and-effect diagrams
- ▲ Mind maps
- ▲ Statistical process control

If members have not been trained in the basic team and problem-solving tools, the PIT should begin with a training class on this subject. Lack of training always has long-term negative results. At the start of team efforts, the level of enthusiasm usually is so high that groups will jump right in and may even achieve some results. In the long run, however, a team lacking training and skills will not completely comprehend the situation it is trying to improve and will not implement the best combination of solutions.

BPI's 10 Fundamental Tools

In addition to such basic team dynamics and problem-solving training, the PIT should have some specialized training to prepare its members for the assigned activities. This training should include, but not be limited to, the following:

▲ BPI concepts
▲ Flowcharting
▲ Interviewing techniques
▲ BPI measurement methods (cost, cycle time, efficiency, effectiveness, adaptability)
▲ No-value-added activity elimination methods
▲ Simulation modeling
▲ Process and paperwork simplification techniques
▲ Organizational Change Management
▲ Process walk-through methods
▲ Cost and cycle-time analysis (activity-based costing)

BPI's 10 Sophisticated Tools

As BPI activities advance, the PIT may feel the need for more sophisticated tools to reach still higher goals. Team members should then increase their abilities by learning and using some of the more sophisticated tools. The tools are

▲ Quality Function Deployment (QFD)
▲ Program Evaluation and Review Technique (PERT) charting
▲ Business Systems Planning (BSP)
▲ Process Analysis Technique (PAT)
▲ Structured Analysis/Structured Design (SA/SD)
▲ Value analysis/control
▲ Information engineering
▲ Enablers identification and application
▲ Comparative analysis
▲ Vision documentation

Providing detailed information about each of the BPI fundamental and sophisticated tools is beyond the scope of this book, but each of them are covered in several other books published by McGraw-Hill.

From the start, the PIT members should be certain that there are possibilities (with regard to the budget, the manpower, and the design of the organization's structure) to change the administrative business processes in the organization. If potential changes are bound to preconditions, they must be made clear to those involved. Management should provide the PITs with detailed information that defines the boundaries and limitations that the recommended BFSS should meet in order for it to be approved.

Finally, it should be clear right from the beginning who in the organization is responsible for the management of particular subdivisions in the administrative organization. The structure and the table of contents of the *Administrative Organization Manual* should relate to the responsibilities for the management of the administrative organization. Thus, the project becomes powerful. The project structure conforms to the management structure, and users will consider the results of the project as their own property. Chapter 7 discusses the organization and management of the *Administrative Organization Manual*.

3 | Phase II—Documentation: Selecting a Documentation Approach

3.1 Introduction

There may be several reasons for an organization or company to document (describe) its administrative business processes. In this chapter, we examine what the objectives for the documentation of administrative business processes are, which factors should be documented, and to what level of detail the processes should be described. The objectives, factors, and level of detail will determine the choice of documentation technique.

DEFINITION | A **documentation technique** is a method by which a description is given of an information system, process, or organization.

Documentation techniques such as the use of form management diagrams, process diagrams, and organizational structure diagrams are further discussed in this chapter. For each technique, documentation enablers such as standard forms, diagrams, macros for personal computer use, etc. are also addressed.

The remaining chapters assume that the process under study has already been documented. A review, with supplementary interviews, needs to be undertaken for each case to determine whether descriptions of administrative business processes are available. You need to start with a series of interviews and inventories relating to the relevant factors of administrative business processes. Defining which starting point is most favorable for the quality of further research is a very important consideration. As soon as documentation is available, the guidance of someone experienced in implementing a similar project should be considered.

3.2 Documenting the Processes

The following steps are used in describing an administrative business process.

A. Inventorying the existing documentation
B. Examining the current procedures
C. Documenting according to the selected techniques
D. Giving feedback to the involved individuals and getting approval by the involved individuals
E. Recording the process descriptions in the documentation set
F. Definitively choosing the processes to be analyzed in the next phase
G. Choosing the final analysis objectives and the analysis techniques
H. Planning the analysis phase
I. Reporting to the project management team

Inventorying the Existing Documentation

In this step, all the available material concerning the administrative business processes to be documented is gathered. Materials such as the accounting system, function and task descriptions, instructions, forms, process documentation, etc. should be considered. Although it may be a little out of date, documentation that was done in the past can be an important enabler in documenting the processes.

The researchers use the gathered materials to define the processes that are to be documented. In addition, the materials determine whether all the steps of the processes that are to be inventoried are also observed and diagrammed. It is important to guard against the impression that the collection of information is completed in this phase. Each time the current procedures are actually studied, new forms and other documents usually appear.

Examining the Current Procedures

In the beginning of the analysis phase, attention will already have been paid to the problem areas and the issues in various processes, such as the time that should be spent on each process, the quantities that play a role, the frequency, etc. Current procedures are examined by holding interviews. It is advisable to review the entire process from beginning to end. The information obtained during the preceding step is an enabler for control of the completeness of the observation. The interview information can be partially filled in by the researchers' observations during the course of the project.

It should be remembered that every transition of a process from one department to another is accompanied by forms. All the forms used during a process come from somewhere and go somewhere. The trail of the copies of the forms can be of importance, and every applied data set should be updated. Appendix XII discusses a number of points that should be considered when conducting an interview.

Documenting According to the Selected Techniques

If the documentation is not done during the interview, then the observed procedures should be set down according to the chosen documentation techniques. It is important to make sure that documentation of all the processes (even though it is done by different individuals) is documented in the same manner and at an appropriate level of detail. The degree of detail can be different for each process and group, depending on the project objectives. Therefore, an exchange of the documented processes among the documentation teams is recommended. In any case, the documents should be approved in regard to the correct application of the documentation standards and techniques by the project leader and preferably also by a quality team chosen for the benefit of the project.

If the documentation can take place according to a number of different documentation techniques, it is recommended that the process be initially documented in accordance with the most general technique. After the documentation has been approved, the details can be defined. This chapter discusses the different documentation techniques.

Giving Feedback to the Involved Individuals and Getting Approval by the Involved Individuals

All the descriptions should be approved by the staff members who perform the process in question. This will be done by presenting the documentation of the different sections of the processes for approval to the staff members who carry out these sections. After approval, the documentation of the process in one department will be presented to the respective departmental manager for further approval. If the processes are carried out by a number of departments and if contact groups have been established, the entire documentation of the process will be presented to the respective contact group for approval. The documentation will be modified on the basis of the comments received.

Recording the Process Descriptions in the Documentation Set

The definitive well-reviewed process documentation will be given a document number and recorded in the documentation sets. These sets are divided according to the processes or the associated departments.

Definitively Choosing the Processes to Be Analyzed in the Next Phase

In the project proposal, it is already specified where the problems regarding the administrative processes are. In this phase of designing the project, the processes that are to be studied are further defined. It is sensible to reconsider whether the choices that were made at the beginning of the project are still relevant. In addition, priorities should be set regarding the order of approach. The definitive choices and the order of approach are determined on the basis of a list of the processes that has been made according to a number of criteria. These criteria are

- ▲ *The frequency with which the processes are performed.* As the frequency increases, the need for an analysis will be greater.
- ▲ *The departments that are involved in the process.* On the basis of reorganization, function modification, etc., it is sometimes specified that particular departments should first discuss the change.
- ▲ *The financial significance of the process.* This significance is expressed by the share that the result of the process has in the turnover of the costs of the organization (for example, the magnitude of the financial transactions as a result of new hires in comparison with those as a result of promotions).
- ▲ *The desired effectiveness of the information management system* (see section 5.4).
- ▲ *The required effectiveness of the administrative product.*

▲ *The cost of the process.* The cost to process an item through a business process can be as important to total cost as the cost per unit of production (in a billing process, for example, the cost of one invoice).

In this framework, it is advisable to give an indication of the possible savings that can be realized if the process is redesigned or reengineered.

▲ *The damage risk involved in a suboptimal functioning of the administrative business process in relation to the primary process.* For example, with processing purchasing invoices, this can be the damage that is done before the discovery of the fact that the invoice was paid twice; with order processing, this can be the chance that a sale is missed because the order was not processed in a timely fashion.
▲ *The speed with which the analysis can take place.* This depends on the availability of manpower for the analysis and the question of whether random sample surveys would suffice, whether extensive observations are necessary, and whether the observations should be spread out over time.
▲ *The expected possibilities for improving the process.*

Choosing the Final Analysis Objectives and the Analysis Techniques

The choice of analysis techniques is to a large degree specified by the nature of the problems that should be investigated. For example, the techniques that are used to solve problems in the area of internal control are different than those that are used for examining processing time problems. For a description of the analysis techniques and the associated criteria that can be used to make the choice, see chapter 4.

Planning the Analysis Phase

After choosing the processes that will be analyzed and choosing the analysis directions, the activities that should be further studied, the amount of time each activity should take, and the individuals who will be involved with the activity should be determined. On this basis, a plan for executing the analysis activities can be drafted.

Reporting to the Project Management Team

The documentation phase is closed with a report to the project management team. Usually, reports are made to the project management team in phases to prevent the project management team from waiting for the reports until the steps mentioned above are completed for all of the processes that are analyzed. These reports are made for each group of related processes.

With projects for which no further analysis is done, the reports should be made right after step E has been completed, since steps F, G, and H are done solely for preparing the analysis phase. These steps are to limit the number of reports given to the project management team, including the reports about the description phase. This causes no objections because the approval of the documented processes by the project management team is still a formal matter, so that the project management team's discussion can be concentrated on the analysis proposal. Sometimes it is advisable to give an interim report to the project management team after step C has been completed. This is necessary if an important change should be made to the previously drawn-up plans.

3.3 Defining the Objectives for Documenting the Processes

Before starting to document administrative business processes, it is important to determine what the information is going to be used for. Every goal or objective dictates different requirements for the content of the documentation. Consequently, the choice of an objective affects the choice of an appropriate combination of documentation techniques. Section 3.9 addresses how different combinations of documentation techniques are chosen.

The following objectives for documentation can be distinguished:

▲ To provide *insight* into administrative business processes
▲ To provide a *basis for the analysis and evaluation* of administrative business processes
▲ To aid in the *transfer of knowledge* between people and over time

3.3.1 Insight into Administrative Business Processes

To obtain a good understanding of the manner in which administrative business processes are organized, a simple description of the processes and their interrelationships is often insufficient. With a description, the researcher is not compelled to systematically represent the factors that should be emphasized in the documentation. In addition, no guidelines are set to determine if the description is complete. Schematic documentation has an advantage over simple descriptions of having a prescribed layout and format and using symbols and signs. A researcher who is comfortable with a particular technique will be able to obtain a good understanding of the ways in which relevant processes are organized without having to reapply the logistics that are essentially not present in verbal descriptions.

In describing the administrative business processes, it is necessary to carefully determine what needs to be understood. Understanding of general concepts such as procedures, cycle times, deadlines, forms required, frequency, and financial interest is crucial. A more precise idea of the factors that need to be understood determines the choice of effective documentation techniques.

3.3.2 Basis for Analysis and Evaluation of Administrative Business Processes

The necessity to accurately document which factors are important also applies to the analysis and evaluation of administrative business processes. Analysis and evaluation are only possible if the factors that are to be analyzed and evaluated are included in the documentation of the processes. For example, if analysis and evaluation are directed toward the distribution of tasks in and between departments, it makes little sense to work with documentation techniques that are appropriate for the circulation of paperwork (forms).

DEFINITION ‖ **Adaptability** is a measurement of an item's flexibility in handling changing customer needs and expectations while still meeting acceptable effectiveness and efficiency requirements.

Effectiveness is the degree to which an item provides the right output at the right place, at the right time, at the right price. Effectiveness is often referred to as quality but goes way beyond standard quality measurements. Effectiveness requirements are defined by the internal and/or external customers and consumers.

Efficiency is a measurement of how well a process uses its resources. It includes all resources, such as people, time, space, and equipment. It often relates to productivity-type measurements.

Timeliness is a measure of how long an output is left unused prior to being consumed in the next activity or how long the next activity is held up due to the lack of an input. For example, parts could be delivered to the production department three weeks before they are used.

The goals for analyzing and evaluating administrative business processes can be roughly divided into four categories: effectiveness, efficiency, adaptability, and internal control. If we break down these categories further, the following analyses can be distinguished.

A. *The effectiveness of information management.* In this analysis, whether the information resulting from the administrative business processes is relevant and whether it complies with the quality requirements that will be placed on it is examined. Stated differently, this analysis determines whether the information is a necessary instrument for the realization of the operations that must be performed in an organization.

B. *The effectiveness and efficiency of the data files.* In this analysis, the effectiveness and suitability of creating, using, and updating data files is examined. How resources are consumed in creating, using, and updating the data files is also considered.

C. *The analysis of timeliness and cycle time.* In this analysis, the timely completion of administrative business processes is quantified by testing against a norm, and the research and assessment of cycle times are included.

D. *The relationship of functions and tasks to the administrative organization.* The analysis of these relationships is directed at defining the most efficient use of data collection and of different administrative technological enablers, the placement of various functions in different departments from the point of view of similarity, and the education and experience required for the tasks performed in the different departments.

E. *The effectiveness and efficiency of the routing of the administrative business process.* With analysis of the routing or path of an administrative business process (as a component of a logistical analysis), it is important to note the order in which activities are executed, how and in which order the physical transfer of documents takes place, and which documents are transferred. Research into the routing of an administrative business process can be aimed at improving the cycle time (processing time), and decreasing the number of errors as a consequence of the transfer and loss of documents, or reducing cost per cycle.

F. *The accuracy, thoroughness, and reliability of the data processing operations.* This analysis is directed toward the internal control of data processing (also called information control).

G. *The productivity of the administrative business process.* By means of this analysis, an attempt is made to form a judgment of the relationship between the costs and productivity of different administrative business processes.

H. *The use of opportunities for standardization.* The analysis and evaluation of the opportunities for standardization in administrative business processes can be focused on the equipment, the office's requirements, and the processes by which similar tasks are performed.

I. *Duplicates and superfluous procedures.* The research for identifying duplicates and superfluous procedures can provide opportunities for eliminating operations in the areas of document collection use and the area of document creation. Moreover, the necessity of each of the procedures is checked.

J. *Adaptability of the administrative business process.* This analysis is designed to define how much input variation the process can stand without having an unacceptable negative impact on effectiveness and efficiency.

K. *The effectiveness and suitability of technological enablers.* This analysis and evaluation is aimed in particular at the enablers that are used for business processes such as microcomputers, word processors, copy machines (copiers), telecommunications equipment, microphotography, etc. This analysis also considers the use of automated data processing equipment and the optimization of the use of administrative technological enablers (including all forms of information technology enablers).

These 11 subjects for the analysis and evaluation of business processes will be extensively discussed in sections 4.3 through 4.12. They will also be treated in terms of the previously mentioned objective to obtain insight into administrative business processes. Understanding of the effectiveness of the information, routing, function, task structure, extent of standardization, duplicates and superfluous procedures, cycle time, accuracy, completeness, reliability of data processing (internal control), etc. can also be accomplished without leading directly to the analysis and evaluation of the processes.

In all instances, it is necessary to accurately determine which factors of the processes should be considered. For example, the concept of internal control can be viewed in several ways. The analysis of type of activity or task distribution in an organization requires a completely different documentation technique than the analysis of financial or production controls.

3.3.3 Transfer of Knowledge

A differentiation can be made between the documentation technique employed for the transfer of knowledge between people and that employed for the transfer of knowledge over time. A combination of both is possible and often required.

After administrative business processes have been inventoried, the documentation will have to be done in such a way that the documenter(s) and/or others will be able to make effective use of the documentation's content. For example, this can be thought of as the effective transfer of information between different PITs in the course of a computerization project or the periodical acquaintance by an accountant of the set up of the accounting system of an organization.

A special form of transfer of knowledge between people is the job training given in organizations. Instruction places particularly high demands on documentation techniques because each instruction can be suitable for only one explanation (can mean only one thing) without causing confusion and differences in interpretation.

The transfer of knowledge over time generally means preparing the documentation so that it will be accessible for consultation and reference. The particular requirements necessary for archiving this will be discussed in chapter 7. The transfer of knowledge is also important to effectively maintain or update the existing administrative system and to maintain the continuity of these systems.

The objectives of administrative business processes determine which documentation techniques will be employed. These choices are not easily made. Depending on the objectives the documentation needs to accomplish, the factors to be documented will have to be determined. In other words, only the documentation techniques that can adequately present the factors needed to achieve the objective should be employed.

Usually, the objectives for documentation have been insufficiently thought out beforehand, which leads to an incorrect choice of documentation technique. In certain cases, it seems that although the objective was determined in advance, the improper technique was selected. This occurs because the analysis of which factors could and could not be adequately represented by the documentation technique was inadequate.

3.4   Documentation Factors

DEFINITION ‖ A **factor** is any item (for example, environment, money, labor, technology, distance, size, etc.) that can have an effect on how a process functions.

In order to make an appropriate choice of documentation technique(s), the factors of the process to be documented must be decided upon. A single or combination of documentation technique(s) needs to be considered based on the factors important to the analysis. The following are several factors that are defined as the different approaches that can be used. The list is not intended to cover all the possibilities, but it provides the reader with the most often used approaches.

3.4.1 The Nature of the Procedures

The nature of the procedures (activities) indicates which (administrative-organizational) procedures are distinguished and why. The level of detail in which the procedures are analyzed depends strongly on the objectives of the project. Whereas in the study of task division in a sales administration department, a designation of "invoice control" would suffice, the documentation of a sales administration project, in which detailed instructions are developed, will need to contain more detail, such as comparing and entering orders, looking up prices, controlling the accuracy of the invoices, etc. (see figure 3.A in section 3.5).

In addition to the level of detail, the level of personnel involvement can be specified in the process documentation. The level of involvement further describes the procedures (activities). For example, the concept of invoices is divided into management, initiation, verification, audit, and technical execution.

Sometimes the analysis of the involvement results in further research. For example, each time an audit procedure is called out in a documented administrative business process, the procedures resulting from the satisfactory or unsatisfactory audit need to be specified (so-called incidental procedures). If the auditing procedure does not deliver satisfactory results, the person who eventually needs to make the corrections needs to be designated.

3.4.2 The Element of Time

The element of time can be divided into questions about deadlines, lengths of time, and the order of time. In connection with deadlines, it is important to indicate when an activity should begin, what the latest starting date is, what the earliest possible starting date is, when the activity should be completed, and what the latest completion date is. With length of time, questions such as how long, at least how long, and at most how long arise. The order of time is based on the order of events or activities in time, the activity time cycles, and the interdependence of other activities. By interdependence, we mean that a procedure can only take place after another has been initiated or completed. Critical-path analysis plays a key role in bringing about improvements.

3.4.3 The Documents

It is important to consider the concept of documents as including every element that can provide knowledge in written, pictorial, or verbal form. Thus, the following should be more closely examined:

- ▲ Forms
- ▲ Charts
- ▲ Records
- ▲ Computer lists

- ▲ Information on screens
- ▲ Photographs
- ▲ Graphics
- ▲ Books
- ▲ Audio tapes
- ▲ Meters/measuring machines
- ▲ Cash registers/calculators
- ▲ Instruments
- ▲ Spoken word, etc.

The spoken word occupies a particular place in this list of documents. Although verbal statements between people (direct or indirect, such as by telephone) are not strictly considered documents, they constitute a part of administrative business processes. It is important to represent them in the documentation of the processes. With further analysis and evaluation of an administrative business process, it appears that the verbal statements form a weak link in the process. If the spoken word is not recognized as a document, then an accurate analysis of the process is not possible.

In using documents, it is also important to determine in advance which characteristics are of interest. Will it suffice to have a general concept of the documents or must the exact content, the format, the scope, the thickness of the paper, and the number of copies also be examined? Once the purpose of the document is known, its effectiveness can be analyzed. Sometimes a document barely plays a role in a single activity. However, a document often fulfills a function in a number of successive activities.

3.4.4 The Information

Typically, information (data) related to how the process is functioning is recorded on forms. Usually the blank forms are included in the documentation. The forms define the information (data) that needs to be recorded and are purposely left blank in the documentation because they are normally used to collect data at various sequences while the process is operating.

For example, the document "sales invoice" can contain the following data elements:

- ▲ Name/address of the supplier
- ▲ Name/address of the client

▲ Delivery date
▲ Invoice date
▲ Number per item
▲ Price per item
▲ Terms of delivery
▲ Item code
▲ Percent discount
▲ Item description
▲ Amount per item
▲ Net invoice amount
▲ Sales tax
▲ Total invoice amount

In addition to this structured information, which is usually recorded on documents, it is important to recognize which unstructured organizational information is present.

3.4.5 The Geographic Location

With respect to the geographic location, the description can emphasize the determination of

▲ The place or location where the operations occur
▲ The time or distance that must be bridged. For example, consider subprocesses that take place in separate geographic locations and the exchange of documents that must occur.

The factor of geographic location plays a role particularly in the analysis of the suitability of a process, which may include the routing or cycle time.

3.4.6 The Organization Location

The concept of organization location (the location within the organizational structure where activities take place) is closely connected with the factor of the individuals and departments that perform particular operations. The reporting channels of departments or staff members, their authority and responsibilities, and many other considerations are important.

3.4.7 The Departments and Individuals

Related to the geographic and organization location is the question of which departments and individuals are involved with a process. Elements for the study of a department include the function of the department, the different activities, the division of tasks, the number of staff members, etc. With individuals, the important elements are the position, the responsibilities, the composition of the responsibilities, the required expertise, the education level, and the experience level.

With the documentation of departments and individuals, particular attention should be paid to the work relationship between the different departments as well as the various individuals involved with the diverse administrative business processes. This relationship can be of many kinds (data exchange, the sequence in the process, cooperation in a process, etc.).

3.4.8 The Frequency

Frequency indicates how often something happens. This factor is particularly important if it relates to the processing capacity of departments, individuals, or administrative technological enablers.

3.4.9 The Technique

Technique indicates how and with which enablers procedures are completed. This especially refers to the method and technique of data collection, processing, and distribution.

In the framework of this book, this list of factors will play a role in determining which documentation technique is appropriate for which objective (see section 3.10). As already stated, this list is not limited: factors can be added as needed. For example, the following factors are important in the analysis of administrative business processes:

▲ Costs
▲ Profits
▲ (Financial) risk and importance
▲ Products
▲ Quantities

Less quantifiable factors can also be important in the analysis of administrative business processes. Factors such as ergonomics, degrees of freedom in processes, employee satisfaction, and even certain cultural and ethical organization elements can be included. As described in section 3.10, each documentation technique is appropriate for accurately describing a particular factor. The number of factors that a documentation technique can sensibly describe is limited to four or five. It often is necessary to choose a combination of several documentation techniques when the number of factors that must be considered in a particular situation exceeds this number.

3.5 The Level of Detail of the Documentation

After deciding on the factors that must be presented (keeping in mind that they must match the objective for which the business process is being documented), the level of detail of the documentation must be decided upon. Each of the factors mentioned in section 3.4 can be documented to a greater or lesser degree of detail.

If a particular objective can be satisfied using a general description and no understanding of the details of the business process is required, it is unnecessary to take the document any further. In practice, this occurs fairly often, since the level of detail required for the accurate documentation of a business process is not specified in advance. Often, the researchers are concerned about not having enough insight into the processes during the analysis stage and will document as many details as possible. This wastes time and effort and may lead to frustration as soon as they realize that too many or too few details were inventoried.

Likewise, the requirement of specifying the level of detail is important in choosing the appropriate documentation technique(s). Although a few documentation techniques are appropriate for presenting both general concepts and details, most techniques are appropriate for presenting either one or the other. Section 3.9 elaborates on which documentation techniques present general concepts and which present details. Section 3.10 addresses the role that the level of detail, together with the objective and the factors, plays in choosing a suitable combination of documentation techniques. A typical organization has five tiers of documentation (see figure 3.A). Figure 3.A also relates the process hierarchy to the documentation hierarchy.

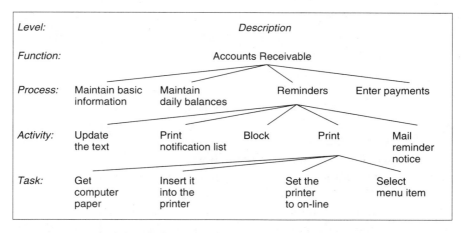

FIGURE 3.A   Level of detail of the documentation

DEFINITION

Tier 1 Documents—Organizational Requirements. Tier 1 documents consist of the organization's mission, values, long-range objectives, critical success factors, and visions. They are the documents that define and direct all the organization's activities and management systems. They are prepared by top management, because setting direction is top management's major role.

Tier 2 Documents—Manuals are documents that define what needs to be done and are conceptual in nature. These documents often define cross-functional strategies and responsibilities.

Tier 3 Documents—Procedures are documents that are used to define the major processes that exist within the organization. They are often called operating procedures. They answer the "four Ws": what, when, who, and where at a department or functional level.

Tier 4 Documents—Instructions are documents that are used to define how an assignment is accomplished. They are written at the task level and provide detailed instructions on how the individual performs the activity. They have many different names, among them work instructions, job instructions, setup instructions, job descriptions, and activity instructions.

Tier 5 Documents—Records are documents that are prepared to provide an audit trail proving that the required tasks or activities were completed. They often also define how effectively and efficiently the tasks or activities were performed.

Documentation structure is a systematic and logical way the different elements of the Business Administrative Organization are described in the *Administrative Organization Manual.* It also contains the processes that are used to update the description of the business administrative organization.

As an example of the way in which the level of detail can be determined in advance, a diagram of the processes of an arbitrary accounts receivable department is given below. The processes used by accounts receivable have four levels of detail specified for the documentation:

▲ Procedures
▲ Activities
▲ Tasks
▲ Work instructions

A major process within the accounts receivable function is maintaining accounts receivable records (see figure 3.A). This process is made up of many interrelated, connected activities; for example, maintain basic information, maintain the daily balances, update reminder notices, enter payments. These activities are further broken down into tasks. For example, the activity "update reminder notices" could be subdivided into such tasks as update the text, print notification list, block reminder notice update, print and mail reminder notices. How to perform a specific task is documented in work instructions. For example, the work instruction for the task of print and mail reminder notices would instruct the employee to

▲ get computer paper
▲ insert it into printer
▲ set the printer to on-line
▲ select menu item

Operating procedures are written flow diagrams that describe the activities that are associated with a specific process. Work instructions are used to identify the specific tasks associated with each activity and to explain how each task is conducted.

DEFINITION ‖ An **activity** is performed within a natural work group (department) by one or more people doing different parts of the activity. Activities are subsets of a process.

Tasks are individual elements and/or subsets of an activity. Normally, tasks relate to how an individual performs a specific assignment.

In most cases, it will also be necessary to determine the levels of detail needed for the other factors (aspects) listed in section 3.4. This is particularly true for the factors of information and technique. For example, specifications such as "with computer" or "manually" will be too vague to properly execute an administrative business process.

3.6   A Few Practical Suggestions

The following provides some practical suggestions on how to define document content and the level of detail within the various documents.

3.6.1   Determining the Scope and Level of Detail in Practice

Each time an administrative business process is to be documented, it is necessary to know in advance which factors must be documented and to what degree of detail. After all, it is impractical and senseless to propose documenting all aspects to all levels of detail.

If the purpose of the documentation of the administrative processes is to be of benefit for educational, training, or reference purposes, the determination of the scope (also called the width of the documentation) as well as the level of detail (extent or depth) is very possible. The nature of the procedures, the documents, the information paths, and the departments and individuals involved in the process are the most important factors in order to understand the processes.

If the purpose of the documentation is also to perform an analysis, a dilemma is created. Ideally, one should already have an understanding of the problems of an administrative business process before directing its documentation activities. For example, if a cycle-time problem is present, factors such as frequency, quantity, starting time, and ending time must be documented. A conflict arises because the understanding of the problems should be clarified by the analysis and that understanding does not or rarely exists beforehand. This dilemma can be prevented by conducting a short orientation study that results in the identification of any major problems related to the administrative business processes before beginning the documentation. In this preliminary study, interviews are conducted with the management of the involved organization and the analysis of appropriate documents (such as management letters from accountants, internal reports, and descriptions of processes). Interviews are held with a standard list of questions. (The documentation technique appropriate for the objective of the analysis can be determined with the figures in Section 3.10). A similar preliminary study should be undertaken to obtain an indication of the time and resources required for the entire project. These will depend on the number of administrative business processes, their complexity, and the number of involved staff members and departments.

3.6.2 Factors and Level of Detail: In Theory and in Practice

Use of the concepts of factors and levels of detail usually results in all sorts of theoretical discussions. With regard to figure 3.A, questions regarding the exact difference between process, activity, task, and operation are frequently raised. The distinction is not very important as long as there is a hierarchy that couples the objectives or goals of the organization unit with the highest level and the work instructions with the lowest level. The first objective is to obtain a good and complete inventory of the functions, activities and tasks, in order to document the processes in the required level of detail (depending on the purpose). Basically, it is important that at the top of the diagram, what gets done (processes and activities, such as "entering invoices," "monitoring of accounts receivable") is identified and that lower in the diagram, how it is accomplished ("print," "mail," etc.) is identified.

Management of the level of detail should also be considered in another respect. In principle, each documentation technique seems to be appropriate for presenting every level of detail. It is not the case that the correct choice of documentation technique will regulate the required level of detail. Supplementary guidelines are needed for this purpose. Thus, the documentation must be evaluated, which can effectively be done by appointing an editor or using a technical writer. However, the choice of a particular documentation technique does control the use of factors (the scope of the documentation).

3.7   Criteria for Selecting Documentation Techniques

The rest of this chapter focuses on the techniques for documenting administrative business processes. An exhaustive summary of all the possible documentation techniques is not given because the number of techniques employed is so large that a thorough discussion of them would undermine the purpose of this book. Moreover, excellent references are available for those who want to study further the complete range of documentation techniques. The techniques treated in this chapter form a knowledge base with which practically all possible documenting objectives can be met. The set of documentation techniques presented at the end of this chapter shows how techniques can be effectively combined for use.

In the following sections, the terms *documentation technique* and *diagramming technique* will be used interchangeably. It is true that the documentation of an administrative business process is not necessarily executed by diagramming the process. However, the documentation techniques in this chapter all belong to the category of diagramming techniques.

By determining which factors are of importance in choosing a documentation technique, we will see that theory and practice are sometimes in conflict.

3.7.1   Objectives and Factors

This chapter presents theoretically how a (combination of) technique(s) for the documentation of administrative business processes is chosen: the objective of the documentation determines the factors and level of detail to be documented. The documentation techniques that adequately present these elements at the desired level of detail are presented.

In practice, other, nontheoretical factors play a role (for example, user-friendliness, maintainability, and the time that it takes to execute diagrams). Moreover, it turns out that available documentation as well as subjective factors are of importance.

3.7.2   User-Friendliness

The term *user-friendliness* in information systems is a fairly current term. Where systems are developed, the word indicates striving for the presentation of the results and products to the final users of the system in the most clear (and acceptable) way. This presentation is accomplished as often as possible by the means of documentation techniques that make it possible for the users to get an adequate understanding of a concept in an easy manner (that is, without having to learn the specific documentation techniques and terminology of the computer science experts in detail).

In the framework of this book, the concept of user-friendliness has a second implication: a technique that is simple for the documenter as well as the user should be employed. However, attention should be paid to the fact that what is uncomplicated for one individual may be complicated for another.

For the documenter, the extent to which a technique is user-friendly is dependent on the speed with which the technique can be mastered, the speed with which the processes can be documented, and the degree to which the technique helps to produce a systematic and satisfactory documentation.

For the user who will be examining the documentation, the amount of effort needed to understand the documentation will determine the user-friendliness. As soon as documentation becomes too complicated, too technical, or too much based on the user's expertise, the user will become less willing to examine the content of the documentation. A resistant attitude is usually already present when documentation is received from other departments or disciplines that employ different techniques. It is important that the documentation be made friendly for the user by using terms that the user is familiar with (see also section 3.8.2).

3.7.3 Preexisting Documentation

You will sometimes determine that the optimum combination of documentation techniques is not being used. In many organizations, one or more techniques are designated as standard techniques in order to simplify the communication between different disciplines. As long as the standard techniques are appropriate for achieving the desired objectives, there are few problems. When the available standard techniques are not suitable, problems will arise. The need to introduce a new and more appropriate documentation technique speaks for itself, yet it often comes up against resistance because the inclusion of another technique makes the internal communication process a little less simple.

More important is that often, a large amount of documentation in an organization may have already been prepared using the standard techniques. Thus, the introduction of a new and better technique could mean that parts of the existing documentation may need to be adapted. However, user-friendliness can also be applied in these situations. It is not sensible to repeatedly confront the users of documentation with different documentation techniques. This applies to documentation that is available in the company in the form of detailed instructions. Out of practical considerations, the path of least resistance is chosen. The customary standard techniques are applied and factors that cannot properly be presented are clarified through the use of appendices and notes. It should be realized that the use of many unnecessary supplements is not user-friendly.

3.7.4 Maintainability

Obviously, the degree to which changes to the existing documentation can be made simply is also a criterion for choosing a documentation technique. As section 3.9 indicates, changes in some documentations are quite simple and in others quite difficult to implement. For a number of documentation techniques, minor changes may even result in having to adjust large parts of the documentation.

In many organizations, the organizational structure and the support documentation are often affected by changes. The requirement that the organizational structure diagram constantly reflect the correct and actual situation is almost impractical. It is also not surprising that in a number of organizations, reclassification of the organizational scheme is automatic with the help of special programs.

3.7.5 Labor Intensity

Labor intensity is closely related to the effort required to develop and maintain a process. When it takes more time to depict a process with a particular documentation technique, that technique is viewed as less attractive. Labor intensity is a factor that must not be underestimated. Some techniques are so simple and so compelling with regard to logistics that they can be used as notation methods during interviews (see appendix XII). Examples include the hierarchical overview and the form management diagram. Other techniques present the desired picture after being reclassified a few times.

3.7.6 Subjectivity

Subjective considerations also play a role in choosing a documentation technique. Subjective considerations are determined using the knowledge that one has of a particular documentation technique. Less rational reasons, such as "that one documentation technique is simply better than another," are not exceptions. Other reasons are often hidden behind these considerations.

For illustrative purposes, the example of an organization where a certain degree of confusion between five departments (such as the internal accounting department, the computer center, an administrative department, an organizational department, and a human services department) is presented. The confusion originated because the same documentation techniques were used in every department, but every department worked with different symbols.

3.8 Characteristics of Documentation Techniques

3.8.1 Common Characteristics

Before moving on to a discussion of the actual documentation techniques in section 3.9, it is of interest to first examine some of the common characteristics of the techniques.

The diagram concept can be described as a visual representation that is aimed at giving a picture of the organization, composition, processes, systems, procedures, and external relationships of the item being analyzed. Symbols are used in diagrams for visual representation. Symbols are all figures, lines, signs, and annotations that are treated as representations of the presented procedures, individuals or departments, documents, information, time, frequency, and enablers. Frequently, a distinction is made between free and bound diagrams.

Free Diagrams

These are not bound by predetermined rules for format and are particularly appropriate because they are suggestive, compact, and can effectively transfer knowledge for quick understanding. Usually, the free diagram includes few symbols. The factors to be highlighted can be emphasized by leaving out the less important aspects.

The classification and use of the symbols are determined by the developer, so the reader must become acquainted with the characteristics of the technique employed in each diagram. The danger then exists that a diagram that is very clear to the developer does not clearly present the subject to the reader unless it is further clarified. Free diagrams are appropriate for illustrating or clarifying texts or explanations. It is difficult to present subject matter in a free diagram without attaching an explanatory text. When drawing a free diagram, each developer should repeatedly ask

- ▲ Will the reader understand this or is an explanatory text necessary?
- ▲ Are the employed symbols clear?
- ▲ Are the important factors emphasized?
- ▲ Are the insignificant factors left out?
- ▲ Does the diagram add to the knowledge of the reader or is it superfluous?

The diagram of administrative business process principles and the general-process diagram are examples of free diagrams.

Bound Diagrams

With bound diagrams, the format, classification, and symbols that are employed are described ahead of time, and the factors to be presented are defined. The construction is such that the diagram is divided into a number of vertical and horizontal columns in which the departments or individuals, documents, data paths, and procedures are presented. Because it forces a thorough description of the presented aspects, the bound diagram is an effective means for describing and analyzing administrative business processes. It is particularly important to work with predefined and accepted techniques in projects where a large number of individuals are involved.

Examples of bound diagrams are the form flow diagrams, the form management diagrams, and accounting system diagrams.

Much more important than the difference between free and bound diagrams is the method by which the specifications and rules are determined. This can vary from rigid arrangements (prescribed language use, prescribed symbols, fixed classification, use of standard forms) to a complete lack of arrangements.

3.8.2 Suggestions for the Use of Diagramming Techniques

With the discussion of the separate diagramming techniques in section 3.9, the requirements for each technique will be presented. In spite of the large differences between the individual techniques, some hints that are applicable for the use of all of the diagramming techniques can still be given.

▲ *The number of factors per diagram should be limited.* Too many factors make diagrams complicated. One should try to restrict the number of factors to four or five, maximum. If the number of factors is larger, then the use of a combination of several diagramming techniques is preferred. It is most important to determine in advance which factors will be represented in the diagrams. The documentation should also be limited to those factors.

▲ *The documentation should be tuned to the needs of the user.* Depending on the experience that a user has with a particular diagramming technique, the technique may be more or less appropriate for that user. In a number of cases, it is necessary to document the same administrative business process with different diagramming techniques, each directed toward a different user group. As a guideline, the amount of detail with which the documentation is executed should increase in the lower levels, down to the level of instructions for the diagrammed organization (for example, a process may be pictured based on how the activities interconnect, and an activity-flow diagram is also presented in another picture that follows the data flow—a data-flow diagram).

▲ *The documentation should be made as user-friendly as possible.* The user-friendliness of the diagrams is determined by the use of text, clear organization, effective layout, and visual clarity.

▲ *The use of symbols must be limited, particularly for the less experienced reader.* If the users have less experience with a particular diagramming technique, it is sensible to work with fewer symbols. As a guideline for an inexperienced user, it is not a drawback to work with eight to ten symbols. The symbols must be easily distinguishable from each other, and they should be drawn in the same format. Otherwise, readers of the diagram could get the impression that a symbol with a different format has a different meaning. Uniformity in the use of symbols should be attempted. One should also try to work with self-explanatory symbols.

▲ *Text in the diagrams promotes clarity, yet the use of too much text is detrimental.* Text is often supplementary in drawn diagrams. As soon as the amount of text threatens to overwhelm the diagram, it should be recorded separately as an appendix or a supplement.

▲ *Diagrams should have a clear visual organization.* The clear visual arrangement of diagrams promotes accessibility.

▲ *Diagrams should use the same format as much as possible.* Because diagrams drawn in the same format can be stored in the same way, the acquisition of similar storage units can result in cost savings. For these reasons, the use of the A-4 format (European paper size: 21 × 25 cm) is recommended for diagrams.

▲ *Diagrams should be designed to be read from top left to bottom right.* The lines that connect the symbols must be easy to follow. Crossed lines should be avoided. Only horizontal and vertical lines should be used.

▲ *A legend should be added to the document.* The symbols used in the diagram should be explained in the legend.

3.9 Discussion of Selected Documentation Techniques

Ten documentation techniques with brief descriptions are discussed below. For each technique, the descriptions address which objective is best met by the technique and which factors and what level of detail can be presented. In this section of the book, the following documentation techniques will be discussed.

▲ Organizational structure diagram
▲ Administrative business process principles diagram
▲ Hierarchical overview diagram
▲ Global overview of processes and divisions diagram
▲ Global process diagram
▲ Detailed process diagram
▲ Instruction diagram
▲ Form management diagram
▲ Form circulation diagram
▲ Accounting system diagram

3.9.1 Organizational Structure Diagram

The organizational structure diagram provides insight into the structure of an organization. This diagram focuses on the formal relationships between departments. These relationships can be just as much hierarchical (with regard to authority) as functional (with regard to regulations and guidelines) in their nature.

A diagram of the organizational structure is not appropriate to represent an administrative business process. The diagram serves as background information for the administrative business processes and is directed toward obtaining insight.

The organizational structure diagram can play a role in various analysis objectives, such as in the analysis of the administrative-organizational function structure and task structure. The organizational structure diagram effectively presents the factors of organization location and the relationship between departments and individuals. The organizational structure diagram is further presented in appendix I.

3.9.2 Administrative Business Process Principles Diagram

The principles diagram is designed to present the core of the administrative business process, a system, or another entity. It is important to note that this diagram presents the essentials or the most important factors in a compact and clear way.

In diagramming the principle factors of an administrative business process, the factors to be diagrammed are not predetermined. It can be a free diagram in the sense that there is no set pattern that is the same for each following diagram. Thus, in the principles diagram, all the factors can be presented, provided that each diagram is restricted to approximately four factors. The administrative business process principles diagram is further addressed in appendix II.

3.9.3 Hierarchical Overview Diagram

The hierarchical overview diagram gives insight into the structure and composition of the overall administrative system. It allows the hierarchy of the administrative business processes to be seen.

In the hierarchical overview diagram, an attempt is made to separate the administrative business processes from the business procedures so that the lowest level of detail of administrative business processes are distinguished and can be studied piece by piece.

The construction of the diagram involves working from top to bottom and from general to specific so that further subdivisions are developed. The subdividing continues for as long as it is desired and useful. The hierarchical overview is used to obtain insight into the transfer of knowledge of administrative business processes. It represents the grouping and connection of procedures in outline form and is not appropriate for presenting processes in detail. The hierarchical overview diagram is further addressed in appendix III.

3.9.4 Global Overview of Processes and Divisions Diagram

The global overview of processes and divisions diagram gives insight into the connections of all the researched administrative business processes and organizational units. The nature of the involvement of the divisions (and/or staff members) in each of the administrative business processes is presented in general terms while the data collections used can be indicated. The global overview is set up as a matrix in which the vertical columns represent the rules of the administrative business processes and the horizontal columns represent the organizational units. At the intersecting points of the matrix, symbols indicate whether or not there is a relationship between the departments and processes and, if there is, the nature of the relationship.

The global overview can be of importance for analysis of the grouping of activities, routing, and internal control of the organization. The global overview diagram can be combined with other diagramming techniques. It can present a number of factors: the outlines and relationships of procedures, the relationships between divisions or staff members, and documents and files. The global overview diagram is further addressed in appendix IV.

3.9.5 Global Process Diagram

A global process diagram is meant to present the general themes within an administrative business process. The diagram is not appropriate for presenting procedures or data paths, but it can be considered for describing the components of which the administrative business process is comprised. The diagram presents the main pattern of the relationships between the various components of the administrative business process. The global process diagram is especially valuable when the components can be presented in a certain order, representing the activities/tasks of each organizational unit without describing the tasks in detail.

The global process diagram plays a role in the analysis of internal control, routing, and grouping of activities. The various factors are not presented in detail. Factors such as the order and relationship of procedures and the divisions and individuals involved with the processes can be depicted. The global process diagram is further addressed in appendix V.

3.9.6 Detailed Process Diagram

The detailed process diagram gives an accurate picture of the order of the work instructions and the path of documents in an administrative business process. With each procedure, the work instruction documents or files can be indicated. However, the order of the work instructions determines their location in the diagram. The department that or individual who completes the work instructions can also be noted.

The detailed process diagram is especially suitable for the analysis of administrative business processes in connection with routing, superfluous processes, and the grouping of activities. A large number of factors can be represented in detail. The relationships between divisions, some facets of internal control, the flow of documents, and the factors of frequency and time will be less clear. The detailed process diagram is further addressed in appendix VI.

3.9.7 Instruction Diagram

Instruction diagrams are meant to give the staff members of an organization insight into the administrative activities and instructions that need to be executed and followed. Instruction diagrams are a special part of knowledge-transfer enablers. The function of communication is difficult to diagram because each instruction may only be suitable for one purpose and should not be ambiguous or leave room for the imagination.

The number of factors that can be presented in an instruction diagram is larger than that in other diagram techniques. Apart from procedures (global and in detail), forms and departments can be recorded in the text or in the specially reserved columns of the diagram's factors, such as deadlines, frequency, and employed techniques. The instruction diagram is further addressed in appendix VII.

3.9.8 Form Management Diagram

Form management diagrams show the use and the route of the forms of an administrative business process. In this context, one should not treat the concept of forms too narrowly. It often proves necessary to depict the route and the use of all types of documents. In addition to forms, books, index files, registers, computer outputs, screen information, and all types of technical enablers, photographs, sound reproducers, light signals, and switchboards can be included. The form management diagram is known as the tic-tac-toe diagram.

The form management diagram belongs to the category of bound diagrams. This analysis can be aimed at the efficient and effective use of forms. The diagrams show the circulation of the forms through the departments, which (copies of) forms are redundant, which data files develop, which of these files are meaningful, and which are not. The presentation of the procedures or work instructions associated with each form also makes it possible to analyze the nature of these procedures, which procedures are duplicated, which are missing, and how the various procedures are grouped among the different departments and individuals. The procedures' order and relationship, the documents' flow, and departments and staff members may be represented in considerable detail. The form management diagram is further addressed in appendix VIII.

3.9.9 Form Circulation Diagram

The form circulation diagram gives information about the use and the route of forms in the administrative business process. This diagram is generally treated as a bound diagram. The arrangement of the diagram is such that the form circulation is depicted by means of symbols, and the forms are grouped in separate columns by department or staff member. Procedures are represented by means of a symbol next to the form upon which the relevant procedure is performed. The form circulation diagram is especially suitable for developing insight into the administrative business process. The diagram plays a role in the analysis of routing, the administrative-organizational function and task structure, and the accuracy and thoroughness of the data processing in an organization. In the diagram, emphasis is placed on the form circulation, the general presentation of the actions associated with each form, and the distribution of the forms and actions to the various departments. This last factor may be particularly important when the division of tasks and functions in the organization is analyzed.

The form circulation diagram highlights a number of other factors. Although actions associated with the forms can be presented, these activity descriptions are limited (for example, comparing, controlling, separating, or joining forms). The technique does not allow for further detail of these actions (although one can indicate that an invoice is being compared with an order form, one cannot indicate which parts of the forms are being compared). Factors of time, frequency, geographic location, and technique used are not presented by the diagram. The form circulation diagram is further addressed in appendix IX.

3.9.10 Accounting System Diagram

The accounting system diagram is a suitable documentation technique for obtaining a rapid and detailed look at the system of bookkeeping of an organization. For a somewhat experienced reader, the diagram can even serve as an instruction guide for the bookkeeping system. The diagram is especially useful for obtaining information about the consequences of possible changes in the bookkeeping system.

The diagram is drawn in the form of a table. The columns present the various accounts and the rows present the different actions that lead to the entries. The method of entry on the accounts is indicated by symbols that are connected by lines. The accounting system diagram is further discussed in appendix X.

3.10 Developing a Set of Documentation Techniques

We will not cover all of the documentation techniques that are used in practice. In section 3.9, a selection of the ten most important techniques are discussed. This set of techniques will satisfy most of the objectives for documenting administrative business processes.

Section 3.7 discusses which criteria play a role in the selection of documentation techniques. Apart from the relationship between the objectives and the technique, the user-friendliness, the existing experience, the maintainability, the work intensity, and the subjective considerations are also limiting factors. User-friendliness, existing experience, and subjective considerations will not be further discussed. These criteria differ from case to case and will have to be determined for each case. The maintainability and the work intensity are treated in the discussion of the particular techniques (section 3.9 and appendices I–X).

This study is limited to the relationship between the objectives and the documentation techniques. The objective and documentation of the administrative business processes will determine which documentation technique will be used. Depending on the purpose for which the documentation is produced, the factors and the level of detail have to be determined.

To select a suitable (or a combination of suitable) documentation techniques, the factors and the levels of detail that can be presented by the chosen documentation techniques need to be determined. Answering four questions helps to further explain the above.

▲ Which factors and what level of detail need to be presented to achieve the objective?
▲ Which aspects and what level of detail can be presented by a documentation technique?
▲ Which documentation techniques are suitable for which objectives?
▲ Which documentation techniques can be combined (the documentation technique set)?

3.10.1 Which Factors and What Level of Detail Need to Be Presented to Achieve the Objective?

The number of objectives that can be formed appear to be so large that a complete, systematic analysis does not prove useful. Following the summary in section 3.3, objectives directed at the analysis of the administrative processes appear to be most suitable for further research. The objectives of "insight" and "transfer of knowledge" are too broad to determine which particular factors are desired. In fact, every factor or every combination of factors can be the object of the insight and the transfer of knowledge. However, if desired factors of insight and transfer of knowledge are determined, then by means of figure 3.B, the suitable documentation techniques can be determined.

The analysis of administrative business processes is aimed at

▲ The effectiveness of the information management
▲ The effectiveness and efficiency of the data files
▲ The timeliness and the cycle time

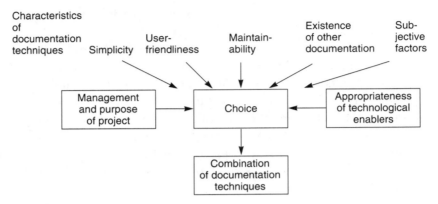

FIGURE 3.B   Selecting documentation techniques

▲ The relationship of tasks and functions to the administrative organization

▲ The effectiveness and efficiency of the routing of the administrative business processes

▲ The accuracy, thoroughness, and reliability of the data processing operations

▲ The efficiency of the administrative business processes

▲ The opportunities for standardization

▲ Duplicates and superfluous actions

▲ The effectiveness and efficiency of applied enablers (see section 4.1.3 for the relationship of and setting of priorities for the objective of the analysis)

Figure 3.C lists which factors need to be presented for a particular analysis objective. The letter *d* indicates whether a factor has to be described in detail. The letter *g* indicates that a general description of the factor will be sufficient. The factors listed in figure 3.C are discussed in section 3.4.

3.10.2 Which Aspects and What Level of Detail Can Be Presented by a Documentation Technique?

Figure 3.D shows which factors can be presented by means of one of the discussed documentation techniques. Sometimes, the documentation technique

Factor Analysis objective	Outline of procedures	Detailed procedures	Relationship of actions	Order of procedures	Deadlines	Length of time	Documents	Document flow	Data flow	Geographic location	Organization location	Departments & individuals	Relationship btwn dep. & individuals	Frequency	Technique	Quantities
Information Management	g	–	g	g	g	g	d	d	d	–	g	g	g	g	g	g
Data files	–	g	g	g	g	g	d	d	d	g	g	g	g	–	g	g
Cycle times/timeliness	g	–	g	g	d	d	g	g	g	d	–	g	g	d	g	d
Grouping of activities	g	d	d	d	–	g	g	g	–	g	g	d	d	g	g	g
Routing	g	d	d	d	g	g	d	d	–	d	–	g	g	d	g	d
Internal control	g	d	d	d	g	g	d	d	d	d	d	d	d	g	d	g
Productivity	g	–	g	g	g	d	d	d	g	–	g	g	g	d	d	d
Opportunities for standardization	g	d	g	g	–	g	d	d	d	g	–	g	g	g	d	d
Duplicates	g	d	d	d	–	–	d	d	g	–	–	g	g	–	g	g
Enablers	g	d	d	d	g	d	d	d	d	g	g	g	g	g	d	d

Legend:
d: presents a detailed description of factor
g: presents a general description of factor
–: does not present the factor

FIGURE 3.C   Relationships between factors and analysis objectives

can reflect more factors than those for which the technique was originally intended. For example, in the detailed process diagram discussed in section 3.9.6, the addition of a whole column for text created a comprehensive documentation by using a process diagram without text. In this text column, factors such as frequency, quantity, and time can be entered.

para-graph	Documentation technique	Outline of procedures	Detailed procedures	Relationship of actions	Order of procedures	Deadlines	Length of time	Documents	Document flow	Data flow	Geographic location	Organization location	Departments & individuals	Relationship between departments & individuals	Frequency	Technique	Quantities	Level of detail
3.9.1	Organizational structure diagram										(x)	×	×	×			(x)	g-d
3.9.2	Principles diagram	(x)	(x)	(x)	(x)	(x)	(x)	(x)	(x)	(x)	(x)	(x)	(x)	(x)	(x)	(x)	(x)	g
3.9.3	Hierarchical overview diagram	×		×														g
3.9.4	Global overview diagram	×	(x)										×	×				g
3.9.5	Global process diagram	×		(x)	×						(x)	(x)	×	×				g
3.9.6	Detailed process diagram	(x)	×	×	×	(x)	(x)	×	(x)	(x)	(x)	(x)	(x)		(x)	×	(x)	d
3.9.7	Instruction diagram	(x)	×	(x)	×	×	×	×			(x)	(x)	(x)	×		×	×	d
3.9.8	Form management diagram	(x)	×	×	×			×				×	×	(x)				d
3.9.9	Form circulation diagram	×	(x)	×	(x)			×	×			(x)	×	(x)			(x)	d
3.9.10	Accounting system diagram		(x)	(x)				(x)										d

Legend:
×　: documentation technique is appropriate for presenting a factor
(x)　: documentation technique is moderately appropriate for presenting a factor
d　: describes factor in detail
g　: describes factor in general

FIGURE 3.D　Relationships between factors and documentation techniques

In figure 3.D, a differentiation is made for how possible it is for a documentation technique to present a particular factor. If it is highly possible, the column is marked with an X. If it is moderately possible, the column is marked with an (X). The last column indicates whether a documentation technique is more appropriate for the detailed description (d) or for a general description of the process (g).

3.10.3 Which Documentation Techniques Are Suitable for Which Objectives?

The combination of the two previous figures ("the factors for each purpose" and "the factors for each documentation technique") provides an overview of the documentation techniques that can be used to meet particular objectives. Depending on whether the documenter has some actual experience in the use of documentation techniques, it will be possible to directly determine whether or not a technique is appropriate for the purpose of the documentation. Figure 3.E reflects the basis of the directions for analysis that will be discussed in chapter 4. An X indicates that a technique is appropriate for a particular objective, an (X) indicates that a technique is less appropriate.

With figure 3.E, it is important to note that it may be necessary to combine the objective-specific techniques with the previously mentioned

paragraph	Documentation technique	Information management	Data files	Cycle time/ timeliness	Grouping of activities	Routing	Internal Control	Productivity	Opportunities for standardization	Duplicates	Enablers
3.9.1	Organizational structure diagram	(×)	(×)	—	(×)	—	(×)	—	—	—	—
3.9.2	Principles diagram	(×)	×	(×)	(×)	(×)	(×)	(×)	(×)	(×)	—
3.9.3	Hierarchical overview diagram	(×)	(×)	—	—	—	—	(×)	(×)	—	—
3.9.4	Global overview diagram	(×)	(×)	—	(×)	(×)	×	(×)	(×)	—	—
3.9.5	Global process diagram	(×)	(×)	×	(×)	×	(×)	(×)	(×)	—	(×)
3.9.6	Detailed process diagram	(×)	(×)	×	×	×	(×)	×	×	×	(×)
3.9.7	Instruction diagram	—	—	—	—	(×)	(×)	—	×	—	×
3.9.8	Form management diagram	—	—	—	(×)	×	×	—	×	×	×
3.9.9	Form circulation diagram	(×)	(×)	—	×	×	×	(×)	—	(×)	(×)
3.9.10	Accounting system diagram	—	—	—	(×)	—	(×)	—	—	—	—

FIGURE 3.E Relationships between analysis objective and documentation technique

diagramming techniques in order to meet the particular objective of an analysis. For example, the analysis of the cycle time of a process requires an understanding of the cycle time of each activity in addition to an understanding of the administrative business process by means of detailed process diagrams (see also section 4.5).

3.10.4 Which Documentation Techniques Can Be Combined (the Documentation Technique Set)?

In discussing which documentation techniques can be employed in combination with others, it appears that every technique can be combined with another technique. After all, each technique can describe several factors of an administrative business process and not influence the contents of another documentation. Most of the combinations are not worthwhile. Most of the techniques overlap in describing factors so that if a combination of two similar techniques is chosen, a lot of duplicate work will be done. Strongly overlapping techniques are the form flow and form management diagrams. Each can approximately cover the same levels of detail and describe the same aspects. At the global description level, the global overview diagram, the global process diagram, and the hierarchical overview diagram are all aimed at creating an overview of processes, although each applies a different point of view. Depending on the level of detail in which the processes are described by the documentation techniques, the techniques can be divided into three categories (see figure 3.F):

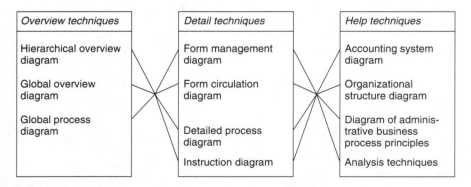

FIGURE 3.F Combination of techniques

▲ The *overview techniques,* which provide insight into the entire administrative business process
▲ The *detail techniques,* which document the administrative business processes in detail
▲ The *help techniques,* which document a specific factor of the administrative business processes

Except for the help techniques, documentation that is based on a particular objective for the analysis of processes can also be included.

Without being strict in setting rules for the combining of documentation techniques, the following instructions can be given:

▲ *As soon as the processes have been documented in detail, a well-developed description of the administrative business processes requires a complete overview of processes.* This overview is especially important in order to be able to determine how the entire administrative system is structured and which relationships or interfaces exist between the separate processes. It is recommended that an overview technique should be combined with a detail-oriented documentation technique. If all the preselected factors cannot be documented with these techniques, they can be aided by the necessary help technique.

▲ *Try to be creative in the use of help techniques.* The documentation of the administrative business processes can be completed with one or more of the factor-oriented documentation techniques. Examples are office floor plans that can help describe the geographic location factor and tables that can help present the cycle times. The analysis of the processes in chapter 4 includes the use of similar, specific, or fixed-factor oriented techniques.

▲ *Whenever overview and detail techniques are combined, use techniques that are complementary to begin with as much as possible.* Combine global process diagrams with detailed process diagrams, global overview diagrams with form flow and form management diagrams, and hierarchical overview diagrams with process diagrams. Since complementary techniques have the same angles of approach, combining overview and detail techniques should not pose much of a problem.

3.10.5 Documentation Technique Sets:
An Example of a Frequently Used Combination

As previously mentioned (section 3.6), before starting a project for the analysis of the administrative organization, it is useful to get an indication of the existing problems of an administrative business process by means of a brief preliminary (orientation) study. The choice of documentation techniques to be applied can be properly based on the analysis objective. It is not always simple to have a concept of the analysis objective. This means that the dilemma of documenting too little or too much exists. The solution is to have a good foundation that can then be further developed. The first step is to ensure that a good hierarchy of documentation techniques is defined (see figure 3.G).

The following is a frequently used combination of techniques. From a hierarchical overview diagram (section 3.9.3) and an organizational structure diagram (section 3.9.1), the complete overview of procedures and departments is developed (section 3.9.4), the so-called matrix. The matrix can serve as the table of contents (the lines of the matrix) for the global process diagrams that will be developed (section 3.9.5). These global process diagrams are used to get a first impression of the processes. The blocks or units of the global process diagram can, depending on the analysis objective, be described in further detail using the detail technique. The depth of the analysis will depend on the analysis objectives.

The method of developing detailed process diagrams (section 3.9.6) from each horizontal line of the matrix is also used (see figure 3.G). These detailed process diagrams can act as the table of contents for the detail techniques. The instruction diagram (section 3.9.7) is often applied with the detailed process diagram. Procedure symbols in the detailed process diagram describe the actions in more detail. In developing an administrative organization manual (chapter 7), this combination appears to be most effective when the detailed process diagram is on the left page and the accompanying instruction diagram is on the right page (mutatis mutandis, the necessary changes having been made). This similarly applies to the layout of screens.

For the analysis of administrative business processes, a complete description of the processes in the instruction diagrams is not needed. It is sufficient to describe in detail only those actions that are required in the context of the analysis. For example, in the context of assessing the internal control of an organization, only the control actions are described in detail.

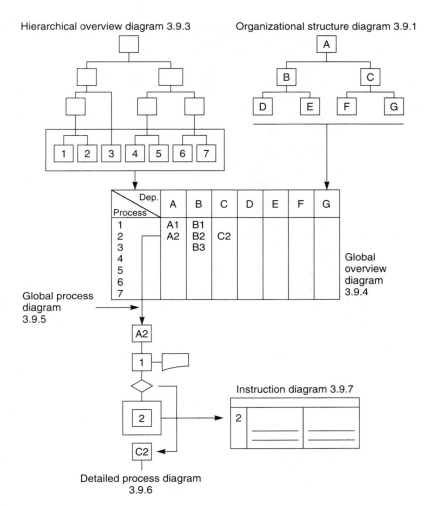

Hierarchical overview diagram 3.9.3

Organizational structure diagram 3.9.1

Global process diagram 3.9.5

Global overview diagram 3.9.4

Instruction diagram 3.9.7

Detailed process diagram 3.9.6

Help techniques

– file descriptions (relationship and content of data files)
– timetables
– accounting system diagrams (section 3.9.10)
– frequency tables
– list of documents
– form flows (sections 3.9.8 and 3.9.9)
– procuration overviews
– function distribution tables
– overviews of control actions/internal control
– network of overall controls
– overview of the movement of money or goods
– office floor plan

FIGURE 3.G   Example of a documentation technique set or combination

Depending on the documentation's objective, various help techniques can be applied (figure 3.G). Help techniques include

- ▲ File descriptions (relationship and content of data files)
- ▲ Timetables
- ▲ Accounting system diagrams (section 3.9.10)
- ▲ Frequency tables
- ▲ Lists of documents
- ▲ Form flows (sections 3.9.8 and 3.9.9)
- ▲ Function distribution tables
- ▲ Overviews of control actions/internal control
- ▲ Network of overall controls
- ▲ Overview of the movement of money or goods
- ▲ Office floor plan
- ▲ Procuration overviews

4 | Phase III—Analysis: Defining Improvement Opportunities

4.1 Introduction

The need to perform an analysis of an administrative business process is usually the reason for documenting the process. The reason for analyzing the process and the analysis techniques cannot be considered independently (as stated in chapter 3). These two factors are major considerations in choosing the documentation technique. In order to obtain a well-executed analysis, the documentation of administrative business process diagramming techniques is often inadequate. Additional activities need to be performed for acquiring and documenting the data necessary to perform the analysis.

The analysis consists of the following three steps:

A. Performing the analysis
B. Discussing the results of the analysis with the involved staff members
C. Reporting to the PMT

4.1.1 Performing the Analysis

The roles that the different staff members (PIT members, contact group members, and administrative staff members) play in the analysis are highly dependent on the chosen analysis direction. It is essential that the respective administrative staff members are involved with the analysis. Administrative staff members are those who will be affected by change. They are close to the activities being performed and can provide many helpful suggestions. In addition, early involvement of the people performing the individual activities facilitates the implementation of future changes. Thus, the PIT should make sure that this involvement can take place. This can be done if the PIT members, on the basis of their analysis, write down a number of points for discussion and discuss them with the respective staff members. On the basis of these discussions, a report documenting the findings can be drafted by the PIT.

4.1.2 Discussing the Results of the Analysis with the Involved Staff Members

The report should be discussed with respective administrative staff members and departmental managers. Depending on the width of the executed analysis, this can be done by conducting discussions with each department or with the contact groups.

In these discussions, those involved should comment on the report and draw conclusions. The discussions will not always result in a collective opinion. However, the researchers retain the responsibility for reporting the final results of the analysis.

4.1.3 Reporting to the PMT

After the discussion of the report with departments or with the contact groups, the PIT will give a definitive report to the PMT. In addition to the analysis, the report can propose that new administrative business processes be started, and it should also indicate how the current administrative business processes should be changed. These recommendations will still be expressed in general terms. The PMT should first give its approval before the definite specification of changes to the existing processes and the design of new processes commence.

After approval by the PMT and consideration of all the conclusions and recommendations from the groups, all the arrangements that are made concerning the modification of processes, the execution of further detailed studies, the setting up of new processes, etc. will be recorded on a record of approved changes. An example of how these arrangements can be recorded is shown in figure 4.A. On the basis of this engagement record, the PMT will be able to monitor the continued execution of activities.

Date:	01 - 30 - 1992 + existence as of 3 - 30 - 1992	Document code:	
Project:	*Adm. organization*	Project phase:	*Analysis*
Project team:	*Personnel*	Subject area:	*Personnel management processes*
Documentarian:	*J. Willemse*	Subject:	*Agreements involving changes*

No.	Process/ sub-process	Objective	Content change	Regulated by	Involved department	Date planned	Remarks
40.3	Take on personnel	Speed up processes	Framework checklist for on-time completion	J. de Wit	Human Resources	Proposal on 3-1-92 Entry on 5-1-92	Completed 3-15-92 Still needs approval
40.3	Take on personnel	Improve control of processing financial transactions	Framework position records in the Human Resources Dept. that can be updated based on computer output	J. de Wit	Human Resources Payroll	Proposal on 3-1-92 Entry 5-1-92	Completed 3-30-92 Still needs approval
40.7	Transfers	Timely reports of transfers	Input management whereby transfers are credited to the budget	R. de Kok	Payroll Human Resources	Proposal 5-1-92	
40.15	Medical expenses	Control the complete receipts from insurance	Supply list of those ill done by Human Res. to Payroll. Framework file for funds received by Payroll	R. de Kok	Payroll Human Resources	Entry 3-1-92	Entered 3-1-92
40.8	Reward corrections	Control of adm. processing and entry of charges in computer	Systematic quantification of verified errors according to causes by Control Dept.	C. Gras	Control	Entry 3-1-92	Entered 3-1-92

FIGURE 4.A   An example of a record of approved changes

An understanding of one or more of the following factors should be obtained from the analysis (also called an *information audit*):

▲ The effectiveness of information management
▲ The effectiveness and efficiency of the data files
▲ The cycle time of the administrative business process and the timeliness of its completion (the effectiveness of the process)
▲ The manner by which different activities in the administrative business process are clustered together
▲ The effectiveness and efficiency of the routing of the administrative business process
▲ The internal control associated with the data processing operations
▲ The productivity of the administrative business process
▲ The opportunities for standardizing the operations
▲ The existence of duplicates (activities or databases) and/or superfluous actions
▲ The effectiveness and efficiency of applied enablers

An assessment of the final results of the administrative business process can also be one of the objectives of the analysis. In that case, the data that result from an administrative business process can be analyzed with regard to their effectiveness as part of the decision-making process (assessing the effectiveness of information management). The structure of the cost calculations or the budgeting system can also be evaluated.

Apart from the factors one wants to understand, a choice of one or more of the analysis objectives discussed in this chapter needs to be made. This chapter includes a limited discussion of the use of data sets as enablers for executing the administrative business process. The discussion is aimed at studying the possibilities for combining data sets. With this study, the results of computerizing data sets are also discussed.

Every analysis starts with the collection of basic information. This information shall consist of the documentation of the administrative business process that is being analyzed and the documents that are part of the documentation. In addition, other available notes and descriptions about the process are important. The different observations that were made and commented on during the diagramming of the administrative business process can also play an important role. First, the administrative business process that is being analyzed needs to be specified (see section 3.2). The collection of detailed information, as a supplement to the basic material already available, must be started. Afterward, the analysis is performed.

It will be necessary to use samples during the collection of detailed information. For example, with the analysis of the cycle time of sales orders, it will not always be possible or necessary to use all of the orders. Documenting a random sample of the orders will suffice.

It is important that the one who will be performing the analysis is an authority on and has experience with analyzing administrative business processes. This expertise and experience needs to be specialized with regard to the objectives of the analysis. The analysis of the efficiency of the enablers applied to administrative business processes requires a specific knowledge of the possibilities for computerizing the existing activities as well as other administrative technological enablers. In addition, the analysis of the reliability of the administrative business processes requires a knowledge of internal control and information control principles.

Chapter 2 discusses how the analysis is organizationally connected to the other activities required for the project (such as documenting and modifying processes). After the discussion of the analysis objectives (section 4.3 to section 4.12), section 4.13 presents a few practical suggestions for managing these objectives. Section 4.2 addresses the question of how flaws may originate in administrative business processes.

4.2 The Causes of Flaws in Administrative Business Processes

Over time, flaws have a tendency to creep into the administrative business processes, making them less effective or efficient and causing some degree of job dissatisfaction. A number of causes can be responsible for this. Some of them are

▲ *The requirements placed on the administrative organization change with the passage of time.* These changes may be caused by changes in new governmental regulations or the markets the organization services. In addition, changes in the organization structure and its associated responsibilities make modifications in the data processing operations necessary.

Shifts in the factors that are essential for the management of the organization (for example, if cost control becomes more important than the degree of service or quality) also lead to modifications in the data processing operations. The choice of critical success factors and the associated control variables for the business processes directly influences the requirements that will be placed on the administrative organization (see also section 5.3.2). At the same time, legal regulations and conditions will constantly place changing requirements on the information system (for example, in the areas of privacy or environmental legislation). The information management system and the resulting setup of the administrative business processes will need to be continuously adjusted because of these factors. These adjustments will be realized through the introduction of changes in or additions to the existing information system. The changes or additions will be applied to the administrative business processes, data sets, and information flows. Because the existing system is continually changing, situations in which the data processing operations no longer satisfy the requirements placed on the system can develop. These situations can be both the requirements that are placed on the system from the viewpoint of efficiency as well as those from changes in effectiveness, internal control, security, etc.

▲ *Developments in the field of automated office procedures and equipment or of automated transaction processing information systems.* Under the most ideal circumstances, a gradual adjustment of the organization to these developments will take place, leading to a gradual increase in efficiency and effectiveness. However, these adjustments do not occur smoothly. In addition, the different technical opportunities are not always optimally applied. Thus, signs of inefficiency and ineffectiveness may gradually appear.

▲ *Autonomous growth symptoms.* There is the inclination to expand the processes still further for individuals who are defining the processes' capabilities and relative support equipment, such as computer programs, because there is a greater degree of visibility and personal satisfaction associated with the development of new information systems than there is related to maintaining systems.

▲ *Staff members, under their own management, will set up data sets that must be updated with the existing system.* This often means that the administrative business processes will constantly expand and will take longer to complete an activity. In addition, this may lead to a situation in which similar activities are completed in a number of different locations within the organization, leading to the creation of similar data sets that must be added to the system.

How do you know you have a problem? Flaws in administrative business processes become evident in many different ways. One indication is the creation of backlogs in the data processing operations. Backlogs are indicated by the development of late or long delivery times, the loss of clients, or the frequent use of backup procedures.

Another sign of inefficiency can be the production of similar overviews summarizing the same procedure in different locations. For example, the management for one oil pipeline receives three different figures on the number of barrels of oil delivered to its storage units each day. Apparently, the data in the different overviews are derived from different data sets, which implies that different assumptions and definitions are being applied. This introduces the subject of unnecessary duplicates. In addition, the process of updating different data sets with the same data is a no-value-added activity.

Flaws can be recognized by the existence of information systems that produce operational information that is not sufficiently used. This becomes evident when users immediately throw away the received information or store it and never use it again. Sometimes this includes all of the distributed information and sometimes this includes only a part of the distributed information or a part of the particular overview. It may even become evident that managers waste a lot of time by doing all sorts of subsequent manual processing of the overviews or by analyzing the information on the overview.

Flaws can also occur because the information is not removed from the database when its useful life is over. This superfluous information needlessly enlarges the database, making it more complex and time-consuming to analyze.

Another indication of the existence of flaws is the introduction of illogical quantitative relationships. For example, this relationship may be between the administrative products that a department produces (invoices, reminder notices, completed ledger records, etc.) and the number of staff members within the department. These flaws may also become evident because the costs of processing the data may be increasing without a comparative increase in production.

A good understanding of the effectiveness and efficiency of the administrative business processes can only be obtained by performing an appropriate analysis of the processes themselves. These key measurements define the important characteristics related to the administrative business processes. Given the infinite number of possible causes for inefficiency and ineffectiveness within most processes, it should be clear that computerization does not offer the solution for all of the observed problems. Although computerization can provide the organization with measurements so that the organization knows if it is performing to expectations, it usually does not define the root cause of nonconformance to expectations. Once again, this emphasizes the importance of thoroughly analyzing and appropriately taking stock of the administrative business processes (see figure 4.B).

4.3   The Effectiveness of Information Management

Administrative business processes are processes whereby data are refined. The processes should not only be efficiently organized, but the information that results from the processes should also be effective. That means that this information should be a necessary tool for completing the functions that must

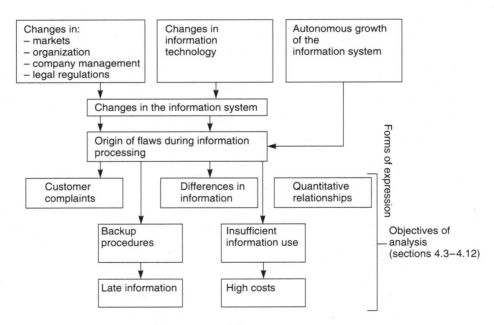

FIGURE 4.B   Overview of the origins of flaws

be performed by the organization. This involves the extent to which and how the information for decision-making processes about the individuals, items, and factors that are relevant for this decision is supplied.

Important questions for the analysis are

- ▲ Are the data supplied about all of the relevant units (departments, sectors, functions, etc.), subjects (employees, suppliers, customers, etc.), and items (end products, supplies, means of production, etc.)?
- ▲ Are the supplied data complete and thoroughly sufficient?
- ▲ Is the frequency and continuity with which data are supplied optimal?
- ▲ Are the data sufficiently critical and is the comparison standard (budget numbers [also over previous periods], area codes, etc.) available?
- ▲ Are enough data about the different phases of the business process (economic position, requirement estimates, current work, etc.) available?
- ▲ Are all the important aspects (information about location, sources, deadlines, capacity, etc.) recorded by the information management system?
- ▲ Are the data sufficiently reliable (see section 4.8)?
- ▲ Is the speed of data processing and supply adequate (see section 4.5)?

The most desirable information management situation with respect to the preceding questions will vary from organization to organization. It is practically impossible to describe a universal model for the information management of an organization. After all, every organization is different because the environment in which that organization operates is different and because the internal organization and management adapted for the environment present different situations.

The environment, the internal structure, and the form of management of the organization are important modifying factors for the desired structure of the information system. First, the organization environment is characterized by the role that the organization occupies in the existing social order (not-for-profit, profit, governmental). The difference between so-called non-profit organizations and organizations that make up a piece of the social order on the basis of market participation plays a role in the environmental factor. Second, the environment is distinguished by the nature of the contribution of the organization to the economic process. Typical important considerations are whether the organization supplies goods or services or whether its activities are concentrated in the area of trade or production. The characteristics of the organization's most important primary process should be specified and are relevant. In addition, the environment is characterized by the industry within which the organization operates. Finally, an important qualifying environmental factor is the structure of the purchasing and sales market; namely, whether the organization operates in one market, in a few markets, or in many different markets.

The internal organizational factors that modify the information system are formed by the scope of the organization, the organizational structure (of divisions, departments, etc.), and the organizational climate, such as the management style (forms of contract management, the employment of management incentives), the methods of communication, etc.

The information system is not determined only by the characteristics of the environment and the internal organization. The information system is also a product of its time, which means that the design is also influenced by factors such as the overall economic situation, developments in the firm, and information technology possibilities. The situation deemed most desirable will also differ for each of the analyses that are to be performed.

Good results are obtained by analyzing the different management processes that take place in the organization. This relates to the management processes that involve

▲ The management of the organization (developing and managing strategies)
▲ The control of the organization and its activities (structuring of functions, tasks, work methods, management techniques, etc.)
▲ The operational performance (performance of activities in the areas of purchasing, sales, administration, supply management, etc.)

These distinctions are important because the different management processes place different requirements on the information used within that process. These requirements can be related to how much the internal and external information is used, reporting, the extent of aggregation and detail, etc.

Each of the three management processes are presented in figure 4.C. The first step in the process is to decide on the desired result, called the standard or norm. The standard is used for comparison with the observed results. If a deviation from the standard is verified, an adjustment to the process is in-

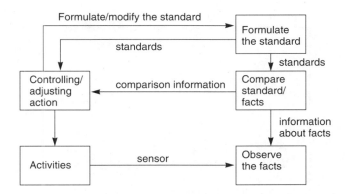

FIGURE 4.C   Schematic representation of the management cycle

dicated. The indicated adjustment can result in modifying the standard and/or correcting the activities. This modified activity is observed again and compared to the standard. The indicated adjustment can also relate to modifying the standard on a subprocess level or to an input to the process. If during the evaluation of the management processes, a decision is made to enter or abandon a particular market (share), such a decision should be followed by specifying the organization's standards for opening or closing a branch, how the branch should be managed, and to whom the manager should report.

Indications for adjustments on the level of controlling activities can have an effect on the management cycle of operational performance. The hierarchy of and between the different management cycles is presented in figure 4.D. Information plays an important role within the individual management cycles and between the subcycles.

The management of information on each of the three levels mentioned for the phases in the management process should be examined. For making policies, sufficient information in the form of market figures, forecasted results per product/market, or estimates of liquidity for the development of a standard/norm (the policy) should be available. The management instructions in the policy should include standards for the amount of control that should take place in the organization. This should be comprised of well-inspected personnel groups, department budgets, prescribed gross margins, or purchasing authorization. The management instructions at this level should include the standards for the level of operational performance. This level should be

Border policy processes

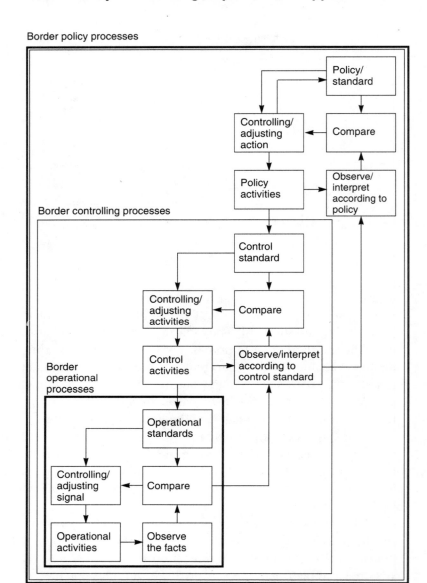

FIGURE 4.D The hierarchy of the subsystems

dictated by the price set for each product, delivery credit terms, or standards concerning the time spent per product.

The standard used for comparison with the actual results and how deviations are indicated is of importance. The standard can be based on the budgets estimated for each task or price versus cost calculations. It can also be based on nonfinancial standards, such as waiting periods, percentage of rejection, or production personnel turnover figures. Sometimes you may not have control over the standard prescribed for a particular task. In these cases, the comparison is done on the basis of historical data. It is interesting to see how deviations between the observed results and a standard are expressed. Additional thought should be given to the presentation of percentage differences.

There should be a balanced distribution between financial information and nonfinancial information. Financial information is necessary for the evaluation of the rate of return and the financial position. In addition, financial comparisons are useful for analyzing issues that are different by nature but still associated with each other.

Quantitative information is usually necessary for managing organizations from specific angles of approach. For example, you can analyze market shares, productivity figures, comparisons with competitors, or information about personnel.

4.4 The Effectiveness and Efficiency of Data Files

In this section, particular attention will be paid to the evaluation of the effectiveness and efficiency of creating, updating, and using files as well as producing and further using documents. In regard to the evaluation of the effectiveness and the efficiency of applied files, it is advisable to make a distinction between

▲ *Files that are stored in the data processing equipment.* This may include files that are stored in large central computers, whether or not they are appropriate for users via terminals, as well as the files that are stored in microcomputers.
▲ *Manual files.* This includes all the files that can be manually updated and in which the information is put into particular forms for the benefit of the administrative business processes (for example, in the form

of card systems or sets of forms and a form that can be used with personal computers).

▲ *Document sets for the purpose of storage.* Sets of documents that are primarily set up and saved for the benefit of storing purposes (for example, to satisfy legal requirements) are counted in this category. References for the benefit of the administrative business processes may incidentally come about.

The evaluation of file application can be approached from two different angles, from the setup of the individual files and from the setup of all the files used with one or more administrative business process.

A. Evaluation of the effectiveness and the efficiency of the design of individual files.

The evaluation of the design of the separate data sets takes place in three subphases. These are

1. *The evaluation of the layout of the screen display and printouts of the computerized files.* This evaluation is aimed at the efficiency and clear organization of the arrangement of the computer printouts. The elements of the documents that should be assessed are discussed in appendix XI.
2. *The evaluation of how the file is organized.* This organization can be based on a number of entries:
   • Name
   • Code number
   • Date of input
   • Geographic location
   • Category

   Many files are not arranged according to any specific criterion but are organized according to a primary category (for example, the geographic location) which is then subdivided into a secondary category (for example, the name). For evaluating the organization of files, an assessment of the costs of the following activities should be made:
   • Storing items in the file
   • Looking up items in the file for reference or updating purposes

- Updating the file
- Thinning out the file

The cost evaluation is expressed per unit of time. The costs of the file are defined by the frequency with which the previous activities occur, the length of time that the activity requires each time it is executed, and the cost per time unit for the staff members who execute the activities (hourly pay rate). As part of the evaluation of the effectiveness of the organization, the consequences of changes to the organization methods for the costs of operating a file should be reviewed. This should be done by thinking of alternate organizational methods and comparing the associated costs with the costs of the existing system. Computerizing files with the help of database packages (both on large computers and on microcomputers) solves most of the selecting and sorting problems. However, the significance of the cost of memory space and processing increases with computerization.

3. *An assessment of the physical capacity of the file.* The influence of changes in the material organization of the file should be reviewed during this assessment. One should consider whether computerization of manual files is practical. As far as the use of computer printouts or forms is concerned, the application of microstorage techniques (microfiche, microfilm, etc.) leading to savings should be reviewed. These savings are achieved in the areas of production, reference, and storage (storage-space savings) of the data sets. Apart from this, thought should be given to the replacement of documents, which must be saved on the basis of legal requirements and are subject to a number of restrictions. Government approval may be required. One of the terms for obtaining this approval is the presence of (manageable) procedures so that complete and accurate documentation of the data is guaranteed.

The (constant) lowering of costs of personal computers may bring the justification for computerization of data files closer. This may also involve files for personal use. Recently released file management software packages are very easy to use and offer a range of sorting and selecting options.

Sometimes it is advisable to change the physical structure of a file without applying advanced techniques; for example, through the implementation of special selection techniques or the conversion of data sets on paper in document files. Thought should be given to the fact that the most important costs in the management of data sets are the personnel costs. The costs of the managed material usually play a lesser role.

B. The evaluation of the efficiency of the organization of files used with one or more administrative business process.

This evaluation identifies unnecessary duplicates in connection with entering data into one or several files within the process under study and other processes throughout the organization. Customer lists are a good illustration of unnecessary duplicates. An analysis of the necessary duplicates and other inefficient activities in referencing and updating the files should also be done. This evaluation should include the files that are stored by the computerized data processing equipment, in both large mainframe computers and microcomputers. One must take into account that inefficiency in the design of the data sets cannot always be corrected in a simple manner. Often with complex applications, the opportunity to change computerized files in the short term is lacking because all these files are coupled with extensive program alterations. On the other hand, geographic or functional distances (for example, the files are located in different departments) that are based on considerations other than efficiency are not the sole consideration related to file locations (for example, the availability of information when data processing capabilities or data files are not available). The performance of these analyses is not always advisable. It is recommended that one form a broad diagram of the possibilities for change before starting the analyses.

The assessment of the organization of a file is found in figures 4.E and 4.F. In figure 4.E, the different applied files are compared with each other with regard to the primary entry (the selection criteria), the items to which the file relates (such as personnel data, data about stocks, etc.), and the characteristics (information) that are stored in the files for each of these items. It is advisable to draft a separate overview for each item. In figure 4.F, the data sets and the characteristics associated with an activity are specified for each activity. A coding system indicates whether the file is updated, the data are referenced or borrowed, or the file is thinned out or data are cleared from it. The sorting activity is represented by the circles, squares, etc. on the diagram. The file that is related to the activities is specified by the letters A, B, C, etc. These letters agree with the file codes in figure 4.E.

Date:	1 - 30 - 1992	Document code:						
Project:	Adm. Organization	Project phase:	Analysis					
Project team:	Human Resources	Subject area:	Human resources management process					
Documentarian: J. Willemse		Subject:	Human resources data file application					

No.	Name / Code ² / Feature	Data set						
		Pers. form.	Pers. chart	Educ. chart	Position sum.	Subj. chart	Salary file	Travel chart
		A	B	C	D	E	F	G
	Primary entry ¹	1	1	2	18	17	2	6
	Secondary entry ¹		1			1		2
1	Employee number	x	x	x	x	x	x	x
2	Name	x	x	x	x	x	x	x
3	Date of birth	x	x	x			x	
4	Place of birth	x						
5	Address	x	x		x	x	x	x
6	City	x	x		x	x	x	x
7	Zip code	x	x		x	x	x	
8	Telephone no.	x			x	x		
9	Nationality	x			x	x		
10	Marital status	x	x		x	x	x	
11	Number of children	x	x				x	
12	Subtract particular expenses	x	x				x	
13	Salary payment method	x	x				x	
14	Education expenses	x		x				
15	Education results	x		x				
16	Current education	x		x				
17	Department/account	x	x	x		x	x	x
18	Position	x		x	x		x	x
19	Salary	x					x	x
20	Travel reimbursement	x					x	x
21	Hours per week	x	x				x	x
22	Rank	x	x			x	x	x
23	Age	x	x			x	x	
24	Date of employment	x	x			x	x	x
25	Education reimbursement	x		x			x	
26	Vacation days	x	x			x		

1. Feature number
2. See Figure 5B

FIGURE 4.E Diagram of the contents of data sets

In the business consulting field, a microcomputer is used for filling in the diagrams. The advantage of this is that one is no longer bound to the physical limitations of the forms in figures 4.E and 4.F. In addition, automated counts can take place and duplicates and omissions are immediately pointed out. Besides, the processing time is decreased because of the use of automated symbols and simple correction procedures.

On the basis of figures 4.E and 4.F in combination with process documentation (in accordance with the techniques described in chapter 3), an opinion can be formed about the effectiveness and efficiency of the design

Date:	30 - 1- 1992	Document code:	
Project:	Adm. Organization	Project phase:	Analysis
Project team:	Human Resources	Subject area:	Human resources management processes
Documentarian: J. Willemse		Subject:	Files applied in processing new hires

Diagram matrix (rows numbered 26 down to 1):

#	Data element
26	Vacation days
25	Education reimbursement
24	Date of employment
23	Age
22	Rank
21	Hours per week
20	Travel reimbursement
19	Salary
18	Position
17	Department/account
16	Current education
15	Education results
14	Education expenses
13	Salary payment method
12	Subtract particular expenses
11	Number of children
10	Marital status
9	Nationality
8	Telephone No.
7	Zip code
6	City
5	Address
4	Place of birth
3	Date of birth
2	Name
1	Employee number

Activity (columns): Fill in personnel chart · Document rank and age · Contract manager · Process position summary · Allowable travel compensation · Allowable educ. compensation · Fill in vacation chart · Fill in pers. chart · Enter into payroll · Etc.

Legend:
⬦ = Change in Data set A.
⌐A⌐ = Remove from Data set A.
Ⓐ = Record in Data set A.
☐B = Refer to Data set B.

Symbols:
1. Should correspond with other documents
2. The letters A, B, C, etc. should correspond to the data set codes in figure 4.E.

FIGURE 4.F   Diagram of the use of data sets

and the application of the different techniques. The possibilities for combining files and for concentrating activities can be analyzed on the basis of this opinion. From the figures, it can be concluded that relevant duplicates exist between the information on the personnel form, the personnel chart, and the computer entry form. Further, it is advisable to see if

- ▲ The personnel chart can be left to expire because the personnel form and the computer output can be used for reference.
- ▲ The few data that are documented on the personnel form but not on the personnel chart can be recorded on the personnel chart or in the computer, or the desired reference can be taken from one of the other files.
- ▲ The education chart (C) or the travel chart (G) can be combined with the remaining data set.
- ▲ The data recorded on the different forms and charts (study, travel, costs, vacation, and personnel data) can be recorded together in one file in a microcomputer designated for this purpose (all of these combining data with the payroll file).

Combining files should result in a decrease in the number of activities associated with the data sets (therefore, less data need to be documented and entered). The process documentation should be used with these techniques to see if geographic or functional positions possibly obstruct the aforementioned changes. If the same information is necessary in different departments (for example, the travel chart is located in a separate department), it should be determined whether one can work with terminals or microcomputers that are attached to each other or with copies or carbon copies of the remaining documentation (personnel chart, personnel form, or computer information).

4.5   The Analysis of On-Time Completion and Cycle Time

The techniques that can be applied with regard to the element of time can be divided into two groups:

- ▲ Techniques for quantifying the on-time completion of an administrative business process
- ▲ Techniques for analyzing the cycle time

These analyses should be performed when there is evidence of processes not being completed on time. The processing operations are backlogged. This becomes evident because of delayed delivery times, cancellations by clients, or the frequent use of emergency or temporary procedures (in the case of a computerized payroll department paying advances or updating extensive manual data sets because the regular computer information is produced later). In addition, the need for performing a time analysis can result from the routing analysis discussed in section 4.7.

An analysis of the on-time completion of the processes should take place first. If from this analysis it appears that there are hardly any delays, there is no direct need to expand the analysis to include cycle time. If processes are completed late, the routing of the respective processes should be analyzed. Whether or not the following occur can be determined from the analysis:

▲ Many departments are involved with the process in which documents are frequently transported from one department to another
▲ Only a few departments are involved with the process but documents are frequently transported between departments
▲ Only one or a few departments are involved with the execution of the process

If only one department or a few departments are involved with the administrative business process, the causes of the delays can sometimes be quickly determined. At other times, an analysis of the cycle time in an individual department should be performed, particularly if many individuals in the department are involved with the process and/or if there are a number of reworked cycles imbedded in the process. The analysis should be developed as a specific study of the cycle time of the process in and between the different departments. This is the case when multiple transfers of documents/information occur between departments. The time that the documents reside in the different departments and the time that is required for the different activities should be documented (in terms of both delays and processing time) as well as the time necessary for transporting the documents (for example, by the internal mail system).

The difference between both analyses is illustrated in figure 4.G. The general process diagram presents the processing of a new hire. The on-time completion is measured by recording a number of new-hire measurements at the start and end of the process (represented by an A). In addition, the on-time execution of the process measurements measures the cycle time (represented by a B).

These analyses are laborious. It is worth processing the observations with personal computers and software specifically developed for this purpose.

Date:	8 - 15 - 1992	Document code:	
Project:	Adm. Organization	Project phase:	Analysis
Project team:	Human Resources	Subject area:	Processing new hires
Documentarian:	J. de Wit	Subject:	Global process overview

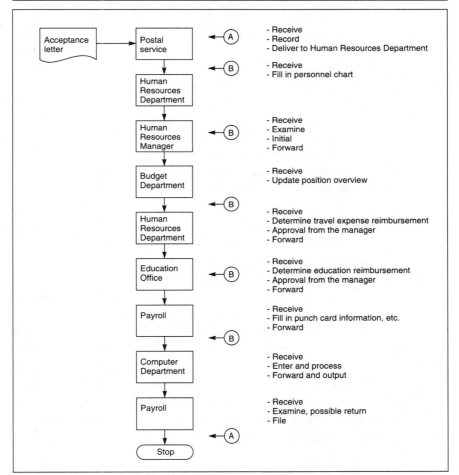

FIGURE 4.G   Example analysis of the on-time completion and cycle time

4.5.1 Analysis of the On-Time Completion of Processes

With this analysis, the length of time between the following is charted:

▲ *The moment at which the process is started (starting boundary).* In a recruiting and selection process, this moment may start when the decision is made to attract a new staff member. In a process for processing new-hire information, this moment may be when the job-offer letter is mailed. In an order management process, the start may be defined by receipt of the order.

▲ *The moment at which the process is completed (ending boundary).* With the previously mentioned examples, the completion time may be the moment that the job-offer letter is mailed, the moment that the data of the newly hired staff member is completely processed in the payroll and human resources departments, and the point in time that the sold merchandise and its associated invoice are mailed.

For every process that is analyzed, the action or occurrence with which the process starts and the action with which the process is considered to be complete have already been established. The activities that form a component of the process that is to be analyzed should be defined (the receipt of the health insurance acceptance letter or the pension insurance can belong to the administrative processing of a new hire).

The analysis can be carried out according to two methods: by performing a random sample survey with regard to the already completed processes, and by recording observations of processes that need to be completed.

If a random sample survey is performed with regard to the already completed processes, links with the documents produced as part of these processes and the dates of the documents should be sought. The study should be performed according to the steps given below.

1. *Define the scope of the random sample survey.* The references at the end of this book are recommended for learning about methods for determining the random sample survey population.
2. *Decide which of the cases from the population should be studied in more detail.*
3. *Standardize the required cycle time.* This standardization can be based on the number of days after the start in which the process

should be completed (for example, the case of processing sales orders) or it can be based on a specific date by which the process should be completed (a new hire should be processed by the time the next payroll is processed).

4. *Execute the random sample survey.* For every observation, the starting date, the actual completion date, and the normative completion date should be recorded. When the process needs to be completed by a certain date, a normative starting date should be noted. This beginning date is necessary to determine whether the cause of a possible delay is due to slow processing or to a late starting date.

5. *Determine the number of work days for each observation.* These should be calculated by the beginning and ending date and for the exceeded cycle time between the norm and the completion date.

6. *Calculate*
   - The average length of time it takes to complete the process
   - The number of times that the norm was exceeded
   - The average excess (the norm period and the number of times that it is exceeded by a particular period [arrange by class])

Although process averages are a good starting point, the major problem related to the process is not always based on averages. Customers are often lost not because of the average cycle time but because of longer-than-average cycle time. This means that the data collected should include a distribution of measurement data and the percentage of items that go through recycled loops. This will allow measurements such as sigma cycle times to be calculated and considered during the process-improvement cycle. Due to the complexity of some of the processes and the related data, computer process simulation models are created to aid in these calculations. Typical commercial programs that can help with these calculations are ones provided by EDGE Software in Pleasanton, California, and Pro-Model in Orem, Utah (for more information on simulation, see chapter 5). If a process should be completed by a particular date, a calculation of the number of times that the norm was exceeded because the process was started late and the number of times that the norm was exceeded because the processing was late should be done.

Time analysis can also take place by observing the process that still needs to be completed. This method should be used in cases when either the basic documents or the dates of these documents are not available.

The observation and documentation can be done by

▲ The individuals involved with the administrative business process
▲ An independent, specifically appointed observer (only if the time interval between the start and end of the process is not too long)
▲ Other staff members or departments that may or may not be involved with the actual process

An objective observation can be guaranteed if the staff members who are directly involved with the process will not be directly influenced by the final results of the study or if the results cannot be influenced by them.

The analysis should take into account any seasonal patterns concerning the amounts that are to be processed. The number of new hires, orders, etc. to be processed can fluctuate per week or per month according to seasonal patterns. Therefore, it may be necessary to subdivide the random sample survey according to weeks or months. One-time backlogs in the complete work cycle should then be accounted for. Figure 4.H is an example of the possible results of a time analysis.

4.5.2 Techniques for Analyzing Cycle Time

Cycle time analyses are associated with the quantification of the on-time completion of processes. If the previous analysis indicates that the processes are not being completed on time, a more detailed study of the areas where delays originated can be performed with the help of a cycle time analysis. An-

Processing / Process	Processed before entry date[1]	Processed on entry date	Number of month(s) processed after entry date			
			0-1 month	1-2 months	2-3 months	3 months
Dismissal	2%	80%	15%	3%	–	–
New hire	–	15%	56%	20%	7%	2%
Promotion	–	30%	22%	15%	15%	18%
Change of work time	–	37%	23%	17%	13%	10%
	1%	40%	32%	14%	7%	6%

1. This means the date on which the dismissal, the appointment, etc. comes into effect based on an agreement among those involved.

FIGURE 4.H Example of the results of a time analysis

other reason for performing these analyses is to define the routing of the workflow through the administrative business processes, as described in section 4.7.

Analysis of the cycle time should first be approached by drawing up the routing diagrams (activity flowchart). The different departments that are involved with the administrative business process and the primary activities of the departments should be recorded on these diagrams. On this basis and with the aid of having studied the documents employed during the process, *measurement points* can be determined. These measurement points are as follows:

- ▲ Data from sending and receiving external documents
- ▲ Initializing data
- ▲ Data from waybills
- ▲ Data from records relating to registers (for example, books containing mailing records)
- ▲ Receipt and mailing data, such as the information (dates) stamped on documents by the various departments

It makes sense to associate the measurement points with the arrival and departure of documents in and out of departments. Within departments, measurement points should be associated with the execution or completion of principal activities. To determine the scope and frequency of random sample surveys, the complexity of the items being studied and the related measurements need to be considered. In collecting data related to cycle time, the time intervals between the different measurement points and related wait time need to be considered. The sum of the average cycle time between measurement points is usually used to define the total process cycle time. In some cases, average cycle time is plotted and a Monte Carlo analysis is used to define average process cycle time. For every observation, the number of workdays between the successive measurement points should be calculated. The complete number of workdays between the first and the last measurement point represents the cycle time per observation. The average number of days between the two measurement points for all the observations represents the average cycle time between both measurement points.

Sometimes, it seems that a particular process is executed according to a number of variables. For example, a purchase order that is less than $1,000 can be written and approved by any manager and sent directly to purchasing. Purchase orders between $1,000 and 10,000 require the approval of both first- and second-level managers. Purchase orders over $10,000 require the approval of the first- and second-level managers and the controller before being accepted by the purchasing department. In these cases, the quantification for each of the variables should be done separately. With the quantification, seasonal influences should be considered.

On the basis of the completed quantification and the associated calculations, a cycle time overview can be drawn up. An example is presented in figure 4.I. For the conclusions made with respect to figure 4.I, see the explanation for figure 4.J.

Although average delay and cycle-time figures provide sufficient information, averages often provide a false sense of security. Organizations lose customers over the abnormal rather than the average. It is for this reason that distribution data are collected and the negative two-sigma value is used to define abnormal cycle times that can have a negative impact on the organization's customers. The complexity of many junction points with the processes that allow only part of the process flow to progress through the different branches can make it very difficult to calculate the cycle time and cost. To overcome these difficulties, simulation models are prepared to perform a Monte Carlo analysis, exercising the process through thousands of cycles to define average and worst-case critical paths, cycle time, and cost. For more information on simulation modeling, see chapter 5.

Activity measurement point	Activity done by department	Cycle time (in work days)[1]	
		New hires	Promotions
1 Receive proposal	Postal service	–	–
2 Complete pers. chart	Human resources	4	2
3 Document rank, etc.	Human res. manager	6	5
4 Approve	Department head	2	2
5 Update position	Budget	3	3
6 Determine travel reimb.	Human resources	4	3
7 Determine educ. reimb.	Education office	2	1
8 Fill in vacation chart	Human resources	3	2
9 Enter into payroll	Payroll	5	5
		29	23

1. This means the number of days that pass between the date the activity on the same line is completed and the date when the previous activity was completed

FIGURE 4.I   Example of a cycle time overview

On the basis of the cycle-time overview, the activities that result in delays can be identified. The analysis still does not provide one with an understanding of the causes of these delays. Therefore, a more detailed study of the departments and the tasks where the delays occur should be performed. First, a connection between larger than average delays or delays beyond the developed norm should be sought. For each of these delays, the reasons behind the long processing times should be studied, resulting in an overview of how often the different delay causes manifest themselves.

If a study of the causes of delays is not possible for processes that are already completed, the activities of the involved departments as well as involved tasks will need to be separately observed.

As with the analysis of the on-time completion of administrative business processes, the study of the cycle time of an administrative business process can also use the observation methods of processes that still need to be completed (see section 4.5.1). The drawbacks specified in section 4.5.1 also apply here. An advantage of this method is that the observation can completely concentrate on the desired analysis results. With the execution of random sample surveys of already completed processes, one should search for links with data that may not always be completely appropriate but are on hand.

4.6   The Relationship of Activities and Functions to the Administrative Organization

In section 4.4, thought is given to the meaning of clustering activities over organizational entities as part of using files efficiently. It was proposed that using files and technical administrative enablers as efficiently as possible could be one of the evaluation criteria in studying the division of administrative activities among different departments. Clustering those activities that make use of the same files or the same enablers should be strived for.

Frequently, similar activities are grouped together within a department to increase the knowledge and resource base. Placing similar activities with one individual or group of individuals promotes the proficiency with which those activities are performed. Grouping activities that require an approximately equal level of education and intelligence is often beneficial. This is inspired by the wish to make optimal use of human capabilities.

The similarity of activities can be analyzed by dividing the activities into a number of activity categories. In defining the activity categories, the following should be considered:

▲ The types of *operations* that are performed, such as typing, coding, controlling, etc.
▲ The kinds of *accounts* that must be updated, such as ledgers, accounts receivable, payrolls, accounts payable, etc.

How the different activity categories are divided among the different individuals as well as departments can then be analyzed.

The activities are then subdivided into a number of categories:

▲ *Policy preparation activities,* such as formulating proposals concerning the administrative organization
▲ *Policy modifying activities,* such as giving direction to an administrative department
▲ *Tasks that require particular capabilities in order to be performed,* such as managing a complex payroll
▲ *Tasks that are easy to perform,* such as updating sales overviews, filing invoices, etc.

The clustering of activities is evaluated by ranking the activities in their appropriate categories and then considering how the different categories are divided among the individuals and departments.

The manner in which different sets of tasks result in optimal job satisfaction can also be a criterion for the evaluation. This indicates whether the set of tasks for each individual or each department provides enough variation and freedom. Likewise, it is also important whether within the set of tasks, a comprehensive part of the administrative business process can be reviewed and performed.

The analysis can also be aimed at the question of whether the degree of association between the different activities is reflected in the distribution of these tasks among departments and individuals. From this point of view, the activities are studied particularly to see if those with the closest relationships are located together. For this purpose, a matrix is used, where for each administrative business process, the different activities are represented vertically and horizontally. In the matrix, the relationship category under which the activity should be grouped is specified. These categories are

▲ *Interrelationship.* This means that if there is interaction between a number of activities, the activities may influence each other. For example, a client orders an item by telephone, the availability of the item is looked up in the stock department, the client is informed that the item is not available, the client orders an alternative item, etc. With interrelationships, the relationship between activities is strong.

▲ *Successive relationships.* The different activities are performed in a particular order. For example, the order is written on an order form, items listed on the order form are retrieved from the warehouse, etc. The relationship of all of the activities performed by the different departments or individuals can vary from weak to relatively strong. The relationship between the activities of interfacing departments should become stronger if the number of times that messages or documents are exchanged between the departments increases. For example, the relationship of procedures in human resource management and storage management tasks in a large organization. For every activity in the new-hire procedure in human resources, the storage management task includes removing the personnel record. After the activity has been performed, the record is put away again. This happens eight times for each new hire. The relationship between the tasks of both units is qualified as being strong.

The objective of the analysis is to obtain an understanding of the extent to which closely associated activities are distributed among a number of departments and individuals. This distribution requires extra approval activities in the form of verbal communication, the exchange of forms, the exchange of data sets, etc. In addition, data related to the approval costs should be collected and studied with the objective of minimizing this no-value-added cost.

By regrouping the activities to correspond more with the extent of their relationships, improvements can be realized with regard to costs and cycle time.

The way in which disposal, performance, storage, documentation, and control functions within one administrative business process or within a group of administrative business processes are divided among different departments can also shape the subject matter of an analysis for evaluating the internal control. More attention is paid to this matter in section 4.8.

You should take into account that a manager of professional staff members cannot function efficiently unless she is given at least five individuals and at the most twelve individuals to manage (span of control). With fewer individuals, there are too few management tasks to fill a complete day. With more than twelve individuals, the manager threatens to be overburdened because there is not enough time to give sufficient thought to all his responsibilities.

The different points of view just mentioned often contradict each other. Striving for optimal task sets from the viewpoint of job satisfaction contradicts the criterion of striving for similarity of tasks. With the evaluation of the clustering of administrative tasks, thought should be given to the fact that improving the clustering with respect to one of the criteria often leads to worsening the clusters with respect to other criteria. For example, if all the engineers are organized in one department and the production personnel are in a completely different function, the production function may not be provided with the proper level of engineering support. It makes sense to include all the criteria while performing the evaluation. Clustering of activities should be done so that the considerations of the different criteria are as much in agreement with each other as possible or at least that as much contradiction is eliminated as possible.

4.7 The Routing of Administrative Business Processes

4.7.1 The Effectiveness and Efficiency of the Routing of Administrative Business Processes

The issues surrounding the routing of administrative business processes are particularly important when considering that the administrative business processes can be greatly impacted based on the physical location of documents. This is because transferring documents is a time-consuming activity and because after documents have been transferred, the administrative processing operations must be resumed. This may result in delays. In addition, documents may be lost in transport. There is also the danger that transferring documents and doing the processing elsewhere may cause errors.

Sometimes the routing can be simplified by changing the order of the activities so that the number of transfers is reduced. This usually decreases the chance that a document will be lost and decreases the cycle time.

Results can sometimes be achieved by changing the routing of different subprocesses. For example, in a large organization, the documents for processing new hires, promotions, awards, and educational allowances followed a route that passed through six departments: recruiting, education and training, housing information, performance reviews, human resources, and payroll. Only one or two departments were involved with many of the (sub)processes. By drafting the individual routing diagrams for each (sub)process, a considerable reduction of the cycle time was achieved because, for each (sub)process, the documents were only forwarded to those departments that applied them.

The initial information about the routes of documents is acquired by studying the filled-in documentation diagrams. The process diagrams, the form management diagrams, and/or the form flow diagrams can be applied in this context. Whether further analysis is necessary can be determined on the basis of these diagrams. These documentation techniques provide understanding of the flow of documents for each administrative business process. Sometimes several pages are used for this purpose. That means that these techniques are not the most appropriate for reviewing the overview of the document flow of all of the administrative business processes together. To obtain an understanding of the flow of documents, see figure 4.J. In this figure, a number of administrative business processes are summarized. The diagram lists the department and the complete number of steps that are performed for each administrative business process. In addition, the number of transfers of documents between one department and another is specified. The quantitative data for each process are recorded in the rows. The number of times that documents are transferred from one department to another combined with the number of departments that are involved with the process gives information about the potential existence of delays in the cycle time of the process.

Process	Number of involved (sub)departments	Number of steps (activities) (sub)department	Number of transfers from one to another
New hires	7	140	35
Dismissals	7	60	15
Extensions	7	40	12
Promotions	7	40	20
Educ. reimbursement	7	20	10

FIGURE 4.J   Example of a routing overview

Thus, one can decide on whether an additional analysis of the cycle time is desired or not. The study can also be an indication of whether it would be advisable to eventually recluster the activities or combine the departments together.

In the example presented in figure 4.J, it was concluded that the performance of an analysis of the on-time completion of processes was desired. This analysis brought substantial delays to light (see figure 4.H in section 4.5.1). One of the actions that was undertaken was to introduce changes to the routing of the involved processes. The processes were split into subprocesses that were executed in parallel. The number of involved departments was limited, and each department received only those documents that were necessary for its own activities. The maximum number of consecutive department document transfers was reduced to seven.

With the analysis of the routing of documents, the efficiency and the costs of applied and possible alternative document transferring methods should be considered (tube mail, PC networks, phone mail systems, etc.). The opportunities for applying forms of electronic mail (E-mail, Internet, etc.) are included in studies about automating an office.

4.8 Determining the Accuracy and Thoroughness of the Data Processing Operations

4.8.1 Introduction

Internal control, aimed at the accuracy and thoroughness of data processing operations, is understood in this framework to be all the controls and checks that are performed by or on behalf of the management of an organization on the information system, administrative organization, and the management of the business processes. This includes the measures of internal control that are built into the administrative business processes and the control actions that are performed by an independent control office.

The primary starting point of these analyses is to evaluate whether the administrative business processes are organized such that the resulting information management system accurately and completely represents the issues with which the information is concerned. For evaluating the internal control, it is necessary that you have a good idea of the organization of the administrative business process. The insight necessary for this evaluation can partially be obtained from the form management diagram (see section 3.9.8) or the form circulation diagram (see section 3.9.9). Both overviews are aimed at further considering the separate processes. The essential overview of all the processes should be obtained by developing a list of control actions of all the processes. Figure 4.K is an example of such a list. If an extra column is added that specifies what must be done if the particular activity is or is not completely executed, it is called a *control structure diagram.*

Date:	03 - 13 - 1992	Document code:	
Project:	Adm. Organization	Project phase:	Analysis
Project team:	Purchasing procedure	Subject area:	Purchasing process
Documentarian: P. Jansen		Subject:	Overview of pur. invoice activities and control

Process No.	Dep. No.	Process Description	Contr. No.[1]	Control description
1	2	3	4	5
16.1	20	Process purchasing invoices	C1	Check invoice
16.1	21	Process purchasing invoices	C2	Compare price, number, description, terms with the order bill
16.1	21	Process purchasing invoices	C3	Check initials of the authorizing staff member
16.1	24	Process purchasing invoices	C4	Compare temporary purchasing book printout with punch card
16.1	24	Process purchasing invoices	C5	Compare temporary purchasing book printout with final printout
12.2	8	Pay purchasing invoices	C1	Compare invoice to payment notice
12.2	8	Pay purchasing invoices	C2	Compare invoice to payment list
12.2	6	Pay purchasing invoices	C3	Compare the payment order authorization letter
12.2	8	Pay purchasing invoices	C4	Compare daily bank account statement with authorization letter
1.4	20	Enter invoices	–	Check the invoice for name, date, address
2.1	41	Receive items	–	Count and compare with package invoice
2.3	41	Inspect items	–	Quality control done by inspector
6.4	21	Approve invoice in purchasing	C1	Check for order bill and bill of receipt
6.4	18	Approve invoice in purchasing	C2	Check inspector's report

1. The numbers should correspond to the numbers of the control activities in appendix IV, figure B.

FIGURE 4.K Typical list of control activities

Understanding can also be obtained by drawing a global overview diagram, discussed in section 3.9.4, of the administrative business process. If only the global overview and neither the form management nor the form circulation diagram is appropriate, then these diagrams should still be drawn up, or the list of control actions should be added to the global overview, as recorded in figure 4.K.

In figures 4.L and 4.M, a second example of a control plan is recorded. It involves a human resources and payroll department. The complete plan of control activities is presented in figure 4.L, and the elaboration of control action C13 is presented in figure 4.M.

4.8.2 Evaluating the Organization of the Internal Control System

The organization of the internal control system should be evaluated according to the following steps:

A.   Formulate the internal control system
B.   Evaluate the internal control system

Contr. No.	Control description
	Appendix
	Introduction
C1	*The formal control of the accuracy, completeness, and reasons for a suggested transaction*
C2	*The programmed input control by the decentral data entry system*
C3	*The verification control of entered transactions by the controller*
C4	*The acceptance control by the central computer system*
C5	*The probability control by the central computer system*
C6	*The user control by means of the logbook overview*
C7	*The control of the total contacts*
C8	*The control of the total route*
C9	*The control of the specific transactions*
C10	*The control of concluding transactions that must still be changed*
C11	*The control of concluding signal lists*
C12	*The control of the calculations*
C13	*The control of managing codes in payroll and human resources information systems*
C14	*The control of recorded data*
C15	*The availability control*
C16	*The control of the functioning and output of the decentral control measures*
	The chain of control
	Schematic overview of the chain of control

FIGURE 4.L   Example of a quality control plan: personnel and payroll department

Contr. No.	Control description
C13	*The control of managing codes in the payroll and human resources information system*
	Objectives : Checking the use of codes in the payroll and human resources information system
	Design : The codes are checked monthly on the basis of the overview of entries
	Operation : The use of codes is checked with the help of the overviews mentioned above and the tables recorded in the Human Resources and Payroll Manual. The H.R. department manager is informed of verified deviations. The H.R. department is responsible for making corrections. The H.R. Internal Control department monitors the progress of the corrections by means of the overviews and the following processing month. See the applicable administrative organization process concerning the management of tables for further information.
	Documentation : The verified deviations are mentioned in the report of the table management project team. This report is stored by the H.R. Internal Control department during the current and following year

FIGURE 4.M   Example of the elaboration of control measure 13

C. Evaluate the complete internal control system (for all of the administrative business processes together)

D. Formulate the basic principles for changing the processes and/or the system

A. Formulate the Internal Control System

The organization of administrative business processes should sufficiently guarantee that

▲ The basic material that is applied is accurate and complete. This basic material should consist of order forms for the sales department, time sheets for temporary employment agencies, warehouse delivery receipts, cash accounts, etc.

▲ The basic material is processed accurately and thoroughly. This processing will involve the execution of calculations, (re)clustering, etc.

▲ The basic material is recorded in the administrative business process and further processed on time.

▲ The decision and performance activities that relate to the administrative business process are done within the framework determined for this purpose. This framework is formed by the qualifications and the rules that should be employed.

These requirements will need to be distinctly and clearly formulated by the PIT. The guarantees that must be present to ensure the thoroughness and accuracy of the data, etc. should be defined for each administrative business process.

B. Evaluate the Internal Control System

The system of internal control should be set up so that unintentional and intentional errors and gaps are ascertained and rectified in an on-time fashion. First, the functional division organizational structure should be evaluated. The use of a functional division structure provides an independent check and balance system. The functional division does not need to be limited to the staff members of departments in the actual organization. Good use can also be made of the interests and operations of third parties (for example, the control of bank account statements by account holders forms an element of internal control for banks, and ISO 9000 registries provide a third-party evaluation).

DEFINITION | **Functional Division** is the dividing of activities between individuals and/or departments from the point of view of opposite interests.

Functional division can be introduced between the different phases of the processing cycle of a transaction so that divisions are introduced between the disposal, performance, storage, documentation, and control functions. The disposal function makes decisions that have repercussions for the administrative business processes, such as closing sales orders, closing purchase orders, or preventing new employees from being hired. Examples of the performance function are the activities in a shipping department, a receiving department, or the recruiting of personnel. The storage function relates to stocking a warehouse with merchandise. At the same time, the storage function can include the deposit or storage of claims and debts (for example, as done by an accounts receivable department or a loan department) and even matters such as patents, know-how, licenses, etc. The control functions include the performance control actions. These are the control actions that are built into an administrative business process (the shipping department compares the delivery receipt of the warehouse with the order receipt of the sales department) as well as the control actions that are carried out by an independent unit (control department).

Functional division can be introduced into the different phases of the flow of merchandise or services through an organization. In a production organization, this functional division can be related to the distribution of activities between the purchasing, production, and sales departments. In a bank, this functional division can be realized by accommodating the recording and putting out of funds in a particular market in two separate departments.

A third possibility for the introduction of functional divisions is formed by splitting the activities for the different services or goods that the organization produces or purchases. In a sales organization, the sale of the various assorted parts can be accommodated in several departments. In banks, the recording of funds in the private market and the recording of funds in the money market can be performed by two different departments. The splitting of tasks in an organization happens on the basis of commercial or other considerations. The promotion of good internal control is merely one of the determining factors.

The use of automated systems in an organization places particular requirements on the measures of internal control due to the following factors:

▲ Documentation of basic data does not occur many times in a number of data sets (manual and located in several places) but happens through a one-time entry in one or a few interconnected (computerized and concentrated in a particular location) data sets (see also figures 4.N and 4.O in sections 4.13.2 and 4.13.3).

▲ The integration of data sets decreases the possibility of having a number of staff members process the data and compare the results.

▲ The integration of successive administrative actions decreases the human interference in an administrative process and thereby decreases the possibilities for building in the functional divisions. This may lead to a decreasing number of links (forms, etc.) that must be understood by the employees or be legible to the employees. Sometimes, the need for functional divisions is eliminated as the process is completely automated; for example, during the exchange of data on magnetic tapes between organizations.

▲ The concentration of activities in the computer center (such as developing programs, data entry, storing and running programs, storing files, looking after the output, etc.) also prompts the use of special control measures.

With regard to the internal control, guarantees should be made that

▲ The programs that are used lead to the desired results.
▲ The correct and complete data are entered in the computer.
▲ The correct programs and data sets are used.
▲ The equipment functions well without undesired interference while programs are being run.
▲ The data sets are protected against disasters.
▲ No improper or illegal corrections are introduced into the data sets.
▲ Reconstruction is possible in case the actual computer breaks down.

These guarantees can also be realized by

▲ Introducing functional divisions between the drafted system requirements and user specifications, the technical system development (programming), the evaluation of the developed systems, and the actual processing of data. The users should be convinced that the developed programs will lead to the desired results. The installation of the functional divisions previously mentioned should help identify unauthorized program use.
▲ Introducing functional divisions with the processing of the data between the entering, the controlling, the storing of data sets and computer programs, and the processing of the data by the computer.
▲ Building in specific control measures in the computerized processing processes, such as programmed controls, application of control numbers, procedural regulations, periodic performance of Electronic Data Processing (EDP) audits, etc.

Often in small organizations, a strict division of functions is not possible or efficient. In these small organizations, one individual may be responsible for the total process, making it impractical to provide value-added internal reviews at the end of individual subprocesses or activities. For example, in a very small organization, one person is often accountable for the entire product design activity and is the only person who is capable of analyzing the effectiveness of the individual activities within the new product development cycle.

Combinations of different functions can always occur. Combinations should be prevented so that data processing errors do not remain unnoticed.

The established functional divisions and control measures should be reviewed with an evaluation to see if they are adequate for satisfying the requirements described in step A. The shortcomings and their causes should be specified.

C. Evaluate the Complete Internal Control System

The internal control system should be logically designed. Even though the internal control of the individual processes can be quantified as sufficient, this does not exclude the opportunity for individual staff members to make errors (example: transactions that are incomplete, inaccurate, recorded or processed late, or illegitimate). The possible occurrence of similar gaps in the overall control system should be brought to light by evaluating the organization of the overall control system. This can be done effectively on the basis of the global overview discussed in appendix IV and the control actions listed in figure 4.K. A global overview of the internal control measures will be covered in chapter 5 (figure 5.E).

D. Formulate the Basic Principles for Changing the Processes and/or System

The way in which the internal controls that are integrated into the administrative business process can be improved is determined on the basis of the outcomes from *B* and *C*.

4.8.3 The Functioning of the Internal Control System

A confirmation that the internal control system is well set up does not mean that it will actually function as intended. It is always possible that the administrative business process will function differently than described by the diagrams. The performance of control actions is often omitted. It is therefore necessary that the actual functioning of the internal control system is evaluated from time to time.

No methodology is presented here for evaluating the functioning of the internal control system because an extensive treatment of the methods and techniques would be necessary. These treatments fall outside the scope of this book. We limit ourselves to describing a number of tools that can be applied in order to assess the functioning of the internal control system. This description is offered to interest the reader in the issues surrounding internal control and to offer assistance for evaluating the actual functioning of the internal control system.

Global relationship controls are applied to compare a series of transactions over a specific period with each other. An example of this is comparing the charges from a particular period for the accounts receivable department with the credits of the sales invoices from the same period. When both accounts are added using separate basic data by separate processes in which a number of control points are integrated, an opinion can be formed, with the help of the global controls, about the size of the recorded sums. The global controls do not show in detail whether the different transaction processes are accurately performed.

The *procedure test* is a study in which the progress of an administrative business process for one or a few transactions is completely followed from beginning to end. On the basis of the documents that are produced during the process and in view of the information in the data sets employed by the documents, you can examine whether the transaction is completely processed according to the instructions. You should pay attention to whether all the control actions are performed in the correct manner. This will occur by again performing the control actions and by reviewing the document to be sure that all of the necessary (control) initials appear on the documents.

With *detailed control,* an activity within an administrative business process that is used with many transactions is analyzed in detail. For example, a detailed control for an order processing process could include reviewing whether the sales invoices are entered correctly, whether the calculations on these invoices are correct, whether the invoices are controlled according to the instructions, etc.

By performing *numeric evaluation,* the PIT forms a numeric opinion about the acceptability of the presented numeric material. The value of a numeric evaluation lies in indicating and assessing the internal difference between different groups of numbers. The numeric evaluation can be done by comparing budgets with the actual results or by evaluating the margins that are realized on the sale of different item categories. The numeric evaluation can also be of importance when analyzing different businesses or parts of businesses.

Account balance statements are used to control whether the balances of accounts receivable, credit department, etc. are recorded correctly. A statement of the balance is provided to the account holders. With positive balance control, the account holder is asked to confirm the accuracy of the balance. With negative balance control, they are asked to respond only if the balance does not agree with their own calculations.

Availability controls are applied to control whether documented assets are available or not. An example of availability control is the inventory of the supplies.

Incidental observation means letting parts of administrative business processes be tested by anonymous groups or individuals. These individuals will usually review a transaction to determine if the activities are completed in the correct manner. An example of incidental observation is conducting test purchases in the different departments of a store to measure how accurately and completely the cashiers enter the sales data. (See section 5.3 for additional information about the design of internal control in information systems.)

4.9 The Efficiency (Productivity) of the Administrative Business Processes

Efficiency (productivity) is a measure of how effectively resources are being used (people, money, space, computer memory, etc). In measuring efficiency, one attempts to form a judgment about the proportional relationship of costs and production in different administrative business processes. The analysis should result in the presentation of a quantity of identifying numbers or ratios that provide an idea of the efficiency of the item being studied.

The analysis is performed by means of the following activities:

1. *Define the products of the administrative business process that are to be studied.* Possible products of an administrative business process are the completed processing of a new hire, an invoice, a reminder/ warning notice, a filled order, etc. It is important to define a small number of products for each process (if possible for each department). The products should be recognizable for staff members. The product must be an independent unit, which means that production of the product should be able to be stopped without affecting other products that are dependent on the output from the process under study. Not all products need to be of a material nature. Products such as participation in consulting or the management of personnel can also be considered.
2. *Define the unit of measurement for each product.* This step defines how the production is measured. With the products mentioned in

activity 1, this can be done by the number of new hires, the number of invoices, the number of reminder notices, the number of filled orders, the number of hours of participation, and the number of personnel who are managed. The units of measurement should be chosen so that they are indicative of the magnitude of the production.

3. *Determine which activities in the administrative business process are associated with which products.* If an activity is performed for a number of products, indicate what proportion of the costs of the activity should be assigned to each of the products.

4. *Determine the costs of the administrative products.* The costs (of personnel, production resources, basic materials, housing, etc.) should be assigned to the activities, and the cost per activity and per product should be added. If costs cannot be directly calculated, cost breakdown techniques should be employed. If personnel costs cannot be directly calculated, the time spent on each activity should be determined by means of time cards, time studies, or time estimates. The personnel costs should then be prorated and divided.

5. *Determine the scope of production.* The scope of production is defined in this activity as the quantity of units processed during the analysis period. Calculate the costs per unit of product. The costs per unit of product are defined by dividing the total quantity of units by the total costs per product. In this manner, the costs per new hire, per invoice, or per reminder notice can be defined.

In each case, quantitative information about the quality of the processes should be analyzed. This information can relate to the number of errors (for example, coding or entry errors as well as the number of missing documents or tools) that are made. This analysis often identifies wasted resources that have a negative impact on the efficiency of the following processes. A quantification of the cycle time may also be necessary (see section 4.5).

4.10 Taking Advantage of the Opportunities for Standardization

The analysis of the opportunities for standardizing administrative business processes will be aimed at studying the equipment that is applied, the office needs, and the ways in which similar activities are performed.

For computerizing the office, standardization of work methods, coding systems, etc. are important conditions for achieving success. An example of performing similar activities in different places is a temporary employment agency, in which the registration of new temporary employees, the recording of customers' needs for temporary employees, and the actual dispatching of temporary employees can happen in about 20 different ways.

Using the techniques to document processes discussed in chapter 3, the similar activities can be localized in different departments. In the individual processes, this is done with the help of the process diagrams.

If the documentation is detailed to the level of activities (see section 3.5), a diagram can be directly formed with regard to the content of the possible differences. With documentation on the level of procedures, more detailed research is necessary. The performance of similar activities within the framework of one process but in different organizational units (for example, the payment of funds in different bank lines) can be indicated by reviewing the organizational structure diagrams and making an inventory of the functions and procedures of each of the separate organizational units. In the analysis of each similar activity, the following should be specified:

▲ Where the activities are performed
▲ In which part of the administrative business process the activities are performed
▲ Why the activities are performed
▲ What the desired outcome of the activities is
▲ Under which conditions the activities should be performed

Using this approach, the PIT can review whether the differences between the departments regarding the objective of the activities, the desired results, and the preconditions are necessary. Thus, you can determine if the activities can be standardized.

4.10.1 Equipment

Standardizing equipment (such as personal computers, standard programs, word processors, copying equipment, etc.) can lead to a number of important advantages; for example, a simplification of maintenance, support, and repair. Less effort is required from the service personnel because the variation in service requirements is removed. Less employee time is required to learn to operate different equipment. At the same time, switching from one machine to another in case one machine breaks down is simplified and therefore sped up.

The study is started by compiling a list of all the equipment that is used in the scope of the administrative business processes. The process, the department, and the activity for which the equipment is used should be specified. If different equipment is operated for these activities, the circumstances in the different departments should be examined to see if the differences are warranted. The purpose of the activities, the speed with which they should be performed, and the extent to which the equipment is used should be reviewed. Based on this information, a picture can be formed of whether it is possible or desirable to standardize the applied equipment.

The analysis will take place with the help of a study about the efficiency of applied enablers, mentioned in section 4.12, and the activities described in section 4.6 as part of the study about clustering activities among departments and individuals.

4.10.2 Office Needs

Standardizing office needs (documents such as forms, charts, storage systems, etc.) aims at reducing their variability and increasing productivity. Lower stocks, simpler ordering procedures, and large-quantity purchases will be made possible. The analysis should be executed similarly to the analysis of standardizing applied equipment.

4.10.3 Work Methods

Often varying work methods are used for performing similar activities in different places. Problems with the exchange of personnel in the case of absence and with the controlling of the activities can originate. In addition, the activities that are performed in different locations can differ. This may obstruct the standardization of equipment or office needs.

4.11 Detecting Duplicates and Superfluous Procedures and Activities

In section 4.4, there is discussion of eliminating superfluous procedures during the use of the files and the production of documents. In addition, it is necessary to discuss the purposes of the different administrative-organizational activities and the need to achieve these purposes. This is necessary because it sometimes develops that activities performed earlier were, but now are no longer, advisable. An illustration of this is the turnover that is recorded daily for each order while the turnover information is documented by an automated system. In almost all organizations, one comes across this kind of situation. This analysis is performed with the help of the form management diagrams, in which the main issues of the administrative business processes are represented. A more detailed study should still be done on the basis of the detailed process diagram that contains broader information than the form management diagram.

The analysis should be done according to the following activities:

1. *The activities should be clustered according to the objectives the PIT wants to achieve with them.* These objectives could be communicating with external authorities by sending documents, distributing internal data about the composition of the sales, etc. It is suggested that a purpose be developed for every process and activity.

2. *A list should be drawn up on which the necessary activities for each objective are reported.* For each activity, the list should indicate whether it also fulfills a function in the scope of achieving other objectives. If this is so, then the possibilities for eliminating the referenced activity are greater than if the activity is performed for only one purpose.

3. *There should be a review to determine if duplicate activities have different objectives.* It is possible that the same activity is performed in different departments to achieve different objectives. These activities can also be spread over different administrative business processes. For example, it is possible that for a review of the detailed sales information by the order handling department, the article codes are grouped as part of the order management function and grouped in the warehouse as part of the warehouse delivery function. A review should be conducted for each of the separate objectives.

4. *The costs of the different activities should be calculated and summed per objective.* This is done by assigning personnel costs and other costs to the activities. For individuals who are occupied with more than one activity, temporary time logs can be used to collect the required data.

5. *A judgment should be made of whether all the activities are essential.* This judgment should be an evaluation of the need to perform all activities for each of the separate objectives. The objectives themselves should not be discussed quite yet. The activities and associated costs should be changed as needed.

6. *An evaluation of the use of automated systems should be undertaken.* If use is made of automated systems during the administrative business process, an evaluation of their use should be undertaken. This activity is aimed at conducting a study of computer applications' ability to eliminate much of the manual data processing operations. Usually improvements in the content and speed of information management are achieved. The training and experience level of the staff members involved with the automated system should be reviewed. The PIT should also determine if the manual files and overviews can be obtained from the computerized system. This is done by using the descriptions of the computer programs, file descriptions, and the overviews produced by the automated system.

7. *Examine whether the objectives could be achieved in any other, less-expensive manner.* Sometimes this may be done by placing less-stringent quality requirements on the information. These requirements may be related to the extent of detail of the information, the frequency, the time frame within which the information comes into being (sometimes detailed manual files are maintained because the computer information will only be ready later), the degree of accuracy, etc. There are cases where the automated computer systems are more expensive than simple manual processes. The just-in-time process used by Toyota manufacturing plants is an excellent example. Try to simplify the process and its activities.

8. *Evaluate whether the separate objectives should actually be attained.* For example, determine if grouping the invoice copies based on the accounts receivable number is really necessary in addition to grouping the invoice copies alphabetically or whether grouping sales by region in the sales overview is really necessary. This evaluation can only be made in this activity, because first, an analysis of the costs of each of the separate objectives must be executed (activity 3 to 7). Only after the execution of this last analysis and the resulting adjustment of the costs for each objective can significant consideration of the objectives take place.

4.12 The Effectiveness and Efficiency of Applied Enablers

Examples of applied enablers are

- Documents and forms
- Computers
- Networks
- Faxes
- Voice mail
- Electronic mail

The analysis of applied enablers differentiates between the following:

- Reorganizing documents and forms
- Evaluating the possibilities for automating administrative business processes
- Optimizing the degree of use of administrative technical enablers

This analysis is one that should be considered within each of the analyses presented in the previous sections (sections 4.4 to 4.11).

4.12.1 Reorganizing Documents and Forms

The PIT should now evaluate the forms and other documents used within the process to identify potential opportunities to improve the effectiveness and efficiency of the administrative business process. This analysis considers whether optimal use is made of

- The production and processing equipment, such as personal computers, minicomputers, microcomputers, or terminals that may or may not be combined with forms of telecommunication
- Appropriate software
- The techniques that can be applied to improve the efficiency of the production of text, such as computerized word processing, magnetic strips, etc.
- The enablers that make the simultaneous production of a number of documents possible, such as duplicate printing techniques (carbon

copies, for example), printing equipment that is connected in parallel, etc.

▲ The techniques for multiplying documents, such as photocopying equipment, etc.

▲ The possibilities for standardizing documents (whether separate documents with a more or less similar text can be combined to form one document)

Analyzing the need for the continued existence of all applied forms, documents, and copies is a starting point for this evaluation. In addition, the PIT will need to determine if all the actions that are performed in connection with the applied documents are actually necessary. These evaluations can, for example, take place on the basis of the form management diagram (see appendix VII) and figures 4.E and 4.F. In these figures, the documents and the files that are employed in relation to them are described.

In addition, an overview is drawn up of the specifics for each document category.

▲ The purpose for the documents
▲ The number of documents produced per time period
▲ The time that is necessary for this production
▲ The associated costs
▲ Standard or nonstandard documents

The analysis can best be started by studying the form management diagram. With the help of this diagram, understanding can be obtained of the place where and the basis on which the documents are created, the quantity used, the purpose for which they are used, and how they are filed and stored. On this basis, a number of provisional conclusions can then be drawn regarding the use of the documents. These conclusions should be adjusted accordingly, and the concrete possibilities for improvement should be examined on the basis of figures 4.E and 4.F. Using these figures, the PIT can determine which combinations of documents can be simultaneously produced, etc. Also, on the basis of these figures, the PIT can understand whether the actions associated with the documents can be combined and/or simplified.

This analysis will also end with a cost assessment of the different alternatives. Analysis of the production of the different documents should include the possibilities for applying word processing equipment. For example, word processing equipment will result in considerable cost savings if large quantities of similar documents are independently produced and the employment of standard documents is not desired or possible.

4.12.2 Evaluating the Possibilities for Automating Administrative Business Processes

With the analysis of data sets and document use, important signs will appear regarding the advantages that can be achieved with the help of computerization and/or information technology. The general evaluation of possibilities for the application and the expansion of computerization will be done in a further study. This future evaluation will consider whether the different activities that make up the administrative business processes should be under consideration for computerization. This study will focus on the number of actions, the scope of the actions, and the time necessary for the actions on the basis of the following activity categories:

- ▲ Calculations
- ▲ Sorting of charts and/or forms
- ▲ Transferring a document to another document
- ▲ Summarizing data from the different documents
- ▲ Comparing data and subsequently making standard decisions and applying standard activities
- ▲ Transferring data carriers (disks, documents, etc.)
- ▲ Storing and looking up documents
- ▲ Processing text

The analysis will focus on the possibilities for realizing the integration of the different actions. Operating automated data processing equipment for the benefit of promoting the efficiency of only one activity in an administrative business process will usually only be appropriate in certain situations.

This phase of the study, a general evaluation of the possibilities for computerization, will be completed. If justified, a more detailed study of the possibilities for computerization will be carried out at a later date. It should be noted that the studies described will only lead to indications about possible computerization from the two approaches of cost and the speed of data processing. In addition, there can obviously be many other reasons for carrying out an additional, more detailed study (for example, a desired improvement in the quality of the information management system and the need to reduce cycle time). Only after the completion of the study can a definite opinion about the possibility and desirability of computerization be formed.

4.12.3 Optimizing the Degree of Use of Administrative Technical Enablers

This analysis is focused on assessing the degree to which the existing administrative technical enablers, such as personal computers, copying equipment, microfiche readers, word processing equipment, etc., are used. By centralizing this equipment, a cost benefit can sometimes be realized, because with less equipment, a larger degree of occupation can be realized than with decentralization.

A list should be drawn up so that for each piece of equipment, the following is set down:

- ▲ The location
- ▲ The purpose for which the equipment is used (processes/activities)
- ▲ The degree of occupation
- ▲ The possibilities for concentrating and combining similar separately located equipment
- ▲ The consequences of potential changes for the personnel, occupation, processing, transportation time, costs, etc.
- ▲ The impact on the individual work flow if an individual needs to go to another location (even within a free flow of their workstation) to use the needed equipment

A great deal of consideration should be given before the organization centralizes equipment. Very often, the amount of lost productivity is grossly underestimated related to the productivity impact of using equipment located in another area. As a general rule, the impact on the work flow is four times the actual travel time. For example, if it takes 3 minutes to go to the copier, the real time lost will be 12 minutes.

4.13 Analysis of Administrative Business Processes: Practical Suggestions

4.13.1 Introduction

For managing the diverse analysis objectives, there are some practical suggestions that can be made. There are many different ways to analyze to what extent the administrative organization satisfies the criteria as described per analysis objective (sections 4.3 to 4.12). Practice shows that experienced staff members can already get a good impression of the quality of the processes during the documentation phase (it should support the impression developed during the preliminary orientation study; see section 3.6). Less experienced employees will need to approach the analysis more systematically by judging each analysis objective.

No matter when or how the analysis is performed, the following should always be kept in mind. You should think about how and with what goal the documentation came about. For example, in the *Administrative Organization Manual* project, in which descriptions are made for instruction or knowledge transfer purposes, documentation can be a sample of the actual results. It does not have to describe all possible factors. The analysis objectives are focused on the issues, not equivalence. These issues involve evaluating the terms, the actual performance, or the products of the administrative business process (see section 4.13.3). A selection from the different analysis objectives should be made ahead of time, and priorities should be set. An all-inclusive analysis usually prevents you from seeing the trees because of the forest.

4.13.2 Limiting the Possibilities for Analysis by Reason of the Documentation Methodology

In an administrative organization project, the processes to be documented and analyzed can be selected by successively drawing up a hierarchical overview (see section 3.9.3), drawing up a complete overview of processes and departments (the matrix; see section 3.9.4), and selecting cells from the matrix for further inventory and analysis.

Accordingly, the analysis of a process occurs on the level of a cell (or row of horizontally bound cells) of the matrix. With the documentation itself, less thought is spent on relationships with other processes or departments because of practical considerations. During the analysis, these relationships should also be included in the evaluation so that the problem of suboptimization can be considered. The level of the analysis of the administrative organization would in that case take place on the too low level of the cell(s). See figure 4.N for clarification.

DEFINITION || **Suboptimization** is defined as the additional resources that the organization expends as a result of changing one activity to save resources at that activity but results in a negative impact on the overall resources consumed by the process.

Departments / Processes	A	B	C	D
1	A1	B1	C1	
2	A2	B2	C2	
3		B3		D3

FIGURE 4.N Department/process relationship matrix

In figure 4.N, cell B2 has the following external relationships:

▲ Data relationships with cells A2 and C2 (these relate to the same administrative business processes)
▲ Organizational relationships with cells in column B (the same organizational unit)

Existing relationships between organizations require that the PIT should continually ask itself whether all relevant facts from the documentation are shown. In other words, is the evaluation, based on the chosen analysis objective, performed on the selected level of the cell. After all, every description of the actual results consciously or unconsciously ignores many aspects thereof, and in principle, all of these results may be important for a thorough analysis.

4.13.3 Differences in the Nature of Each Analysis Objective

The following analysis objectives are summarized in this chapter:

A. Effectiveness of the information management
B. Effectiveness/efficiency of the files
C. Cycle time and on-time completion
D. Clustering of activities
E. Routing
F. Internal control/information control
G. Productivity

H. Opportunities for standardization
I.   Duplicates/superfluous procedures
J.   Effectiveness/efficiency of the enablers

The analysis objectives can be divided according to analysis issues. Analysis issues are

▲ The *conditions* within which the administrative business process occurs (analysis objectives B, D, E, F, and J).
▲ The actual *performance* of the administrative activities (analysis objectives C, F, G, H, and I).
▲ The *end products* of the administrative business process (analysis objectives A, C, and F).

This can be presented as in figure 4.O (the letters correspond to the analysis objectives).

It is inefficient to carry out an investigation of the administrative organization completion without differentiating the nature and influence of the objectives related to each activity. You will quickly notice that the observation of flaws is repeated with an applied analysis objective, etc. From figure 4.O, it seems that inadequate preconditions often lead to inadequate processing and end products.

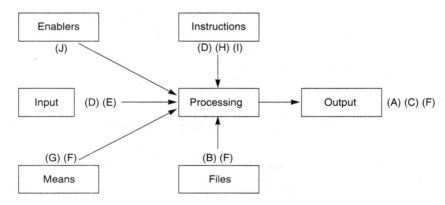

FIGURE 4.O   Analysis issues

An example of an analysis hierarchy with which the analysis objectives can be classified according to significance can be presented as follows:

1. First, determine the *end products* (A, C, and F) and the effectiveness of information management. If this is in order, determine if they should be studied.
2. If yes, determine whether the *conditions* for efficient performance are satisfied. (For example, with respect to the use of the files, consideration should be given to computerization, or with respect to the function and task structure, consideration should be given to the distribution of activities among organizational units.)
3. After the evaluation of the *effectiveness* of the output and the *conditions* for efficient work methods, the actual performance of activities should still be considered to determine if duplicates appear, if the routing within the department is adequate, if standardization possibilities are made use of, and if the productivity is sufficiently high.

Section 4.13.2 indicates that not all data for an analysis can be taken from existing received documentation. This may make it necessary to prioritize the items being analyzed, creating a hierarchy in the analysis objectives. Suppose, for example, that a situation arises in which only an organizational structure diagram (section 3.9.1) and detailed process diagram (section 3.9.6) of the administrative organization are appropriate. As stated in section 3.10, not all the required factors can be charted with a combination of both documentation techniques. In this case, the necessary supplementary data required for an adequate analysis (see figure 4.P) can be presented for each analysis objective. So, for example, an analysis of the productivity of the administrative business processes will require further specification of diverse quantities, costs, and standards. Usually, one should look past the borders of the relevant administrative business process.

4.13.4 Opportunities for Improvement

The indicated limitations for the performance of an analysis obviously also have repercussions for the possibility of proposing improvements. Suppose that in an early stage, the effectiveness of the information management is indicated to be inadequate; for example, because of the lack of enablers. A proposal for improvement can then be drawn up after the examination of the or-

Objective	Priority	Supplementary information needed for a good analysis
A. Information supply	1	Information plan, goal, judgment about receiving department information plan
B. Files	2	
C. Cycle time/ on-time completion	1	On-time completion analysis
D. Clustering activities (among departments)	2	Understanding of the work in other departments (cells)
E. Routing (within departments)	3	
F. Internal Control	1	Relational controls; Functional divisions; Safeguards; Specific measures
G. Productivity	3	Costs, standards, quantities
H. Possibilities for standardization	3	
I. Duplicates	3	
J. Enablers	3	

FIGURE 4.P   Priority of the directions of the analysis and the necessary supplementary data

ganizational data relationships (see section 4.13.2) or, more extensively, from an information plan.

Every increasingly detailed analysis can lead to a new solution. You should realize that if the solution that results from the more detailed analysis uses computerization as an enabler for the first time, it will result in a completely different picture.

4.13.5 Automated Enablers

In addition to automated enablers that are appropriate for describing (usually with the help of personal computers) the administrative business processes (see section 7.5), there also now exist programs in which automatic overviews for analyses (in addition to documentation) can be made. These programs start from a complete overview of processes/departments (the matrix; see section 3.9.4), in which a number of factors are entered into each cell of the matrix to be used for the analysis. Factors such as procedures, document/ information paths, time involvement, frequency, quantities, organizational relationships, etc. should be considered as cell headings. In addition to the development of various types of overviews, all sorts of desired analysis overviews can be made automatically (horizontally and vertically in the matrix).

In practice, these enablers seem to make the documentation, but particularly the analysis work, much more efficient and effective, particularly if related standard question lists are employed in addition. It should be noted that this does not mean that holding interviews as part of a project is unnecessary. Most organizational cultures do not lend itself to being documented in automatic ways!

5 | Phase IV—Design: Designing the New Administrative Business Process

5.1 Introduction

This chapter will present ways in which administrative business processes can be designed and how they can be improved. Before starting the design phase, two initial situations can exist:

▲ An analysis of the existing administrative business processes has already been done.
▲ Building new or improved processes is being considered.

Assuming an analysis of the existing processes has been done, the description of the problem areas can indicate whether an entirely new organization of the administrative business processes (reengineering) is necessary or whether improving the existing processes (redesign) will suffice.

The conclusions from Phase III form the basis for the modification of administrative business processes or the setting up of new processes. Understanding the current processes and their support documentation is very helpful in redesigning the process. On the basis of this, the following activities can be developed:

▲ Development of the changes according to the selected documentation methods

▲ Specification of the organizational conditions that should be fulfilled and the organizational changes that should be made. In this context, thought should be given to the possible availability of technical administrative enablers, manpower, etc.

▲ Specification of the differences between the current processes and the proposed processes. It should be clearly identified how the modified process solves the problems that were revealed during the analysis phase.

▲ Approval of the proposals by the departmental managers and by the respective contact groups

▲ Presentation of reports to the PMT

▲ Final approval of the proposals by the PMT

When one proceeds to draw up entirely new administrative business processes, it is easy to miss the connection with the current situation. The design of the new processes should therefore be done in an analytical manner. The starting point for this design will be determined by the objectives that were formulated in the analysis phase. The design of the administrative business processes can be determined using the following steps.

▲ Formulate the basic assumptions (design variables).

▲ Describe the information to be delivered.

▲ Determine the basic activities.

▲ Determine which information is necessary.

▲ Determine the order of the activities.

▲ Develop the process details.

▲ Calculate the costs.

▲ Specify the organizational conditions that should be met in order to successfully switch the administrative business processes.

▲ Have the proposal approved by the involved staff members.

▲ Give reports about the proposals to the PMT.

▲ Obtain final approval of the proposal by the PMT.

This chapter discusses the methods and techniques with which the development of new administrative business processes can be accomplished in more detail.

Even though automated data processing equipment will be used for modifying the existing processes or developing new processes, the PIT should concentrate their efforts on performing a suitability study. When the information technology enablers are defined, the PIT can be involved with the development of design specifications.

In designing administrative business processes, a top-down approach is followed: From general to specific. The process design must be based upon the requirements that management and the process's customer place upon it. The way that this is accomplished, the techniques that are to be applied, and the documentation are discussed in section 5.2. The approach to the design and the associated techniques are discussed in section 5.3. In section 5.7, attention is paid to the methods for implementing changes in the existing administrative business processes.

Few if any administrative systems are still completely manual. With the design of new administrative business processes and the implementation of changes to the existing processes, the application of computerized data processing should always be considered. Discussion of the connection between the design of administrative business processes and the development of computerized systems is found in section 5.8.

Automated enablers are going to play a large role in designing administrative business processes as the relationships between different processes become stronger and as the entire administrative system becomes more complex. Automated enablers for documentation, analysis, and design are discussed in section 7.5.

In this chapter, exclusive attention is paid to the methods for designing and modifying administrative business processes. The organization of the project is discussed in chapter 2. The management of the constructed documentation is discussed in chapter 7.

5.2 Methods, Techniques, and Documentation in Designing Administrative Business Processes

The design of new or altered administrative business processes is often considered too lightly. In practice, it is regularly observed that someone gets an assignment "to modify the administrative business processes so that the problem areas are eliminated" or "to improve the efficiency of the administrative business processes and/or the effectiveness of the process." The chances are that in those situations, the existing problem areas will be eliminated by the modifications. Often, other problems will be introduced because the various design approaches that should be considered are not clear.

Problems can also be created when a completely new design (reengineering) for the administrative business processes is being considered. It is more difficult than it seems to keep reviewing all the new angles together with and among the organization, management processes, files, documents, information to be distributed, etc. The problems with designing administrative business processes can be decreased or even eliminated by using a top-down approach, in which the design is built up roughly and then in more detail. During each phase, the team that is designing the improved process returns to explicit principles and purposes.

Techniques are used with the design in order to describe the different relevant aspects of the administrative business processes in an unambiguous manner. With the help of documentation design techniques, a model of the administrative system is built in such a way that it can be developed in a manner that ensures the descriptive requirements are met.

DEFINITION | **Administrative system** is the combination of the administrative business processes and the organization.

The approach to designing administrative business processes is discussed in the following sections. You will learn that starting points and relationships should be established before the design is implemented. With the design, a logical structure is defined before the physical structure is built. This entire process is supported by a set of related techniques.

The approach for designing the administrative business processes consists of four activities. They are:

1. Determine the organizational starting point
2. Specify the application of information
3. Design the logical structure
4. Design the physical structure

Figure 5.A displays the thought process upon which this approach is based. The letters of figure 5.A will be referenced in the following paragraphs.

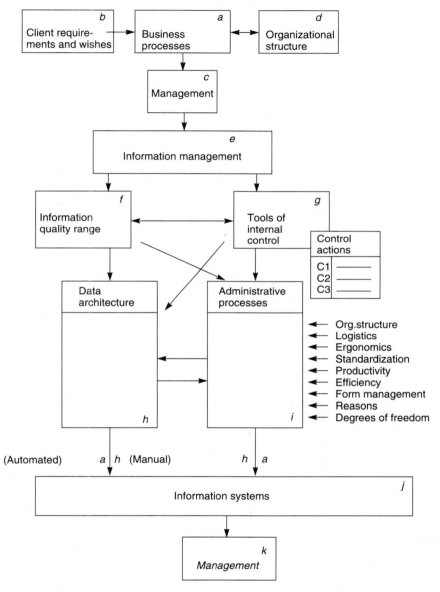

FIGURE 5.A   Thought process for designing administrative business processes

5.3 Activity 1: Determine the Organizational Starting Point

5.3.1 Specifying the Basic Organizational Principles

The administrative business processes are aimed at producing the information that is required for operating, completing, and managing the daily affairs of the organization and the associated responsibilities that are assigned. One of the first requirements of specifying the basic organizational principles is to think about how the information is used in daily activities. This use of information is dependent on

- ▲ Primary processes (*a*)
- ▲ Management method (control) (*c*)
- ▲ Organizational structure (*d*)

DEFINITION A **primary process** (critical process) is a major process that is critical to the successful operation and/or performance of the entire organization.

Primary Processes

Figure 5.A starts with the business processes (*a*) of the organization. These primary processes result in products that are delivered by the daily activities. For each product, it is possible to indicate which effectiveness requirements the product (and therefore the process) must meet to satisfy customers' requirements and/or legal specifications (*b*). It is likewise possible to define which efficiency requirements the primary process must satisfy, given internal objectives such as costs and stocking levels. The measurements related to the primary processes are derived from the main objectives of the organization and from the critical success factors. These measurements will be used to help define the process' key objectives.

DEFINITION **Critical success factors** (CSFs) are those factors that are of decisive importance related to the achievement of the organization's business plan.

Management

Once the primary processes requirements have been defined, it is important to determine how these processes should be managed (*c*). The management will naturally be directed toward satisfying the client requirements, legal requirements, and internal objectives. The risks, frequency, and financial significance of the business processes are therefore extremely important factors that should be analyzed and their exposures minimized during the design phase.

Standards should be specified for the aspects of the primary processes that need to be managed. These standards are important because they are the factors that will drive the design of the new administrative business processes. The administrative business processes will need to produce data that can be compared to standards.

Organizational Structure

The chosen organizational structure (d) is also important as a basic consideration. It involves the methods by which authority is delegated and rules are set. The delegation of authority creates obligations at a higher level to keep an eye on the delegated activities and to adjust them as necessary. In the event of delegation, standards (such as budgets) should be established that performance at lower levels must meet.

Once the organizational structure has been determined, it should be documented in the form of an organizational structure diagram (see appendix I). The organizational structure diagram helps to provide an understanding of the design of the organization's formal relationships. The organization diagram clarifies the relationships in the organization but conveys little information about the functions and activities that are within the different organizational units. The functions and activities are described in supplements to the organizational structure diagram, often in verbal form or documented in operating procedures and work instructions.

The relationship between the business processes, organizational structure, and management method provides the basic information required to design the logical structure of the administrative system. It is now possible to broadly indicate which staff members should be responsible for each risk related to each business process. The information that is required for the management and the responsibility of the business processes can be derived from this information.

5.4 Activity 2: Specify the Application of Information

The content of the information management system in the organization can be specified based upon management choices, organizational structure, and operational and management methods. This includes

▲ The information that is used for the operation, the completion, and the management of the daily activities and for the associated responsibilities that are assigned
▲ The quality criteria for this information
▲ The appropriate set of internal control tools

5.4.1 Required Information

Figure 5.A indicates that initially, the information that is needed for each function (for example, production control, quality assurance, product engineering, etc.) is significant for making strategic, tactical, and operational decisions. The day-to-day operational needs required to manage the function are used to define and develop the management reports consisting of financial and nonfinancial information. In addition, actual performance measurements must be specified for

▲ Accountability, both within the organization and outside it
▲ The actual performance of the process (such as the location in the warehouse where particular goods are stored)
▲ The external communication (such as the information that must be distributed to pension insurance services, health services, tax services, etc.)

It is important that the subjects for which the information is necessary are well defined. Determining the required information can be done according to a method that consists of five activities (see figure 5.B):

▲ Identify the critical success factors (CSFs).
▲ Identify the business processes.
▲ Determine the interrelationships between the CSFs and the business processes.
▲ Specify or make the control variables operational.
▲ Determine the form and frequency of management reporting.

Two things are of importance for the development of the form and content of the information management system. (1) This information management system should, on the one hand, be derived from the realization of the organizational objectives. These objectives follow from the chosen strategy or

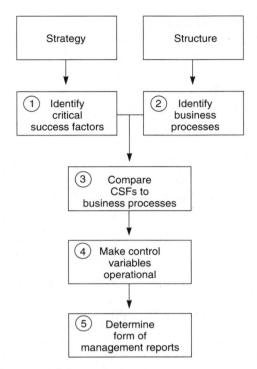

FIGURE 5.B   The five steps of the method

the formulated policy and the associated CSFs. (2) Operationally oriented internal reporting should be based on the business processes of the organization. The business processes should, after all, be managed and operated.

In the first activity, CSFs are identified. Critical success factors can be derived from the strategies and objectives chosen by the organization. The effectiveness of information management is to a strong degree determined by the understanding and reporting of the factors that are critical to the functioning of the organization. For example, it is not critical that a governmental organization in charge of maintaining monuments deplete its annual budget allowance. A financial statement says little about the handling of policies and the realization of objectives. An overview of the different monuments, their ages, and the number of subsidized projects provide a much better view of how the organization is performing. Too often, management focuses on the financial considerations, ignoring the resulting impact or improvement upon the organization's objectives.

In the second activity, business processes are identified. With the help of a functional organization chart, a hierarchy is introduced into the inventoried business processes. With this hierarchy, the structure and composition of all processes in the organization can be understood. The detail of the business processes should be defined to the level at which there is an unambiguous connection to the responsibilities and qualifications of the respective managers. The technique for this purpose is described in appendix III. A way of illustrating the interrelationships between the organization's CSFs and typical administrative business process can be found in figure 5.C

The CSFs and the business processes are associated with each other in a matrix developed during the third activity. With the matrix, management should ask itself where the CSF influences the business process; in other words, where the performance of a business process relates to (achieving) a CSF. In the third activity, interrelationships between CSFs and business processes are determined. In figure 5.C, this relationship is represented by an X. The process of purchasing is associated with the CSF of efficient production. In the figure, the quality of the purchase material to a large degree determines the defects in production.

CSF

1. Maintaining market share				
2. Spreading financial risk				
3. Wide variety of products				
4. Efficient production				

Business processes

1. Purchasing	X	X	X	
2. Production	X		X	
3. Sales			X	X
4.				

FIGURE 5.C   Determining the interrelationships between CSFs and business processes: example of an industrial company with a consolidation strategy

DEFINITION ‖ **Control variables** are variables as indicators that provide an understanding of the quality with which a business process is carried out.

In the fourth activity, control variables are specified or made operational. Management chooses, on the basis of the method of operational, financial, and organizational importance, which Xs from the matrix should be specified.

Each X can be expanded to include one or more control variables. The variables should be clearly described, norms and source data should be specified, and their operation should be determined by a random sample test. Familiar logistic control variables, including the reliability and speed of delivery, are used.

A set of control variables or performance indicators give insight into the integral performance of the business processes and all the associated elements (input, processing, output), and these indicators should also tie into the responsibilities and qualifications of management.

In the fifth activity, the form and frequency of management reporting are described. These reports consist of the value of the control variables regarding the standard, the plan, and/or the forecast. Financial reports are used to indicate if the processes are in keeping with the plan of record.

Tables in management reports often are supported with graphics. The report text gives a short explanation for the observed discrepancy and other relevant information (action taken to correct problems, explanations for out-of-control points, etc.). Together, tables and text should by preference not be longer than three standard pages.

Asking the proper questions at the right moment is the essence of the approach. One should first know something about the objectives and processes and then something about the necessary information.

5.4.2 Range of Quality of the Necessary Information

With respect to the defined information requirements, the quality requirements (f) that the information must satisfy should be established in terms of relevance, reliability, form of presentation, and efficiency (see figure 5.D).

The quality requirements that are associated with relevance are specified by a number of criteria. The relevance of the information is defined, among other factors, by the speed with which the data are distributed after the period is over, the period during which the information is distributed (length of the information interval), and the thoroughness of the data.

Description	Information management	Data processing	Data collection and documentation
A. Relevance			
1. Degree of abundance	+		+
2. Degree of thoroughness	+		
3. Degree of detail	+		+
4. Critical quality	+		+
5. Degree of quantification	+		+
6. Degree of accuracy	+		+
7. Degree of information delay	+		+
8. Speed of information distribution	+	+	+
9. Length of information interval	+		+
10. Degree of continuity	+		+
B. Reliability	+	++	+
C. Form of presentation	+	+	+
D. Efficiency	+	++	+

FIGURE 5.D Range of information quality

With the help of columns labeled "Information management," "Data processing," and "Data collection and documentation," information about the requirements that are placed on the data set, starting with the requirements that are placed on the management of information, can be documented. The diagram can be read from left to right. If the user wants detailed information, the information must be set down in detail.

It should be remarked that the requirements that can be placed on data processing from the point of view of relevance are only of consequence to the speed with which the data is processed. The primary requirements for data processing are based particularly on reliability and efficiency.

5.4.3 Information Control Objectives and Tools

The basic measures of information control (also called internal control) (g) are aimed at the reliability of the collection, the documentation, and the processing of data. The objective of these measures is to guarantee the desired degree of reliability for the management of information. The information control requirements that result from client requirements or issued regulations and rules are also identified.

The explicit specification of basic information control measures often occurs late in the course of the design of the processes. But it is important to specify the information control measures during an early stage, because they influence the data architecture (for example, by creating redundant data documentation out of concern for not having enough) and process architecture (for example, by integrating the control operations).

The measures that need to be chosen for information control must be tuned to each other. The information control measures can be referred to as a system (see also section 4.8). Thought should be given to the information control factors presented in figure 5.E.

Controls for forming judgment *ex ante*:
1. Control of expectations

Control for the actual business occurrences:
2. Management control
3. Authority control
4. Output control
5. Progress control
6. Efficiency control
7. Quality control

Control for the actual business situation:
8. Storing control
    – protection
    – account reports
    – material contract controls involving sacrificed and acquired business matters
    – inventory

Control for data processing:
9. Information control
    – inclusive control of the use of material contracts (BETA formulas)
      • control technical functional divisions
      • authority control
      • supplementary measures
      • determining numbers
    – checking *ex ante* data
    – duplicating documentation and further processing
    – supervision

Control for the standards used with controls:
10. Control of standards

Control for the design and compliance with the internal control system:
11. Do the rules form an efficient and effective whole?
12. Are the rules sufficiently complied with?

FIGURE 5.E   Information control factors

5.5 Activity 3: Design the Logical Structure

In this design activity, the administrative-organizational system is reviewed. The use of information, the requirements placed on the information management system and the associated information control tools define the ultimate process design. We are now concerned with processing the requirements into the design of the administrative system. This logical design includes, starting with figure 5.A, the following:

▲ A conceptual data model (*h*)
▲ A hierarchical overview of the administrative business processes (*i*)
▲ An additional, more detailed analysis of the links between the data model and the administrative business processes (*j*)

5.5.1 Conceptual Data Model

Section 5.4 indicates how data definitions (*h*) are made. These will be further specified in the logical design phase. At the same time, during this activity, the attributes of the applications for which data are needed and the relationships between the applications will be established. For the purpose of this book, it is unnecessary to examine extensively the issues of data modeling; a lot of good literature has been published on this subject.

5.5.2 Hierarchical Overview of the Administrative Business Processes

The hierarchical overview of the administrative business processes (*i*) can provide one with an understanding of the structure and composition of the administrative system. It shows the internal hierarchy of the administrative business processes in relation to the functions of that system. With that function, the information management objectives are exclusively reviewed (see also appendix III).

We are now concerned with the fact that from the business processes, an organized hierarchy of the data processing processes is described in order to be able to anticipate the application of information (described in section 5.4). Processes that are components of the set of information control tools (described in activity 2) are also specified.

5.5.3 Links between the Data Model and the Administrative Business Processes

The data model and the administrative business processes together form the whole information system (j). During the phase of the logical design, a clear connection must exist between these two. The administrative business processes are data processing processes in which the basic data are collected and recorded. They are immediately processed or they are stored and processed. After being processed, they can be distributed or they can first be stored before being distributed.

The process is thus comprised of an input of basic data and an output of processed data. The process must be organized so that on the basis of input data, the required output can be delivered. The activities of the administrative system can be specified by this method in connection with the data model.

The technique applied for this process is a data flow diagram. This technique became known as an enabler during the development of automated systems. The diagram of administrative business process principles (see appendix II) is fairly often used as a data flow diagram in the same manner.

With the help of data flow diagrams or diagrams of principles, the methods by which the data output (information requirements) are created from previously input basic data are analyzed. The diagram is drawn up so that the input and output of data are drawn as arrows toward and away from the administrative business process. The actual process is drawn as a circle. Storage of the data is indicated by a small "container." Entering data into a file or recalling it from a file is reproduced by an arrow.

The storage of data, the data flows, and administrative business processes are each assigned a unique name. The definitions of the stored data and the data flows must be defined in a data catalog (data dictionary). The processes must be included in the hierarchical overview of the processes so that the internal relationships are evident.

If a diagram on a certain level does not provide enough insight, the details of the processes and data flows should be further defined in a new diagram. Thus, the consistency between broader, more general diagrams and detailed diagrams is continually maintained.

The detail of the diagrams is continued until the data processing activities are described in a concise and unambiguous manner at the lowest required level. Figures 5.F.1 and 5.F.2 give an example of the application of data flow diagrams.

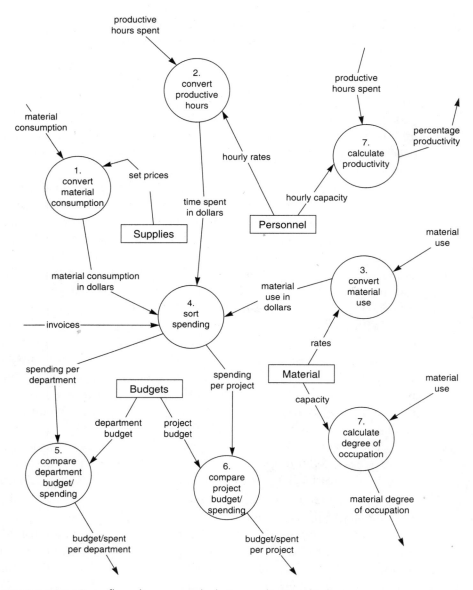

FIGURE 5.F.1 Data flow diagram: calculating realization budgets

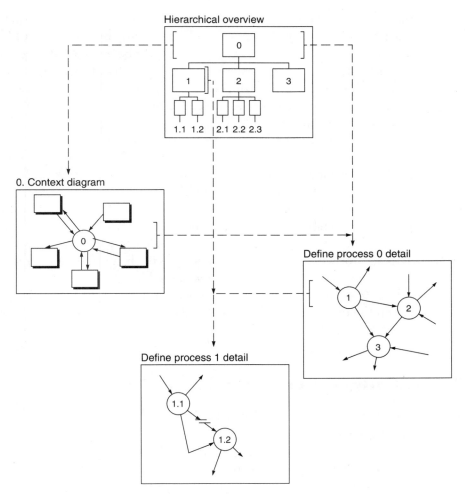

FIGURE 5.F.2 Defining the detail of data flow diagrams

5.5.4 Other Elements of the Processes

For each process, the event that starts the administrative business process and the point at which the process is considered to have ended should be indicated. The start can be the receipt of an order, an invoice, a solicitation form, or a termination of employment notice. The end point of the process can be the mailing of an order, the mailing of a payment, an announcement that the solicitation is over, or the mailing of the final remuneration to the departing employee. Sometimes an administrative business process branches out. Sometimes a particular activity may never be completed. With an incoming order, the mailing information will be recorded, the merchandise will be mailed, the invoice will be drawn up, but an error in the accounting department may cause the invoice to be sent to the wrong organization, and as a result, the invoice may never be closed.

The frequency with which a process must be performed should be specified for each process. A frequency table should be applied for this purpose. An estimate should also be made of the quantities for each process. For this purpose, a quantity overview should be drawn up.

The use of enablers with administrative activities should be considered in situations where they will enhance the efficiency, improve the reliability, or shorten the cycle time of the data processing procedures. In evaluating the activities for which enablers could be effectively used, the use of the quantity overview and the frequency table is advisable. One of the possible enablers relates to automated/computerized data processing. For the relationship between the design described below and the system development, refer to section 5.8.

5.6 Activity 4: Design the Physical Structure

The design of the physical structure of the administrative business processes (see figure 5.A) includes

▲ Which organizational units should perform the data processing activities
▲ Which activities should be included as part of an administrative business process and what the sequence of activities should be in the administrative business process
▲ Which data files and forms are necessary
▲ A detailed description of the process, the associated work instructions, and the layout of the forms and files
▲ The costs and cycle time of the designed process

It is important to have a good illustration of the different approach angles (design variables) for the physical development of the administrative business processes. The decisions mentioned above directly influence the fulfillment of the set requirements. The entire spectrum of possible design variables is quite large. A selection that seems to work in practice is presented in figure 5.G. These variables are a result of activities 1, 2, and 3 (see section 5.2).

Date:	1 - 16 - 1992	Document code:	
Project:	Adm. organization	Project phase:	Design administrative process
Project team:	Human Res. proc.	Subject area:	Design adm. new hire processing
Documenter:	G. de Korte	Subject:	Basic activities

No.	Basic activity	Description	Outputs	Form. no.	Performed by
A	Fill in registration form and tax form	The registration form should include all the data that is needed for processing the new hire	Filled in: – registration form for employee – tax form	1 2	Human Res. employee
B	Fill in registration form and contract	Fill in the data involving the department and initial the agreement involving placing the employee	Registration form filled in for dep. data and initialed	1	Dept. manager
C	Control completeness	Control of the completeness of the filled in registration form	Control initial on registration form	1	Human Res.
D	Request medical examination	Request medical examination from the company's medical service	Request form	3	Human Res.
E	Agreement letter	Set up agreement letter	Typed but not yet signed letter and copy	4	Human Res.
F	Receive medical results	Return received request form with examination results	Filled in request form	3	Human Res.
G	Set up personnel records	Assign file number and prepare the file	Records file	5	Human Res.
H	Apply for health insurance	Fill in and mail health insurance form	Insurance form	6/7	Human Res.
I	Monitor budget	Update the position board, check whether the vacancy is approved	Updated position board	8	Budgeting.
J	Enter payroll	Fill in time card Record in payroll charts	Time card Payroll chart	9 10	Payroll
K	Apply for pension insurance Enz.	Fill in and mail application letter	Application letter	11	Human Res.

FIGURE 5.G   Example of a basic activity overview

It regularly seems that the different design variables are in contrast to each other. In that case, a good choice must be made with respect to the priority with which the various design variables will be applied. It is also sensible to indicate the minimal requirements with regard to the other design variables. The mix of priorities will be dependent on the client requirements and legal specifications, the nature of the management process, the organizational structure, etc.

5.6.1 Allocating Activities to Organizational Units

When the hierarchical overview is combined with the organizational structure diagram, a complete overview of the organizational units is formed (see the matrix in appendix IV). With the help of this matrix, the involvement of a particular organizational unit in a particular administrative business process can be specified.

It is possible that particular administrative-organizational conditions are formed in relation to particular activities. In the first place, these conditions may be related to the location where the activity occurs. The following conditions should be included and specified:

▲ Particular activities should be performed by previously determined individuals or departments.
▲ Certain activities should be combined with each other in one department.
▲ Certain activities should not be combined in one department or for an individual.
▲ In the administrative business process, certain data sets must be updated or referenced.

In addition, the administrative-organizational conditions could be related to the creation, processing, referencing, and removal of particular data sets.

Taking the design variables into consideration, the matrix can indicate in which location (workplace/department) the referenced activity will be performed. The location (department) in which a particular activity is executed is indicated in figure 5.G. If it has been determined beforehand that activities are performed by several departments, a further branching of the activities will occur in this stage.

In order to indicate the location in which activities are performed, one should already have some understanding of the organizational clustering of the different activities. If a new process is set up that must replace a previously existing process, links within the existing structure must be considered. With a completely and newly developed organization, one will find links with the descriptions of the business's characteristics and, on this basis, the expected layout of the organizational structure.

A few criteria that can play a role in determining the location of the activities are

▲ Achieving the most efficient use of the applied data sets
▲ Realizing an optimal use of the enablers that are used with the administrative business process
▲ Placing the activities so that those with the largest organizational interrelationship are located together as much as possible
▲ Placing similar tasks and tasks that require an approximately equal level of education together as much as possible
▲ Separating disposal, performance, storage, documentation, and control functions to realize optimal control ratios
▲ Compiling sets of tasks such that a good degree of job satisfaction is realized. The content of the work and the work conditions should include the optimal amount of variation and autonomy. To have motivated employees, you should strive to create well-rounded sets of tasks so that as much use as possible is made of the abilities of the involved staff members. It is also important that groups are formed of individuals who fit together based on their interests, dispositions, and educations.

The various criteria can contradict each other. Sometimes, one or a few criteria prevail. Thus, the others play a lesser role in the organization of the structure. If few or no criteria prevail, a balance is sought. The characteristics of the business process and the required information for its management ultimately determine the priority of the criteria.

You can obtain some understanding of how a balance is reached by evaluating the extent that each criterion is satisfied for each of the alternatives. The alternative with the highest overall score is the preferred one as long as this alternative does not score below a minimum level for any of the individual criteria. Determining the location of the activities has a provisional character, for it is possible that on the basis of the following design steps, the location of the activities will be defined.

5.6.2 Determining the Order of the Activities in a Process

Activities that are initiated by the same event (triggering event) and that have the same frequency can be included as part of the same administrative business process. Other times, it makes more sense, from the point of view of cycle time, to design the processes to flow in parallel rather than serially.

The order of the administrative business processes is derived from the logical structure and processing of the data that are inputted into the following activity. They can be represented in figure 5.H. The order can be read from the data flow diagrams. Whenever these are relatively complex, for each frequency and triggering event, the activities should be mentioned in a diagram such as that in figure 5.I. This diagram indicates (once again) which

```
* Effective information management:
  – relevance
  – range of quality

* Data files

* Position and task structure

* Ergonomics

* Internal control:
  – tools
  – measures

* Routing

* Possibilities for automation

* Efficiency factors

* Productivity

* Enablers

* Degrees of freedom
```

FIGURE 5.H   Basic principles for designing administrative business processes

Date:	1 - 15 - 1992	Document code:	
Project:	Adm. organization	Project phase:	Design administrative process
Project team:	Personnel	Subject area:	Adm. processing set-ups
Documenter:		Subject:	Information features

Data set	Nr	A	B	C	D	E	F	G	H	I	J	K	L	M	N
Output doc.no.	29	1+2	1	(1)	3(+1)	4(+1)	3(+1)	5(+1)	6+7(+1)	8(+1)	9+10(+1)	11(+1)	4(+1)		alle
Input doc.no.	28		1	1	1	1	3	1	1	1+8	1+4	1	1+4	9+12	3+5
Initial of control	27			O									X		
Initial of budget	26										O		X		
Initial of manager/director	25		O										⊗	X	
Date of payroll	24										O		X		
Date of health fund	23								O						
Personnel file number	22							O							X
Date of appointment letter	21					O							X		
Examination results	20					X	O		X				X		
Travel expenses	19	O	X	X		X						X	X	X	
Salary	18		O	X		X			X	X	X		X	X	X
Date of request examination	17				O		X								
Hours per week	16		O	X		X			X	X	X		X	X	X
Department	15	O	X	X		X		X	X	X	X		X	X	
Position code	14		O	X	X	X	X	X	X	X	X		X	X	
Date of employment	13		O	X	X	X	X		X	X	X		X	X	X
Filled positions	12	O	X	X											
Military service	11	O	X	X	X					X	X		X		
Education followed	10	O	X	X											
Current education	9	O	X	X											
Additional jobs	8	O	X	X					X	X	X		X		
Salary payment method	7	O		X							X		X		
Subtract particular expenses	6	O		X		X					X		X		
Number of children	5	O	X	X							X	X	X		
Marital status	4	O	X	X					X		X	X	X		
Nationality	3	O	X	X	X				X	X	X		X		
Date of birth	2	O	X	X	X		X		X	X	X		X	X	X
NACZ	1	O	X	X	X	X	X	X	X	X	X		X	X	X
Basic activity		Fill in application form and tax form	Contract dept. manager	Control for completeness	Request medical examination	Agreement letter	Medical examination results	Open personnel file	Medical insurance	Monitoring budget	Payroll entry	Pension fund letter	Signature	Input control	Collect documents etc.

FIGURE 5.1 Example of the first analysis of the information features

data are necessary as the input for a specific activity (O) and which data are created or processed by the activity (X). The order of the activities can now be read from figure 5.G, because each activity and each information feature, whether use is made of the information originating from a previous activity or not during the performance of the activity, is recorded (by means of an X and O).

An activity can only be executed after the completion of the activities, that have an O in the feature column, has an X. The order of the activities is entered in the last column of figure 5.J.

5.6.3 Specifying the Necessary Data Files and Forms

If figure 5.J is filled in, the documents that are necessary to bring about the transfer of data between the different activities can be specified in figure 5.I. The data that are created by the first activity are set down in document 1. This document is noted in the column "output documents" (column 29 of figure 5.I). In addition, where the information of the document is applicable, it is noted in the column "input documents" (column 28). The input documents for all the activities are noted in the same manner. If, for a particular activity, data sets are noted, this information must also be noted in the output column. Existing documents should be noted in the overview wherever they are used in the administrative business process.

If more specific data (initials, date of activity, etc.) are given on one of the input documents, the number of the filled-in documents is noted between parentheses in column 29. With activity E, the offer of employment letter is drawn up (no. 4) and the date of the letter is noted on the registration form (no. 1), which provided the basic data for the letter. With activity L, the director signs the letter, and the date on which the letter was signed is specified on the registration form. Filling in figures 5.I and 5.J is an iterative process. Processing the elaboration of the basic assumptions of figure 5.G in figure 5.I leads to the adjustment of figure 5.J and vice versa. Often, it is necessary to once again complete the document figure 5.I (this time in more detail). In principle, the order of the different activities and the documents and data sets used with them should be clear after completing the aforementioned exercise. On the basis of the figure 5.J overview, the global process diagram of the administrative business process can be drafted. Appendix V further describes this diagram.

Date:	1 - 15 - 1992	Document code:	
Project:	Adm. organization	Project phase:	Design administrative process
Project team:	Personnel	Subject area:	Adm. processing setups
Documenter:	G. de Korte	Subject:	Sequence overview

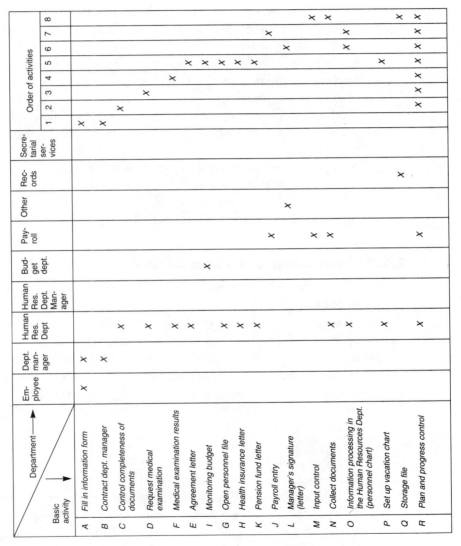

Basic activity	Employee	Dept. manager	Human Res. Dept	Human Res. Dept. Manager	Budget dept.	Payroll	Other	Records	Secretarial services	1	2	3	4	5	6	7	8
A Fill in information form	X	X								X							
B Contract dept. manager		X								X							
C Control completeness of documents			X								X						
D Request medical examination			X									X					
F Medical examination results			X										X				
E Agreement letter			X											X			
I Monitoring budget					X									X			
G Open personnel file			X				X							X			
H Health insurance letter			X											X			
K Pension fund letter			X											X			
J Payroll entry						X										X	
L Manager's signature (letter)						X									X		X
M Input control						X											X
N Collect documents			X												X	X	
O Information processing in the Human Resources Dept. (personnel chart)			X														X
P Set up vacation chart			X											X			
Q Storage file								X									X
R Plan and progress control			X			X				X	X	X	X	X	X	X	X

FIGURE 5.J Example of an overview of the sequence of activities

5.6.4 Defining the Detail of the Future State Process

In view of the information received from the previous activities, the administrative business processes in figure 5.A can be elaborated. This elaboration will consist of

- ▲ *The detailed process diagram.* This defines the detail to the level of activity/task. For each activity, the information necessary for the activity, where this information can be found, and where it is passed on to are accurately described. See appendix VI for a more detailed description of the detailed process diagram.
- ▲ *Form and file design.* The layout of the data set and the documents used with the administrative business process is now established in more detail. For guidelines that can be used in designing documents, see appendix IX.
- ▲ *Other administrative business process documentation.* Drawing up an instruction diagram (see appendix VII) is also recommended. Any other possible documentation of the new administrative business process is also drawn up in this activity.

5.6.5 Calculating Costs and Cycle Time

A time estimate is made for each of the defined activities during the design of new administrative business processes. In addition, the category of employees (or staff members) who will perform the activity is also indicated. Thereafter, for each category of employees (or individual staff member), the costs per time unit are calculated. Multiplying the time units per activity by the costs per time unit results in the costs per activity. By adding all the costs, one gets the total cost for the administrative business process as a whole. These costs should naturally increase with the addition of the costs of the enablers, materials, overhead, etc.

If an estimate of the cycle time per step needs to be made, an estimate is made of

- ▲ The time that is required to carry out the particular activity
- ▲ Possible delays that exist because overtime work can accumulate
- ▲ The time that is necessary for communication between the different activities. This includes the time needed for internal transportation, the time that is needed for external authorities to react to letters sent

by internal units, etc. On the basis of these estimates, one can get an idea of the expected cycle time duration of the process.

5.7 Making Changes to Administrative Business Processes

The methods by which required improvements are realized are not often specified in the analysis of the administrative business process. It is important that a measurement system be established that can be used to measure the effectiveness of major changes that are applied to administrative business processes. It is also important that a clear definition of expected performance is defined before the change is implemented so that results can be quantified and the change evaluated.

As part of the design of the recommended changes, the extent to which an existing process is changed is particularly important. In the simplest situation, the changes will be confined to a process and to the execution of that process in one department. The global documentation of the process (such as the complete overview of the processes and departments, the global process diagram, and the hierarchical diagram discussed in chapter 3) does not need to be modified. Modifying the detailed documentation (detailed process diagram, instruction diagram, etc.) will suffice. The situation becomes more complex if the change extends to a number of departments and possibly to a number of processes. In this case, not only should the detailed documentation be modified, but the global documentation should also be changed.

The extent to which the existing process is changed determines how much of the existing descriptions can be used. The magnitude of the change and its impact upon the organization influences the way the process is modified. The consequences of the suggested modifications can be understood more quickly from small changes than from changes that involve quite a few departments or processes. Making changes to the existing design of the administrative business processes should be done according to the following steps:

▲ Formulate the principles for the changes.
▲ Determine the essence of the changes.
▲ Define the BFSS.
▲ Develop the details of the changes in accordance with the chosen documentation method.

Developing the changes is followed by a description of the conditions that should be met in order for the changed processes to function successfully. The differences between the current processes and the future state processes will also be specified. The way in which the future state processes provide a solution for the problem areas that occur with the existing processes should also be described.

5.7.1 Formulating the Principles

What the changes in the processes will achieve needs to be further defined. For each (sub)process, the following should be put next to each other:

▲ The degree to which the objectives are achieved in the current situation (as-is model)
▲ The description of the gap that is found between the desired and actual situation

The objectives that one can achieve with the changes should be stated. Not only should the objective of the change be defined (in terms of improving the accuracy and completeness of the data processing, decreasing the cycle time, etc.), but also concrete standards should be specified. With a desired improvement of the data processing procedures, the data for which the improvement is to be made and which concrete criteria are involved (in terms of completeness, accuracy, etc.) will need to be indicated. In the case of a desired improvement in cycle time, the cycle time that is projected to be realized must be specified (in hours of work days).

Changing a process can be subject to a number of organizational conditions. These conditions may be related to the location where the activities should be performed (for example, the personnel files must be maintained by the records department), the selected combination of activities (for example, the accounts payable department must authorize the deliveries), the involvement of particular staff members in a process (for example, the manager must approve the expenditures), etc. The conditions may also concern the use of the data sets and the use of computerized data processing equipment (for example, if the invoicing of different sales departments is done on one central computer and strict rules are applied to the input documents and procedures). Such organizational conditions, as part of the formulation of basic principles, need to be resolved. Sometimes the organizational conditions are so stringent that unless they are satisfied, the drafted objectives will not be able to be achieved. In this situation, it would obviously not make sense to continue drawing up the modifications. Before additional efforts are expended on modifications, either the organizational conditions or the process objectives need to be changed.

After the process objectives and the organizational conditions are aligned, the further development of the modifications can be continued. The essential components of the current processes that should and should not be altered are initially identified.

5.7.2 Deciding the Essence of the Modifications

For determining the essence of the modifications, documentation should exist about the existing processes that will be modified. The documentation should mention

- ▲ The activities and tasks that make up the process
- ▲ The order in which these tasks and activities are performed
- ▲ The location of the activity
- ▲ The data that should be delivered by the process
- ▲ The information that is used with the process
- ▲ The process' measurement data

All of these tasks will have been recorded in the documentation activities of the project. On the basis of these documents, the changes that should be implemented in the processes can be examined with the help of the formulated problem areas, basic assumptions, and objectives.

Sometimes, from the results of the analysis activities, it will be clear which of the factors mentioned above should be changed. If the evaluation of the information controls establishes that the functional division is unsuitable, the activities or tasks should be moved from one department (or individual) to another.

The relationship between the desired outcome and the change that must be introduced is not always clear. Sometimes, another study should first be carried out regarding the nature of the change that must be introduced to achieve the desired objective. This is particularly true for situations in which a number of alternative changes to the administrative business process are possible. In developing a future state solution, many combinations of improvement approaches should be considered (for example, solutions are sought for increasing the processing capacity, the impact of all types of these enablers, the simultaneous performance of tasks or activities, the elimination of activities, etc.). In some situations, a number of alternative future state solutions will be developed and analyzed.

For each potential future state solution, the extent to which the change contributes to the realization of the formulated objective is specified. In addition, the consequences for the tasks and activities (place, order, etc.), the use of information (is other information necessary or is the same information necessary in a different phase?), the information to be produced, etc., should be considered as well as the cost and implementation cycle time required to install the potential solution.

The organizational consequences of the change should be charted. At the same time, one should attempt to form a picture of the effects of the changes on the costs and the speed of processing.

It is best to develop a number of conceptual future state solutions. Each potential future state solution can be analyzed by constructing a preliminary model of the process and exercising it to ensure that

- ▲ There are no interface problems
- ▲ It performs as expected
- ▲ No unforeseen problems develop

Typically, modeling at this stage will be either computer simulation modeling, physical modeling, or a combination of both.

Computer simulation modeling provides many advantages in today's environment. There are a number of excellent programs available that can help you build a replica of the future state process without machining a part or moving a desk. Computer simulation programs in hardware design and manufacturing flow applications have been popular since the mid 1970s, but business process simulation did not become popular until the mid 1990s.

Layout simulation modeling allows the designer to build a dimensionally correct 3-D model of each activity and assemble the activities together, statistically varying inputs to help define process performance and to identify problems.

Typically, process simulation modeling is an expansion of the flowcharting process used to characterize the as-is item and the revised flowchart used to define the future state process. Today's simulation models are very sophisticated. They use icons to simulate process flow to define

- ▲ Bottlenecks in the process
- ▲ Critical paths
- ▲ Cycle times
- ▲ Processing times
- ▲ Workload problems

In these process simulation models, the product is depicted as moving through the process while icons of little people answer phones, take breaks, attend meetings, and yes, even do some work. Most programs allow the process flow to be sped up or slowed down. Days or months of process flow can be reduced to minutes in the simulation model. Worst-case scenarios can be created and analyzed without upsetting the process or your customer. A well-designed process simulation model takes the theoretical and converts it into the harsh reality of your organization's everyday activities. Initially, it may take some time to prepare a computerized simulation model, but if the change is significant, the time will be well spent, and the model can eliminate many false starts.

In many cases, it is necessary to prepare physical models of the future state process to prove the concept. This is particularly true when the process is a product or an item that does not lend itself to computer simulation. Computer programs such as Computer Aided Design (CAD) and Computer Aided Manufacturing (CAM) greatly aid in reducing the time required to build hardware models. Typically, these hardware models will be subjected to a series of performance evaluations and stress tests to verify projected performance.

Administrative business processes can be physically modeled. This type of modeling is called conference room modeling. In these cases, mock-ups of the layout, terminals, keyboards, forms, and equipment are prepared. If commercial software is included in the future state solution, it will be exercised during this modeling operation. New, noncommercial software will be simulated manually, creating the superficial illusion that it has been written. Process modeling often requires substantial behind-the-scenes support in order to create the illusion of the future state process.

As a result of the modeling activity, a number of problems and improvement opportunities have been defined that require the future state solution to be upgraded and improved. By the end of the modeling phase, the feasibility of each future state solution should be well defined, and the risks associated with its physical implementation understood. If physical modeling is used, many of the human and emotional risks in the implementation will also be defined.

Future State Solution Validation

Now is the time to validate each of the potential future state solutions with the item's stockholders and to determine which solution they prefer. This means that the PIT needs to get out of its ivory tower and meet with customers, employees, managers, and suppliers. This validation can be done with focus groups; holding mixed focus groups (management, suppliers, customers, etc.), however, is not recommended. The purpose of these focus group meetings is to determine if the participants have any suggestions for how they can further improve the solutions and to get their assessment of which future state solution best meets their needs. The customer/consumer focus groups are the first sounding boards, because one of the major reasons for conducting a BPI study is to improve customer satisfaction. If the future state solution does not meet the customer's needs, there is little use in going further. The customer focus groups should concentrate on how the item's improved performance will impact them.

The next series of focus groups should consist of middle managers. Select managers who will be responsible for making the item work. With these focus groups, the PIT should present all the benefits of each of the potential future state solutions. These meetings are followed by meeting with the employees and suppliers. In both of these cases, the PIT should present all of the benefits of each of the potential future state solutions, but the major focus should be on how the individuals in the focus group will be impacted by each of the potential future state solutions. Suppliers are often a particularly rich source of improvement ideas.

All of the potential future state solutions should be presented at these focus group meetings so that the participants can evaluate and rate each of them. This is extremely valuable data and will be of great help in selecting the BFSS.

Sometimes, changes to processes can have consequences for other processes. This is particularly relevant if changes are introduced to data sets that are used by a number of processes. For techniques that can be used to examine the consequences of the proposed changes, the reader is referred to chapter 3. If a number of solutions are available for a particular problem, a decision on the basis of the collected and examined data should be made about which alternatives are the BFSS for the organization.

5.7.3 Best-Value Future-State Solutions

In today's competitive environment, it is difficult to select the best solution when redesigning an administrative business process because there are many options in designing a process. If the PIT had only one measurement to consider, the job would be relatively simple. If the PIT were only expected to design a process that had minimum cycle time, and no other factors were to be considered, the project would also be relatively simple. They would only focus on automation, mechanization, and information technology that would minimize cycle time. The problem is that processes are rarely designed to optimize one measurement without considering the other process-related measurements. In reality, a whole series of factors must be considered before an organization can understand the benefits that the stakeholder will derive from an individual future state solution. Some of the most common measurements that should be considered are

- Effectiveness of the future state process
- Efficiency of the future state process
- Adaptability of the future state process
- Cost to implement the future state process
- Cycle time to implement the future state process
- Risks related to the future state process

It becomes obvious that with these six factors, which impact almost all administrative business process future state solutions, it is difficult to determine if an individual future state solution is truly the best one for the organization if it is the only one being analyzed. If you delete bureaucracy from a process, you reduce cycle time and cost, which can have a negative impact on the quality of the output from the process. A more sophisticated example is the future state solution that completely automates the process, reducing cycle time and error rates but costing $3 million and 24 months to implement, when an improved manual process could be implemented for $50 thousand and be in place within six months. The manual process would provide 80% of the benefits realized from the automated future state solution. So which of these two is the future state solution that the organization should implement? In truth, there is no one right answer. It all depends on which process is being improved and the impact of the change on the entire organization's performance. What is right for one organization is often wrong for another.

A series of future state solutions based upon different objectives can be developed. Typical examples of different objectives for the same process are

▲ How much improvement can be obtained in cycle time and cost if the future state solution has to be implemented within a 90-day period?
▲ How much improvement in output quality can be obtained while reducing cycle time and cost by a minimum of 20%?
▲ How much improvement in cycle time, cost, and output quality can be obtained if the implementation cost and cycle time is not an important factor?
▲ How much improvement in cycle time and output quality can be obtained if the return on investment is a minimum of 12 to 1 over the next three years?
▲ How much improvement can be obtained by streamlining the present process and incorporating current proven techniques?
▲ What is the future state solution that will provide the best three year ROI?

Value, like quality, is in the eye of the beholder. With value, however, there are many more factors that the beholder evaluates than when she evaluates quality. The future state processes that represent best value to one organization often are the wrong processes for another organization. With the onset of the concept of best-value future-state, the concept of best practice has been replaced with a more comprehensive view of the administrative business processes. Today, very few, if any, best practices are the best-value solutions for the majority of the situations.

5.7.4 Defining Detail

In the framework of the design, the original schematic descriptions are modified and supplemented. The conclusions during the preceding activity (see section 5.2.2) regarding the consequences of the changes, are evaluated to determine if they are still consistent with the change objective or should be changed, supplemented, or defined in detail. The possible changes to the existing documents and files should be specified, and new forms, charts, etc. should be designed.

It is worth recommending that in the design phase, the changes should take the recording of the descriptions in the *Administrative Organization Manual* (see chapter 6) into consideration after approval.

5.8 Administrative Business Process Design and System Development

At first sight, it seems that a noticeable difference exists between the design of automated and manual administrative business processes. These differences are also present as we study the physical differences between manual and automated data processing.

▲ With the physical design of manual administrative business processes, departments in the organization, geographical locations, routing, document transportation times, and card trays and forms are considered.
▲ With the physical design of automated administrative business processes, processors, terminals, printers, cables, operating systems, database management systems, and so on are considered.

With the development of computerized systems and the design of manual administrative business processes, the designer tries to make as much use as possible of the available processing capacity. The physical characteristics of people are entirely different than those of machines. In all respects, this should be taken into consideration. It is at this point in the improvement cycle that the organization change management activities start to pay off.

There are also, however, clear similarities between manual and automated administrative business processes. In both cases, the administrative business process has as an objective: the distribution of information to those who need it. The manner by which this information is created is unimportant to the user. In other words, whether the data on which the information is based is collected, documented, and processed by computers or by people makes no difference to the user; the user will continue to ask the same questions. (Of course, one difference is that automated techniques make it possible to satisfy the information distribution requirements because of the higher speed and lower cost associated with the use of computerized information techniques to process the data, whereas with manual data processing, these requirements may not be met.) It is not surprising that the first three activities in designing administrative business processes do not differ much from the similar activities in the system development method.

With the development of automated systems, at the end of the phase called *designing the logical structure,* the so-called people and machine boundary is determined. The details of whatever lies within the boundary are further defined by system analysts and programmers. They are the specialists in making optimal use of the capabilities of computers. The details of whatever lies outside of the boundary are further defined by specialists in the field of manual administrative business processes. They are the specialists in the area of designing administrative business processes in organizations. The internal coordination of the activities of both fields of expertise is very important. The complete administrative-organizational system should function as one unit.

Experts in designing manual administrative business processes are often called in late by the system developers. This results in the experts having to construct the processes around the already setup computer system. Not infrequently, the results are suboptimization and frustration, both for the designers and the users of the administrative business processes. The process designer, not the programmer, should be in charge of all business process-improvement activities. Information technology should be used to further improve the process after the process has been streamlined.

6 | Phase V—Implementation: Installing the Future-State Solution

6.1 Introduction

The payback for all of the PIT's work is realized during Phase V. This is where the results of all the data analysis and creative thinking that went into the development of the future-state solution are transformed into real performance improvement. Although a great deal of care has been taken to ensure that the future-state solution is complete and the projected costs and savings are correct, if the solution is poorly implemented, the entire project can become a failure. In fact, this is the phase that is most often responsible for BPI project failures. There seems to be an excitement and dedication to the creative part of the administrative BPI activities (Phases I through IV) that gets lost during the more mundane implementation activity. Too often, management's interests get sidetracked to a new project, and they don't establish the correct priorities that drive the project through to completion.

The other factor that causes the BPI project to fail during the implementation activity is that the individuals living with the current process have not been properly prepared for the change. Here again, we want to emphasize the importance of the Organizational Change Management (OCM) activities that should have been going on in parallel with Phases II through IV. If the PIT has waited until this point in the administrative BPI activities to start its OCM activities, it is asking for problems, as it is too late to get the real

203

support and help of the people who need to change. The difference between doing a good or bad job of OCM can be seen in the attitudes of the people who will be living with the change (changees). If the PIT did a good job, the changees will be saying, "Let me show you how to make this change work," instead of, "Let me show you why this change will not work."

The modified or new processes will be introduced by the respective departmental managers or contact groups. The project leader will fill a supporting role during this phase. Initially, it should be ensured that the different organizational conditions are fulfilled. Thought should be given to

▲ The availability of sufficient manpower to execute the respective administrative business processes
▲ The availability of sufficient enablers such as equipment, documentation systems, etc.
▲ The modification of the existing organization structure
▲ Consideration of the staff members involved with the process (It should be noted that the considerations of staff members directly involved with the process are discussed in the previous phases. Here, the consideration is of giving information and instruction to the indirectly involved staff members.)
▲ The control of the change from the old to the new process
▲ Delivering reports to external authorities who are also involved with the administrative business process

After the introduction of the process, it is important that departmental managers, the contact group, and the project leader monitor the process to make sure that it is functioning well. Possible unanticipated problems should be solved using a separate group or subgroup of the PIT.

In many situations, a test-run phase is performed before a new process formally starts functioning. During this phase, the new as well as the existing system (in part) will be run simultaneously. If, after the execution of an acceptance test by the future users of the system, it seems that the new process functions according to expectations, the old process will be retired definitively. The issues surrounding the test-run phase should naturally already have been considered during the design phase. During this phase, additional pressure will be placed on the organization because extra manpower and enablers are needed.

When the new process has been run for some time, an evaluation should be done. In this evaluation, which is performed by the departmental managers as well as the contact groups in cooperation with the project leader, whether or not the newly started process fulfills all the expectations will be examined. Adjustments will be made as needed. The evaluation report should be given to the PMT.

Phase V is made up of eight activities. They are

1. Form the future-state solution implementation team
2. Develop the implementation plan
3. Implement the first 90-day plan
4. Implement the long-term improvements
5. Measure and report results
6. Hold periodic reviews
7. Compare results to goals
8. Reward team members

6.2 Activity 1: Form the Future-State Solution Implementation Team

In phase IV, the future-state solution implementation team may or may not be made up of the same individuals who created the future state solution. (Note: The best-value future-state solution [BFSS] was selected during the previous phase. Throughout the remainder of the book, BFSS will be used interchangeably with future-state solution.) Often, specialists are required to

▲ Define the process design
▲ Provide the required software and IT equipment
▲ Provide the training
▲ Complete the detailed documentation

As a result, the team that will implement the future-state solution takes on additional support personnel. The future-state solution implementation team (hereafter referred to as the implementation team) is responsible for three tasks. They are

▲ Implementing the future-state solution
▲ Implementing the OCM plan
▲ Measuring the impact of the future state changes

In most cases, the members of the team are excellent technical change agents, but they seldom understand their role as a change agent in the OCM process.

The first activity that the implementation team must undertake is one of educating its members in the improvement process that the PIT has just completed so that the implementation team has a thorough understanding of the approved future-state solution. The next phase of their training is OCM training with specific emphasis on their role as people change agents. Each implementation team member must learn how to facilitate change within the organization. During this training, a change-project role map will be prepared and the following roles defined (see chapter 3):

- ▲ Initiating sponsors
- ▲ Sustaining sponsors
- ▲ Change agents
- ▲ Changees
- ▲ Advocates

6.3 Activity 2: Develop the Implementation Plan

Although an overview implementation plan is often prepared during phase IV, a very detailed implementation plan should now be prepared by the implementation team.

The implementation team should focus its efforts on developing a detailed plan for the next 90 days. A less comprehensive plan is then prepared for the remainder of the project. It is important that implementation and OCM detailed plans are well integrated, combining both the technical and OCM activities. Great care should be taken to ensure that the activities assigned to different functions are integrated and coordinated. Each function has a tendency to work as a stand-alone entity on most projects. This approach is inappropriate when the future-state solution is being implemented.

The following is a checklist that should be completed in support of every change.

- ▲ Have the employees been notified in advance of the change and have all of their questions been answered?
- ▲ What experiments have been made that prove the change will produce the desired results?

▲ Are there any negative side effects? If so, what are they?

▲ Has all the documentation been updated to reflect the change before the change is implemented?

▲ Has the employee training program been developed and the training scheduled to support the change? How will the implementation team measure the effectiveness of the training?

▲ What measurements will be impacted either positively or negatively? Do you have data that give these measurements before the change is implemented?

▲ How long should the implementation team wait after the change is implemented before the change impact is evaluated?

▲ What OCM activities are required to support the change and are the activities scheduled?

▲ How long after the change is implemented will outside support be required and what is the nature of that support?

The long-range implementation plan is used to constantly update the next 90-day detailed plan. Every month, the first month's activities of the 90-day detailed plan are dropped off, and the next month in the long-range plan is expanded and used to update the detailed 90-day plan. For example, if the detailed 90-day plan covered June, July, and August, then at the beginning of July, the June part of the plan is dropped and a detailed plan for September is added to the detailed 90-day plan, making a rolling detailed 90-day plan.

6.4 Activity 3: Implement the First 90-Day Plan

The implementation team should now concentrate on implementing the first 90-day plan. This is probably the most important part of the implementation project, because it will set the pace for the rest of the implementation process. Usually, the improvements that are implemented during the first 90 days are the quick fixes and the less complicated improvement solutions. Seldom are the major technological changes implemented during the first 90 days, because the technological changes require extensive planning, scheduling, and modeling. On the other hand, the OCM activities during the first 90 days are critical to not only the successful implementation of the first 90-day improvements but also the implementation of the total future-state solution. Great care should be exercised to establish functional, open communication systems from the beginning. The first month is the start of the transitional phase and is a high-stress period for all the targets. It is a period where sustaining sponsorship must be in place and any black holes quickly identified and corrected.

To add to the stress level, this is a period when the rate of improvement is usually the greatest. It is also a period when the executive surveillance activities run very high because they are evaluating the accuracy of the PIT's estimate. Successful completion of the first 90-day projects will greatly reduce the performance stress on the implementation team during the remainder of the cycle.

As each change is implemented and its impact measured, the project plan and the database should be updated. Particular care should be taken to keep flowcharts and simulation models up to date.

6.5 Activity 4: Implement the Long-Term Improvements

The long-term (greater than the first 90 days) implementation plan is the more technical part of the future-state solution. This is where new equipment and software are introduced into the process. The new application of information technology, other computer applications, and automation techniques require very careful evaluation and modeling before being adapted to ensure compatibility with the existing activities and the organization culture. An individual improvement can go through the following evaluation phases:

- ▲ Paper-level evaluation. A comparison of the performance specifications of the computer system or automation equipment to the application requirements. This often results in customizing the software and hardware before they can be modeled.
- ▲ Simulation modeling. Often a computer simulation model can be prepared that will provide a vertical picture of the improvement. This model is then exercised to define potential problems with the proposed improvement.
- ▲ Conference room modeling. A model is set up to duplicate a proposed solution. This model is used to verify that the solution will provide the desired results and to define additional changes that may be required. Normally, this is a very manual process with many people running around behind the scenes simulating the hardware and the software.

▲ Pilot test. A portion of the total organization is used to exercise the proposed improvement. This limited experiment is designed to detect any unforeseen problems and to verify the solution's effectiveness before it is implemented throughout the organization.

As the future-state solution implementation continues, the long-term implementation plan will be detailed and made part of the next 90-day plan. This process will be repeated every 30 days until the implementation is completed.

6.6 Activity 5: Measure and Report Results

At regularly scheduled intervals (about once a month), the implementation team should issue a status report. The report should cover

▲ Progress made compared to plan
▲ The updated, detailed 90-day plan
▲ Improvement results compared to projections. It is important to realize that many of the improvements have a learning curve associated with them, so that the maximum improvement level may not be reached until the operational effectiveness has peaked.
▲ Expenditures compared to budget
▲ Results of any OCM surveys
▲ Any unexpected problems

These status reports should be distributed to the executive team and the sustaining sponsors.

6.7 Activity 6: Hold Periodic Reviews

The implementation team should hold very short periodic progress reviews with the sustaining sponsors and the interested executive team members. At the beginning of the implementation process, this review should be held monthly. After the first 90 days, they should be held immediately following a major milestone or at a minimum of once every 90 days. These meetings should focus on the progress made in implementing the future-state solution and the measured results.

6.8 Activity 7: Compare Results to Goals

At the completion of the implementation process, the results should be compared to the goals and project improvement objectives. In addition, a detailed three-year return on investment should be calculated. This is also the time for the PIT and the implementation team to perform a postmortem of the administrative BPI (Business Process Improvement) project. The postmortem should concentrate on defining any creative approaches used by either team that could be applied to other administrative business processes and the mistakes that were made during the improvement process. The results of the postmortem should be documented.

6.9 Activity 8: Reward Team Members

It is very important to reward desired behavior if management wants to see the behavior pattern repeated. Most TQM books talk about rewarding people using the three *Ps*. They are

- ▲ **P**laques on the wall
- ▲ **P**ats on the back
- ▲ **P**resentations to management

These are all good, but in the BPI projects, a fourth *P* should be added— a **P**at on the wallet. A BPI project should result in a major dollar performance improvement, and this newfound wealth should be shared by the organization and the members of the two teams that made it possible.

Rewards should be given out as close as possible to the time that the desired behavior was observed, for it is at that point in time that the reward has the most effect. With this in mind, the PIT should be rewarded as soon as the executive team has approved the future-state solution. The problem with giving the PIT a financial award at this point is that the executive team does not know how good the solution is. As a result, one or more of the first three *Ps* are used to reward the PIT when the future-state solution is approved, and a financial award is given when the first 90-day solutions are evaluated. The implementation team's financial award usually comes at the end of the implementation cycle, with the first three *Ps* used as each major milestone is successfully completed.

6.10 Summary

With the completion of Phase V, the future-state solution has been transformed into the as-is process, and the impact on the process' performance has been measured. If the project was properly followed, management is happy with the results and has properly rewarded the members of the project and the implementation teams. Congratulations—but you cannot stop here. The organization has realized a major breakthrough in the process' performance, and now the organization should enter the management and continuous improvement phase, Phase VI.

It is important to note that although the future-state solution has been implemented and its effectiveness measured, the OCM process is not complete. For most major process changes, the OCM activities will continue for months and even years, depending on the degree of commitment that the organization wants from the changees in support of the future-state solution.

7 | Phase VI—Management: Managing the Administrative Business Process Organization for Continuous Improvement

7.1 Introduction

Now that the documentation, analysis, and design of the administrative business processes have been discussed in the previous chapters, this last chapter focuses on the ways in which the entire administrative business process is managed.

In order to have a well-managed administrative organization, it is necessary to have a continuous understanding of the ways in which the processes are organized. The administrative business processes are frequently analyzed and modified, if necessary, as a result of increasing automation or modifications in the operation and/or in the internal organization. For this, a good description of the processes is indispensable. The description must be complete and up to date.

The management of the administrative organization also includes a review of the setup and operation of the administrative organization. This review happens on the basis of the process descriptions. Similarly, four elements are considered to be important for a well-managed administrative organization.

- ▲ The setup of a documentation system
- ▲ The maintenance of the documentation

▲ The procedures for introducing changes
▲ The clarity of the responsibilities for the management of (parts of) the administrative organization for the involved staff members

We will first concentrate on the setup of the documentation system. Documentation contains the word *document*, which is any item that can provide us with knowledge or information in written or pictorial form, or by verbal communication. A documentation system is considered to be a systematically ordered collection of documents.

The purpose of documenting is to record and supply information by means of documents. A distinction must be made between the documentation of administrative business processes and project documentation. The project documentation that was also briefly discussed in section 2.6.3 (defining the details of the project) is recorded in the different project files (see section 7.2). The documentation of the administrative organization is included in the *Administrative Organization Manual* (see section 7.3).

7.2 Project Documentation

The project documentation involves all the documentation that originated during the execution of the project. The project documentation partly satisfies the following objectives:

▲ *Communication.* With the documentation, all those who were involved with the project can be informed about the development of the project from beginning to end.
▲ *Instruction.* With the project documentation, task assignments can be handed over from the project management team to the project team and the user, from the project team to the contact group, etc.
▲ *Assigning responsibilities and exercising control.* The project documentation exists as a means for assigning responsibilities for the activities that must be performed by staff members for the project. The project documentation can help the project team leader and the project management team determine if the decisions that were made were put into effect, and control can be exercised on the progress, costs, and quality of the activities.

▲ *Recording history.* The documentation can, while evaluating the project, be used as a reference

For every phase of the project, the project documentation includes

▲ Overviews of the activities in the project phase, such as activity plans, detailed time plans, and suitability plans (see section 2.7.1)
▲ Work plans and financial plans involving the activities in the various phases of the project (see section 2.7.2 and section 2.7.3)
▲ Progress reports about the time and cost spent on each of the phases of the project (see section 2.7.5)
▲ Reports to and approval by the contact group(s) and project management team of the applicable project documents
▲ Documentation about the administrative business processes (such as process documentation, analysis documentation, proposals for modifying or redesigning processes, and the final proposals)

See the overview of a project in section 2.6.1 for the relationship between the diverse project documents.

The project documentation is stored in diverse files within specific projects. These files are designed for each project and are organized according to the phases. The project files can be set up according to the type of project. Four project files (see below) are shown in figure 7.A.

▲ A project management file, in which work, detailed time, availability, suitability, and cost plans are recorded together with progress reports
▲ A decision-making file, in which the formulation of assignments, approval by contact group(s) and project management team, and decision-making are documented
▲ A development file, in which the information regarding the documentation, analysis, and evaluation of the processes is recorded
▲ A user file, in which the documents approved by the user are recorded. These documents include the final description of the modified or newly developed administrative business processes. These descriptions are recorded in the *Administrative Organization Manual* together with the forms that will be used, the function and task descriptions, a list of the employed concepts, etc.

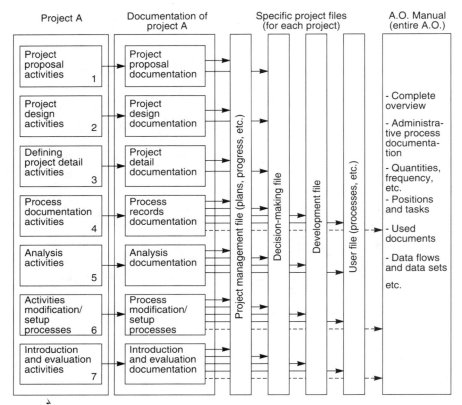

FIGURE 7.A   Relationship of the *Administrative Organization Manual* to the project documentation

Also as presented in section 2.6.3 (defining the details of the project), the various documents that originate during the project are coded and filed according to the project, the phase, and the subject. All the project documents are given a five-number code in which the following is recorded:

- ▲ The name of the project
- ▲ The phase in which the document originates
- ▲ The subject-matter number
- ▲ The number of the order of the document within the subject matter
- ▲ The version number

The documents in the *Administrative Organization Manual,* in which the documentation concerning the administrative business processes is recorded, are coded according to the organizational unit and the process; thus, the manual does not overlap with the contents of the project documentation. Documentation for the manual can nevertheless originate during the project. The documentation, in addition to the five-number project code, should also be assigned the codes needed for recording the document in the manual.

The relationship between the project documentation and the *Administrative Organization Manual* is represented in figure 7.A. In the two left columns of the figure, the successive project phases and the documentation from these phases are diagrammed for an arbitrary project. The project documentation is filed in the four different project files. Documentation for the *Administrative Organization Manual* comes particularly from the user file.

7.3   Documentation of the Administrative Organization

A different system is required for the documentation of the administrative organization. First, it is important that the documentation be accessed under the category of responsible organizational unit (division, department) and for the category of administrative business process or groups of processes. It is not important to know in which projects the processes were developed or how these projects were executed.

We will first focus on the objectives of a documentation system for an administrative organization, called an *Administrative Organization Manual.* In the manual, all of the documentation regarding the administrative organization is recorded. In addition to the descriptions of the processes, the task divisions, rules, standards, background information, and explanations should also be included.

A number of objectives for an *Administrative Organization Manual* are distinguishable.

▲ By means of the manual, the structure of the administrative organization is made clear. The manual clearly documents how the administrative business processes are organized and which guidelines must be followed. The documentation thus also serves as the basis for reviewing the operation of the administrative business processes. The documentation can also help to maintain the existing administrative-organization systems.

▲ The manual forms the basis for the analysis and the evaluation of the administrative business processes.

▲ The documentation in the manual makes comparison of existing and proposed designs of the processes possible in case of modifications.

▲ With the help of the manual, knowledge can be transferred between individuals (see also section 3.3) both over time and over distance. The manual can be used as an aid for training and helping new personnel understand the processes, while at the same time, because of the clear interpretation of the accepted process documentation, a uniform performance method can be brought about throughout the organization. The formal communication between the staff members involved with an administrative business process is also recorded, because the when, with whom, how, and what is communicated is indicated.

▲ The functions, tasks, and responsibilities within the administrative business processes are defined. A well-delineated task is particularly necessary for those processes in which various departments of the organization must successively or together perform specific tasks.

A few criteria, also noting the objectives, are important for managing the manual. These criteria should for each separate case be formulated in more or less detail. One can infer that as the organization becomes larger and more complex (more departments, more staff members, more processes, etc.), the work must be done in more detail.

The criteria for managing the manual are

▲ The management of permanent systems

▲ The coding of all the documents. It is stated in section 2.6.3 (defining the details of the project) that coding all of the documents, departments, subdivisions, processes, and forms requires quite a lot of time, but that it is still necessary to reach the objectives of the *Administrative Organization Manual.*

▲ The use of updating procedures designed to provide documentation control needs to be in place (see section 7.4.3)

▲ The organization of the management of the manual (see section 7.6)
▲ The association of the amount of detail with use. Depending on the ways in which the manual is used, the level of detail of the documentation in the manual must be specified (see section 3.5)
▲ The organization of the distribution of parts of the manual to the users (see section 7.4.3)

7.4 Content and Layout of the *Administrative Organization Manual*

All of the documentation concerning the administrative organization is recorded in the *Administrative Organization Manual*. Below, the content and structure of as well as the instructions for the manual are discussed.

7.4.1 The Content of the *Administrative Organization Manual*

The *Administrative Organization Manual* plays an important role as a tool for the management of the administrative organization. All of the documentation is also used with

▲ The analysis of the setup of the administrative organization
▲ The review of consequences of the proposed changes to the administrative organization
▲ Transferring knowledge involving the administrative organization
▲ The instruction of personnel

The documentation should be all inclusive. Attention must be paid to what is necessary for analysis (see chapter 4), and the construction of the manual must fit in with the thought processes that were used for designing the administrative organization (see chapter 5, in particular, figure 5.A). This combination of requirements leads to the next chapters of the *Administrative Organization Manual;* their content is further explained in figure 7.B and listed below.

Administrative Organization Manual	
	Page: 1
Section: *0. Instruction for the Manual*	Version: 2
Chapter: *2. Content of the Manual*	Author: *T.H. Koster*
Paragraph: *3. Explanation of the content*	Completed: *06-10-1991*
Subpar.:	Date: *01-13-1992*

0. Introduction and key word index
- a general brief introduction about the content, organization, work methods, and reasons for the manual
- an explanation of the control methods of the administrative organization in the organization
- a key word index to promote the manual's accessibility
- a tutorial (programmed lesson instructions) if necessary for quickly learning the content of the manual

1. General
- the context; the location of the organizational units/business processes in the environment
- a brief indication of the business processes, for example by means of a hierarchy of the goals
- the manner in which the control of the business processes is organized, as well as the selected control tools
- the relationship with the strategic information system plan in the organization
- risk analysis

2. Organization
- the organizational structure and its occupation
- the relationships with other organizational units
- the function of the involved organizational units
- the position, tasks, qualifications, and responsibilities of the involved staff members
- the procuration rules and design rules
- the relationship with the possible organization manual

3. Information management (internal communication)
- an overview of the most important management information (regarding guidance and responsibility)/internal reports, as well as a specification of the information systems/administrative processes from which these are created

4. Administrative processes
- a hierarchical overview of the administrative processes
- a complete overview (matrix) of the administrative processes and the organizational units
- a description, for example, in the form of global process diagrams or detailed process diagrams of the administrative processes
- a clarification of the administrative processes if necessary
- the relationship with system and user documentation of the automated systems

FIGURE 7.B   Contents of the *Administrative Organization Manual*

Administrative Organization Manual	
Section: 0. *Instruction for the Manual* Chapter: 2. *Content of the Manual* Paragraph: 3. *Explanation of the content* Subpar.:	Page: *1* Version: *2* Author: *T.H. Koster* Completed: *06-10-1991* Date: *01-13-1992*

5. *Work instructions:*
   Textual, in the form of instruction diagrams, processed collection of work instructions for those situations which is worthwhile, as a result of the complexity of the processes, the associated importance, or the necessity for using changing or inexperienced personnel. These work instructions are usually recorded on the right-hand side pages of the manual, next to the associated detailed process diagrams on the left-hand side.

6. *Internal control:*
   An overview of the recorded internal control measures for control as well as for the reliability of the information, one and another can be distinguished in:
   - specific relational and complete controls
   - network of control totals
   - organizational measures such as functional divisions, etc.
   - qualification rules
   - unique measures (quasi-merchandise, file of existence, creation and delegation files, etc.)
   - (detail) controls within the administrative processes, for example, in the form of an overview of the control actions

7. *Various aspects (enabling techniques):*
   - time table
   - frequency table
   - office layout
   - quantity overviews
   - particular fiscal factors
   - particular legal factors
   - particular administrative rules
   - (ledger) account use rules, for example, in the form of an account use diagram

8. *Data carriers:*
   A chapter in which the data carriers (documents) and their characteristics are recorded

9. *Data definitions:*
   A chapter in which all the definitions of the entities as well as the relationships between these entities are recorded

FIGURE 7.B—Continued

0. Introduction and Key Word Index
1. General (context, business processes, method of operation)
2. Organization
3. Information management (internal communication)
4. Administrative processes
5. Work instructions
6. Internal control
7. Various aspects (enabling techniques)
8. Data carriers
9. Data definitions

This content fits in with the definition of a basic administrative organization. The manual addresses the systematic collection, documentation, processing, and distribution of data aimed at producing information required to manage the daily activities and to choose alternatives.

In practice, the chapter layout is customized to meet the needs of each function. In the part of the manual in which the financial administrative processes are documented, specific room is reserved for the ledger accounting system, the entry regulations, the agenda, periodical entries, the budget and annual accounting cycle, assessment regulations, and so forth. The human resources and organization section provides separate space for training rules.

Apart from the exceptions mentioned above, it is important that the layout of the chapters for all the sections in the *Administrative Organization Manual* are as similar as possible if different organization subdivisions exist in which (parts of) the administrative organization are managed. This makes it possible to group different subjects together in the different sections of the manual. Thus, a combination of all the fifth chapters (administrative business processes) and the third sections (detailed process diagrams) will give one an understanding of all of the administrative business processes.

7.4.2 The Structure of the *Administrative Organization Manual*

The *Administrative Organization Manual* is an important management tool. The structure of the manual must therefore tie in with the organization's management structure (see section 7.6). The manual also provides direction to the process designers (PITs) that helps them establish common single-data models with uniform data definitions that can be used for all of the administrative business processes.

Two structural models for the *Administrative Organization Manual* are discussed below. One model is for situations in which there is a relatively high degree of integration among the administrative business processes and the other is for situations with a relatively low degree of integration. In general terms, cases are also explained in which these models are considered to be applicable.

Organizations with a relatively high degree of integration among the administrative business processes are small to medium sized organizations in which the interdependence of the different organizational units is relatively strong. A consequence of relatively strong organizational unit interdependence is that those units exchange data and make use of the same data collections relatively often. That is why in these situations, many of the aspects of the administrative organization are centrally coordinated and managed. This central coordination can be necessary from the point of view of strategic, management, expertise, consolidation, and efficiency considerations. It leads to central management and therefore to an *Administrative Organization Manual* in which there is a similar layout for all the organizational units. To keep sections of the manual for each of the organizational units accessible, during distribution, the relevance of the different sections for the organizational units should be considered.

The structure of a manual in the case of a relatively high degree of integration is presented in figure 7.C. It involves a manual for a medium to large production company with divisions of purchasing, sales, shipping, production 1 and 2, warehouse, and laboratory, and the staff departments of control, business administration, information management, general affairs, and human resources and organization. Figure 7.C shows that the contents of the sections of the manual that include the departments are for the most part the same and yet the descriptions of the administrative business processes are only distributed to the involved departments.

The *Administrative Organization Manual* looks completely different for an organization with a relatively low degree of integration among the administrative business processes. This second type can be characterized by the existence of a central, relatively small management system with a number of practically independent business units. In this situation, the question is what should be managed centrally and what can be decentralized?

Chapter of the manual \ Sections of the manual	Main departments					Staff departments				
Introduction/key words	X	X	X	X	X	X	X	X	X	X
General	X	X	X	X	X	X	X	X	X	X
Organization	X	X	X	X	X	X	X	X	X	X
Information management	X	X	X	X	X	X	X	X	X	X
Administrative processes	see the diagram below									
Work instruction	X	X	X	X	X	X	X	X	X	X
Internal control	X	X	X	X	X	X	X	X	X	X
Diverse aspects	X	X	X	X	X	X	X	X	X	X
Data carriers	X	X	X	X	X	X	X	X	X	X
Data definitions	X	X	X	X	X	X	X	X	X	X

Administrative processes	Departments									
1		X					X		X	
2	X			X						
3	X				X					
4			X	X		X		X		
5	X			X	X		X			
6			X	X		X		X		
7		X	X				X		X	
8				X	X					
9					X	X				
10						X	X			
11							X	X		
12							X		X	
Etc.										

FIGURE 7.C *Administrative Organization Manual,* relatively high degree of integration among the administrative processes

Figure 7.D presents the structure of a manual based on an organization with independent organizational units, such as divisions, business units, and/or results-oriented units.

Sections 0, 1, and 2 of the manual are centrally managed in this structure (for section 0 of the manual, see section 7.4.3). In section 3, the regulations

Section / Chapter	0 Instruction manual	1 Data management	2 Data carriers	3 Financial dept.	4 H.R. & O.	5 Organizational units	6 etc. Organizational units
0	Introduction	Introduction	Introduction	Introduction/ key words	Introduction/ key words	Introduction/ key words	Introduction/ key words
1	General	General	General	General	General	General	General
2	Content of Manual	Data definitions	Data carriers	Organization	Organization	Organization	Organization
3	Control	Etc.	Etc.	Information management	Information management	Information management	Information management
4	Distribution			Administrative processes	Administrative processes	Administrative processes	Administrative processes
5	Documentation techniques			Work instructions	Work instructions	Work instructions	Work instructions
6	Automated enablers			Internal control	Internal control	Internal control	Internal control
7	Rules for change			Various aspects	Various aspects	Various aspects	Various aspects
8	Rules for layout			Data carriers	Data carriers	Data carriers	Data carriers
9	Terms and concepts			Data definitions	Data definitions	Data definitions	Data definitions

FIGURE 7.D   *Administrative Organization Manual,* relatively low degree of integration among the administrative processes

from the financial administration (the so-called accounting manual) are given. Section 4 contains the similar regulations from the human resources and organization units. In section 5, a–n, the remote, decentralized organizations' managers document their own administrative organization for all activities that are not managed out of the central office. This can involve documenting remote locations' parts of the information system plan and the conceptual data model. This means that the *Administrative Organization Manual* for the manager who is responsible for section 10 includes sections 0–4 (filled in and managed by other positions) and his own section 10.

In practice, diverse variables are recognized for the two situations described here. The situation of the remote, decentralized organization should not be confused with the situation in a branch organization. In a branch organization, there is no mention of a decentralized authority for managing and designing the primary processes nor of a deconcentration of the execution of centrally managed processes or centrally managed administrative business processes. In this case, it is a matter of a relatively high degree of administrative business process integration.

Intermediate forms are also possible. For reasons of expertise, standardization, legal equality, and efficiency, the situation may be one in which the transaction processing information systems are centrally managed while the authority over the design of the operation method is decentralized. In this case, the structure of the *Administrative Organization Manual* will be a mixed form of figures 7.C and 7.D. It should be clear that assigning a section of the manual only makes sense if a centralized or decentralized controller can be indicated for that section.

7.4.3 Instructions for the *Administrative Organization Manual* (Section 0)

The objectives of the *Administrative Organization Manual* (see section 7.3) are a uniform layout of the different sections and a uniform use of symbols. Promoting the uniformity and arranging the management and the distribution of the manual are the most important objectives of the instructions for the *Administrative Organization Manual*. In practice, they are for the most part indicated in section 0. The contents of section 0 are given in figure 7.D. A few comments about each chapter will be made below.

Chapter 2 of section 0 contains the table of contents for the entire *Administrative Organization Manual*. The following are indicated in this chapter:

- ▲ The contents by sections (with reference to chapter 3 of section 0)
- ▲ The layout used for the chapters and sections
- ▲ The content of the chapters (figure 7.B provides an example of two pages from chapter 2, section 0)

Since the administrative organization is constantly being adjusted, it is advisable to set up the manual as a loose-leaf binder or to computerize it. In case of changes, the manual will not have to be completely redistributed each time. The distribution of the changes will be sufficient. Each page must therefore be uniquely identified. The header of each page serves this purpose. The contents of the header, as presented in figure 7.E, makes the unique identification of each page possible regardless of the selected manual structure.

The table of contents of the manual must be updated to reflect changes that are recorded during the documentation phase. On the basis of these changes, one can quickly examine which changes were implemented and whether the prescribed procedures were followed. If the documentation standards are not recorded anywhere else in the organization, they should be recorded in the manual, in chapter 7 of section 0 (the rules for change).

Chapter 3 of section 0 indicates how the management of the administrative organization and the manual are built into the organization. This will be further discussed in section 7.6, in which management is treated in detail.

In chapter 4 of section 0, the distribution of the manual is arranged. The distribution of the manual is looked after by the unit that is responsible for maintaining the manual. The names of the individuals who have a copy of the manual should be documented on a distribution list. The changes are given to those individuals on the basis of the list.

It is possible that staff members only receive certain sections of the manual. In this case, the sections that are in the possession of staff members should be marked on the distribution list and only the changes for the relevant sections should be distributed.

Administrative Organization Manual		
Section: *0. Instruction for the manual* Chapter: *2. Content of the manual* Paragraph: *4. Page identification* Subpar.:	Page: *1* Version: *2* Author: *Noordam* Modified: *06-10-1991* Date: *01-13-1992*	

FIGURE 7.E   *Administrative Organization Manual* page header

An accompanying list is sent along with the updates for the manual, on which, among others, the following is included:

▲ The pages to be added
▲ The pages to be removed
▲ The date of distribution
▲ The date of the previous changes
▲ The number of these changes
▲ The number of previous changes

In all cases, the new table of contents of the manual is sent along.

A step-down distribution, whereby a number of the manuals are given to the heads of the departments, who can, according to their own views, distribute it to their staff members, is also possible. Several conditions are placed on using a manual; namely, that the content be reliable and that it is only used in the scope of the activities of the organization. The staff members are thus obliged to turn in the manual when they are no longer employed. Arrangements whereby manuals are distributed by room are not advisable unless the staff members are made responsible for the management of the copies for each room.

A few rules for documenting the descriptions in the manual are recorded in chapter 5 of section 0. These diagramming conventions must tie in with the selected choices regarding the width and depth of the documentation (see sections 3.4 and 3.5). For examples of the rules for the use of the documentation techniques, the reader is referred to the appendices. The computerized enablers used for documentation (see section 7.3) can, by their operation, be of influence on the rules that are to be made. For the application of computerized enablers, chapter 6 of section 0, see section 7.6.

Chapter 7 of section 0 contains the rules for changing the manual. In principle, all the users of the manual are authorized to make proposals for change or additions to the administrative business processes. Good procedures, such as those that make sure that all the consequences have been reviewed, must be used for implementing changes. The following steps are important:

▲ Filing proposals for change or additions to the administrative business processes with a central department—the Administrative Organization Department
▲ Setting up an initial orientation between the initiators, the involved departmental managers, and the Administrative Organization Department about the change/adaptation

▲ Examining the results of the change for other administrative business processes, efficiency, internal control, automated systems, etc.

▲ Recording who should approve the change and making a proposal for the completion date (done by the Administrative Organization Department)

▲ Making a conceptual description of the administrative business process, in which attention is paid to the relationship with other processes, the effectiveness and efficiency, control factors, and automation

▲ Assessing the conceptual description (by the departmental heads and internal and external accountants)

▲ Proposing the final process description (by the Administrative Organization Department)

▲ Delivering the description to the documentation department (This department confirms whether the description satisfies the form requirements, is responsible for recording it in the manual, and is also responsible for distributing the description to the organization.)

▲ Introducing the administrative business process to the involved departments (with guidance from the Administrative Organization Department if necessary)

To control the completion of all the steps for introducing a change, the changes can, from the moment that an initiative for a change exists, be recorded in a change file in which the completion of each step can be noted. The tables of the change files can contain the following columns:

▲ Number
▲ Initiative description
▲ Process number
▲ Approval date
▲ Date of introduction
▲ Approved by
▲ Recorded in the manual
▲ Evaluation
▲ Final initials

Chapter 8 of Section 0 presents the word-processing rules for the manual. The definition of the type size, page layout, the use of letter types, the use of predefined macros in the word processing software, and the use of special paper can all be considered in this context. In this chapter, how the word files and the files of the computerized tools must be prepared, changed, and filed can also be presented.

In chapter 9 of section 0, the definitions and concepts of the terms applied in section 0 and their relationship with other terms and concepts are specified.

7.5 Computerizing the *Administrative Organization Manual*

It is advisable from the point of view of quality and productivity to computerize the *Administrative Organization Manual.* This can be done on a personal computer. In this context, programs for the following are important:

▲ Word processing for the text of the manual
▲ Diagramming with the help of the documentation techniques described in the appendices

The word-processing program enables the text to be rearranged, changed, etc. The word-processing tools make it simple to quickly make changes to the text of the manual in the case of changes in the administrative organization.

The diagrams documented in the *Administrative Organization Manual* can be drawn manually. Templates and previously printed forms are employed. Drawing the diagrams manually nevertheless has a few drawbacks: it requires a lot of time, the diagrams are more difficult to update, and the consistency between the different diagrams must be monitored manually.

There are also computer programs that automate the drawing of diagrams. These programs work on personal computers or networks. Drawing diagrams with the help of such a computer program has a number of advantages.

▲ For experienced users, the drawing goes much more quickly.
▲ The diagrams can be saved in computerized data files and updated later.
▲ The layout is frequently of high quality because the diagrams can be printed on a laser printer, the letter type can be made to fit the diagrams, and the programs can control various layout functions, such as centering text and symbols.

The ease with which the text or the diagrams can be updated is an important advantage of having a computerized versus a manual version of the manual. In documentation, analysis, or design projects, a diagram will not be good after the first effort because it is improved by means of an iterative process. A computerized documentation enabler can result in a considerable increase in productivity.

The application of computerized enablers for documentation also has disadvantages. A certain amount of time is necessary to learn how the program operates. However, the programs available on the market are quite user-friendly and can often be operated with a mouse. A second disadvantage is that an investment in hardware and software is needed. It is true that these days, personal computers are common property. Yet investments in the necessary software can increase quite a bit, particularly for more advanced enablers. Whether this investment is warranted depends on the advantages that can be realized in the case-specific situations.

There are roughly three groups of computerized enablers for documentation that can be distinguished:

- ▲ Free-style drawing programs. These enable the user to be completely free in selecting an illustration. A hierarchical overview can be drawn with these programs, as can houses and trees. The fact that these programs are completely free-style makes it somewhat complicated to diagram the administrative organization.
- ▲ Structured or restricted drawing programs. These are programs that have been specifically developed for making certain kinds of diagrams. These programs include standard symbols that can be recalled. The restricted drawing programs have a number of advantages over the free-style drawing programs. A fixed layout can be prescribed and controlled with respect to the location of symbols (always right under or next to each other). Restricting the ability of the user to draw freely helps to ensure the uniformity of the diagrams. The structure also results in greater productivity with documentation.
- ▲ Integrated enablers for documentation. This constitutes a unique category of structured or restricted drawing programs.

Integrated documentation enablers are particularly aimed at building an integral model of the administrative organization. Integrated documentation enablers belong to the Computer Aided Software Engineering tools (CASE tools). With these programs, the diagrams are in-between stations. Symbols, by means of a diagram, are entered into an encyclopedia by the user. This encyclopedia is stored in the central database. In calling up a diagram, it is not recalled from a disk but is put together from the symbols and relationships that are stored in the encyclopedia. In saving a diagram, the symbols and relationships that appear in the diagram are read into the encyclopedia. Each symbol is only represented once in the encyclopedia. Each time that a diagram is called up in which this symbol appears, the symbol is copied from the encyclopedia to the diagram (see figure 7.F). Thus, if the name of a docu-

Free-style of structured enablers for documentation

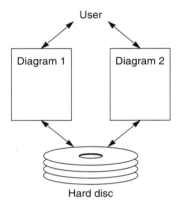

Integrated enablers for documentation

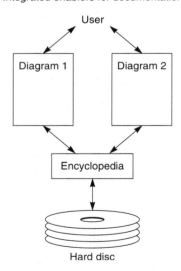

FIGURE 7.F   Free-style, structured, and integrated documentation enablers

ment is modified, the modification is also transferred to the encyclopedia. The name of the document is also changed in all the other diagrams in which this document appears.

The specific advantages of integrated enablers are

▲ The ability to document large and complex administrative organizations as a whole without losing the overview. This is particularly important if the administrative processes are integrated to a high degree.

▲ For each of the symbols, all sorts of features, definitions, and comments can be stored.

▲ Productivity will improve because the data and the data modifications only need to be entered once.

▲ The consistency of complex documentation is monitored by the documentation enabler.

▲ Reports about the administrative organization as a whole can be made in an easy way.

7.6 Responsibility for the Administrative Organization

The problems discussed up to this point in the book have in each case been insufficient in one respect: the question of who in the organization is responsible for administrative information management systems/administrative organization as a whole has only been indirectly discussed. In this chapter, we talk about an Administrative Organization Department that is responsible for the management, maintenance, and distribution of the *Administrative Organization Manual.* This department can also be responsible for the documentation, analysis, and evaluation of the administrative business processes. It is the department where a good overview of the administrative organization exists and where the consequences for possible changes can be studied. This set of tasks, however, does not cover all the responsibility for the administrative organization: what is the validity of an administrative organization manual, to what extent can the procedures be undone, which sanctions are present when not following the rules? The manager responsible for individual sections and/or parts of the manual is held accountable for the content of the manual, for the good design of administrative business processes, and for their introduction, compliance, and functioning. The administrative staff department is responsible for coordinating, disseminating, and controlling the manual content but is not responsible for the credibility of the manual's contents.

7.6.1 The Controller and the Administrative Organization

Often, the Administrative Organization Department is part of the controller's organizational structure.

The controller in this situation also has the responsibility for the

▲ Business economic analyses and recommendations
▲ Forecasts, estimates, and budgets
▲ Calculations
▲ Financing and credit reviews
▲ Treasury
▲ Taxes
▲ Insurance

The administrative support activities may also be included in the controller's function. This type of organization structure unites the entire administrative information management system within a single function. The controller can make use of the different departments that are experienced in that particular field (such as an Administrative Organization Department). Various interpretations are presented in the literature about the composition of the position and tasks of a controller.

Note: Depending on the organization, the responsibilities for the *Administrative Organization Manual* can be placed in many different functions. (For example, we have seen the responsibilities assigned to the human resources, information systems, quality assurance, production control, or accounting functions.) To demonstrate how the manual can be maintained in an organization, we will present the case where it has been assigned to the controller's function.

7.6.2 The Information Manager and the Administrative Organization

The responsibilities of the administrative organization are still being developed, due in part to the influence of process computerization, office computerization, etc. Counted among those positions partly responsible for the administrative organization (such as the internal accountant, internal control department, administrative organization experts, system developers, controller) is the recently developed position of information manager. The information manager is considered to be responsible for

▲ Monitoring the consistency between the organization, information policies, and information plans (and subsequent automation policies and plans)
▲ The changeable aspects of the above
▲ Describing the future information needs in consideration of the long-term information policies
▲ Developing and managing a conceptual framework for the administrative information management system (with emphasis on the user specifications for the system)
▲ Monitoring the rejection between individual projects (partly determined by the information management system)

The information manager is kept busy on an abstract level with the aspects of the information system aimed at the users. We recommend that the information manager position should not be at the official management level within the organization, irrespective of users and a possible computer center. This is frequently a nonmanagement staff position. A combination of the positions of controller and information manager is not unheard of.

7.6.3 Functional Divisions between the Controller, the Management, and the Information System Manager in the Area of Administrative Organization

As noted at the beginning of this section, the tasks that must be completed in the scope of managing the administrative organization go substantially further than those for only managing the *Administrative Organization Manual.* It is advisable to differentiate between technical management and functional management with the management of the manual. Functional management involves the content of the manual and the applicable concepts and definitions. Technical management involves writing the descriptions for the manual and updating the manual.

Tasks that are included in the functional management of the manual are

▲ Designing the structure of the *Administrative Organization Manual*
▲ Defining the terms and concepts used with the *Administrative Organization Manual* and updating them
▲ Controlling the quality of the definitions
▲ Monitoring the application of the documentation standards
▲ Defining, documenting, and improving the documentation standards

Tasks that are associated with the technical management of the manual can be summed up as follows:

▲ Proposing rules for word processing
▲ Ensuring that good computerized enablers are used for documenting and analyzing
▲ Updating the manual (process changes)
▲ Organizing the distribution of the manual and the updates
▲ Filling a supporting role for the initiation and realization of changes

Of course, a number of additional advisory and executive roles can be distinguished in the scope of the manual, such as

▲ The execution of the descriptions and the analysis or the delivery of the expert manpower
▲ The organization of the description and analysis projects
▲ The actual implementation of improvements in the administrative organization

The tasks in the scope of the management of the administrative organization also include tasks such as those defined for the *Administrative Organization Manual*. In addition, the tasks of the management (in the broadest sense of the word) of the administrative organization include

▲ Setting up the information structure of the organization
▲ Defining future information needs and indicating how these needs can be met
▲ Setting up and designing the administrative organization
▲ Monitoring the efficiency, effectiveness, and reliability of the administrative organization

▲ Testing whether the administrative organization functions as prescribed
▲ Taking care that there is sufficient knowledge about the setup, design, and desired work methods

The question of which positions in the organization must take the different administrative management tasks is a complex one, particularly when the organization grows, when specialization within the organization increases in the field of administrative information management systems, and with the discussion about the advisability of centralizing and decentralizing the tasks.

Originally, the administrative-organizational position was filled within the financial function of the organization. With smaller and medium-sized organizations, administrative organization, computerization, information processing, and analysis are still for the most part combined in one department. Defining the tasks of the operational departments, such as purchasing and sales, results in few problems. The responsibility for the tasks in the area of administrative organization management as defined above lies with the staff members in the financial department.

Dividing the tasks of administrative organization is generally sensible when the financial functions are divided into functions of management and controller duties on the basis of considerations about efficiency or internal control. In this way, a separate administrative department can exist that operates in addition to the controller's department and that continues to perform the tasks, except those of financial administration, summed up in section 7.6.1.

As soon as a certain size is reached, it becomes effective for the organization to establish a separate administrative organization. This organization will define the data processing structure within the individual departments and the guidelines that the supplying departments must satisfy regarding uniformity and consolidation requirements.

For writing and analyzing the administrative organization, the central Administrative Organization Department will provide support, although not in the form of manpower, training, etc. The department manager who prepares a section in the manual is usually assigned to determine when that section of the manual should he updated and is given the responsibility for managing that section of the manual.

The situation becomes more complex if in addition to the controller's position and the management function, the position of information manager is present. Because the task of the information manager is not limited to the administrative organization regarding the financial management and the systems that deliver to it, the information manager includes in his area the complete information processing and distribution systems in the organization. In other words, information management for the benefit of the financial office is only one of the sometimes many areas needing attention. Here, the question arises of how the task divisions among the controller, the administrative organization staff department (whether differentiated or not), the information manager, and the users should be carried out.

In the area of the administrative organization, the task of the information manager should at least be to create common frameworks and monitor consistency. This means that in the area of administrative organization, the information manager, in addition to his tasks in other areas, should

- Indicate the overall structure of the *Administrative Organization Manual*
- Indicate the pattern of functional and task divisions concerning the administrative organization and describe the associated responsibilities and needs
- Maintain the methods and techniques for describing and analyzing the administrative organization
- Manage computer systems for describing and analyzing the organization and support the users of the systems
- Train staff members in the areas of describing and analyzing the administrative organization
- Support the users (possessing manpower)
- Maintain at least one complete copy of the *Administrative Organization Manual* of the entire organization in which all the descriptions are recorded
- Maintain the (overall) data management
- Indicate the information structure (information architecture) for the entire organization
- Monitor the consistent use of the prescribed methods and techniques throughout the entire organization
- Identify, in the framework of the management of the *Administrative Organization Manual*, unnecessary duplicates and/or overlaps in the organization. This means that the different responsibilities of the management should be clearly defined.

Assuming that for the entire organization, a central controller function exists, the following tasks in the area of administrative organization management can be defined:

▲ The general setup and design of the administrative organization for the functions that come under the controller functions (business economic analyses, planning, calculations, treasury, etc.). This involves the setup and the design of functions within the controller's own department and those of the authorities that deliver information.
▲ Checking the data processing in the appropriate areas
▲ Carrying the responsibility for the quality of the distributed information. In this area, the controller must also be able to give guidelines to the departments that supply the information.

It makes sense that the management of the section of the manual that involves activities conducted by the controller function is managed by the controller. This means that in practice, the controller will analyze and describe the relevant sections of the administrative organization. She will also be responsible for analyzing the documents produced in or by the departments that deliver information.

With respect to the initial setup of the manual, the controller will prioritize the order in which the different divisions of the administrative organization are described. The section of the manual that involves his functions will be maintained and distributed by him. He should also make sure that the departments that deliver information operate according to the rules recorded in the manual. Through this work organization, the controller also performs a few tasks that are part of the internal control processes.

The management department will, on the basis of the guidelines and requirements set by the controller, design the detailed layout of the business processes within the management department. In accordance with the rules of the information manager and the controller's office, it will design and describe in detail the administrative organization within its own department. In addition, the management office should also make sure that the processing of the data is done in accordance with the prescribed methods.

These practices result in a task division whereby the information manager is occupied with the main structures, the rules regarding the methods and techniques, and the full support of the information system. She produces a hierarchical overview, the (main) diagram of administrative process principles, the context diagrams, and the complete overview of the entire organization. The controller is responsible for the design of the internal communication administrative organization, and he monitors the effectiveness and describes the administrative organization on the level of the global process diagrams and the detailed process diagrams for his own department. He also writes the guidelines and the instructions for the departments he supplies with information.

The management office describes the administrative system in its own department according to the detailed process diagrams and the necessary instruction diagrams. The management office also documents its own information processing activities for the benefit of the departments it supports and its own employees.

7.6.4 Conclusion

A good definition of the responsibilities of the management of the administrative organization is very important. In the very beginning of the project, it is important to record who the responsible users are and who is responsible for the management (in a broad sense) of the administrative organization. Clearly defining these responsibilities avoids a great deal of confusion that can exist when the individual detailed processes are being defined and documented. In addition, it is preferable to prearrange the project organization in accordance with the eventual management situation: a manager of a section of the *Administrative Organization Manual* will need to be a member of the project team that describes that section of the manual.

The administrative organization should schedule an audit for each section of the manual to periodically test whether the documented procedures are being followed and whether they meet the organization's ever-changing business needs. The chairperson of each audit team should be the manager who is responsible for that section of the manual. The objective behind this is to involve the user as much as possible with the maintenance of her own section of the manual, with guidance from a central technical coordination unit or person. After all, the *Administrative Organization Manual* is prepared to provide help and guidance to the people who work with and use the organization's administrative systems.

I

Organizational Structure Diagram

I.1 General

The organizational structure diagram serves to give insight into the structure of an organization. In particular, the diagram focuses on the formal relationships between individual units and departments. These relationships can be of both a hierarchical (with regard to authority relationships) as well as a functional (with regard to the rules and guidelines) nature.

The organizational structure diagram is not appropriate for diagramming the administrative business processes; the diagram serves as background information for the administrative processes and is aimed at providing insight. In particular, the organization location factors and the relationship between departments and individuals can be presented in the diagram.

I.2 Features

Of all the possible diagramming techniques, the organizational structure diagram is applied the most in practice. In almost every organization, a need exists to clarify the formal hierarchic and functional relationships, and probably some form of documentation of the organizational structure is available. Reproducing the organizational structure, therefore, does not initially involve the questions of which individuals hold which particular positions and which tasks they fulfill. Of more significance is how certain positions interrelate. To reproduce this, it will often suffice to document the interrelationships between the various departments, subdepartments, contact groups, commissions, or project teams without indicating the individual positions within each group.

The objective of a reproduction of an organizational structure diagram is limited: in addition to the formal lines of authority and responsibility, it shows the groups, departments, or individuals into which the operations are divided. The squares in the diagrams represent these units.

Something can be reported about the nature of the operations in these diagrams by means of definitions. The set of tasks of an administrative department in a trading company, for example, can be subdivided into updating the accounts, controlling purchasing invoices, controlling sales invoices, monitoring accounts receivable, drawing up budgets, and managing reports in which the facts are compared with the budgets.

It is advisable to limit the organizational structure diagrams to the factors mentioned above (the hierarchical relationships, the division of operations among the departments). One should realize that the diagram may suggest relationships that in practice do not exist: the numerous informal contacts and relationships are not represented. The information organization does not appear in the diagrams. In addition, one can indicate in the diagram that there is some hierarchical relationship between two business divisions, yet the extent to which this relationship is valid is not diagrammed. In general, it can be stated that the organizational structure diagram is not appropriate for representing the degree of authority and responsibility of the different positions as well as the different staff members.

Although an organizational structure diagram is present in most companies, the diagram is not always up to date. The number of changes that are regularly made in some organizations makes it nearly impossible to remodify the diagrams each time. Still, it is of the utmost importance, particularly in somewhat more complicated organizations, to have an accurate impression of the structure of the organization at one's disposal. With these kinds of companies, one also sees that new diagrams are published fairly frequently and distributed within the organization, or at least that only those pages for which changes have been made are modified. The organizational structure diagram then usually makes up a section of an organization guide, in which, in addition to the structure of the organization, the names and positions of all the staff members, addresses and telephone numbers, as well as geographical layout of the company is recorded.

To meet the drawbacks of the repeatedly redrawn diagrams, one can see that simple computer applications should be used. After implementing a change in the organizational structure file (for example, by the position code, name, and immediate manager), the computer programs immediately modify the diagrams and reprint them. (The applications are also a part of the computerized tools for describing the administrative organization.)

This application can become more interesting when, in addition to the hierarchical relationships, the functional lines of consultation can also be diagrammed. In small organizations, this application is usually not advisable, and new manual modifications of the diagrams will be necessary each time.

I.3 Rules

I.3.1 Layout

There are two variations for the layout of the organizational structure diagrams: the *vertical* and the *horizontal* diagrams.

The Vertical Diagram

In the vertical diagram, the vertical lines indicate the hierarchical subordination and the horizontal coordination. This method of drawing is traditionally the one most applied. In figure I.A, a management secretarial staff department that reports directly to management is drawn. In the circle, a computerization steering committee is indicated.

In general, it is true that commissions, consulting units, and project teams are indicated by similar circles as part of the organizational structure. The circle is drawn next to the department or units that had the initiative for starting the commission or the consulting unit. On the bottom right side in

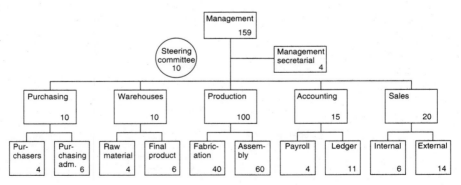

FIGURE I.A   Organizational structure diagram (vertical): Type 1

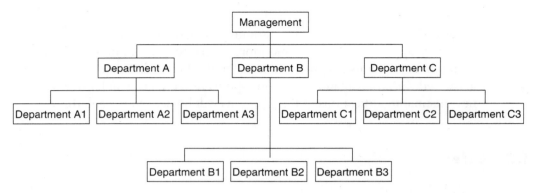

FIGURE I.B   Organizational structure diagram (vertical): Type 2

the squares, the number of personnel including the management level in each department is recorded and totaled. The above example covers the entire width of the page. With more complex diagrams, it may be necessary, because of a lack of space, to construct the diagram in such a way that the reproduction of the equality of the diagrams on a horizontal level is dropped.

Examples of these less accurate (of necessity) diagrams are reproduced in figures I.B and I.C. Figure I.B gives the impression that departments A1 to A3 and C1 to C3 are located higher in the organization than departments B1 to B3. In figure I.C, A1, B1, and C1 seem to be respectively higher in position than A3, B3, and C3.

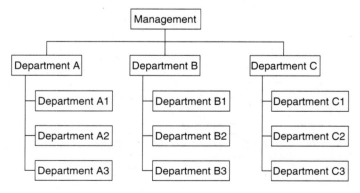

FIGURE I.C   Organizational structure diagram (vertical): Type 3

The Horizontal Diagram

This form of diagram is attractive from the viewpoint of a surface division (particularly when the organization is fairly broad). For the benefit of saving space in the length of the page, the individual departments are represented by lines rather than squares (see figure I.D).

A third layout, the circular layout, in which equal hierarchical ordered positions are drawn in concentric circles, is also used in practice.

I.3.2 Drafting Rules

The number of rules for drawing the organizational structure diagrams is, in general, limited. The draftsman should follow the following rules as much as possible.

▲ A hierarchically higher staff member should be drawn above a lower one (in a vertical diagram), left of the lower one (in a horizontal diagram).

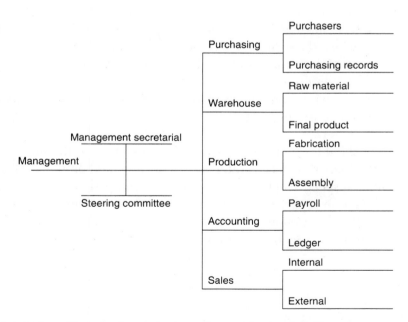

FIGURE I.D Organizational structure diagram (horizontal): Type 4

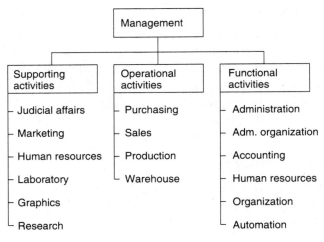

FIGURE I.E   Organizational structure diagram

▲ The specification of names, strength of the departments, position classifications, names of the positions, ages of the staff members, etc., should be allowed.

▲ Commissions and consulting units should be drawn on the level at which the commission comes into being.

▲ Staff departments should be drawn next to the departments to which the staff is assigned.

▲ A square should be used for departments and staff members; a circle for consulting units.

It should be noted that in some businesses, the difference between line and staff departments can often not be documented properly. All the departments, irrespective of their nature, are then grouped together as much as possible and drawn next to each other in the diagrams. Figure I.E gives an example of this by grouping the departments under the so-called operational, functional, and support activities of the organization.

APPENDIX II

Administrative Business Processes Principles Diagram

II.1 General

The principles diagram is intended to reflect the principles of an administrative process. It is important that the diagram give a clear and brief presentation of the essential factors. The diagram of administrative business processes principles is in general not appropriate for showing factors in detail.

II.2 Features

The principles diagram should be completely self-explanatory so that a further explanation is unnecessary. The diagram can give a good idea of the processes.

The principles diagram is a free-form diagram in the sense that there is not a permanent pattern that is the same for every subsequent case. If required, agreements can be made about the symbols that are to be used, the number of symbols, the use of text, the maximum number of factors that can be presented, etc.

Each diagram will be evaluated according to personal taste. The most important thing is that the diagrams are kept simple. In addition to the use of few symbols, the following count as advantages.

- ▲ Effective transfer of knowledge
- ▲ Suggestive effect
- ▲ Conciseness
- ▲ Presentation of the main concepts

The advantages are only valid if, in the right cases, use is made of the principles diagram. Using the principles diagram as a means for transferring knowledge is not always advisable. It is recommended that the following should be questioned in each case.

- ▲ Does it actually add to the knowledge of the already existing descriptions or diagrams?
- ▲ Can the diagram's purpose be better served by a different diagram or text?

II.3 Rules

The rules for using the principles diagram, as a free diagram, are limited. Of importance are the guidelines that are generally employed with free diagrams. These involve, among others

- ▲ Ensuring the clear presentation and readability of the diagram
- ▲ Limiting the number of factors that are presented in the diagram to four or five
- ▲ Adapting the diagram to the knowledge level of the reader
- ▲ Using simple symbols, such as squares, circles, and arrows, each with a single meaning; the symbols are explained in the diagram
- ▲ Limiting the text in the diagram
- ▲ Using standard paper sizes

II.4 Examples

As examples of diagrams of administrative business processes principles, a hospital administration is presented in figure II.A and a temporary employment agency in figure II.B.

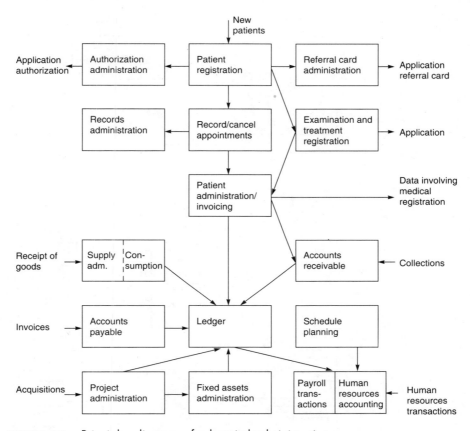

FIGURE II.A   Principles diagram of a hospital administration

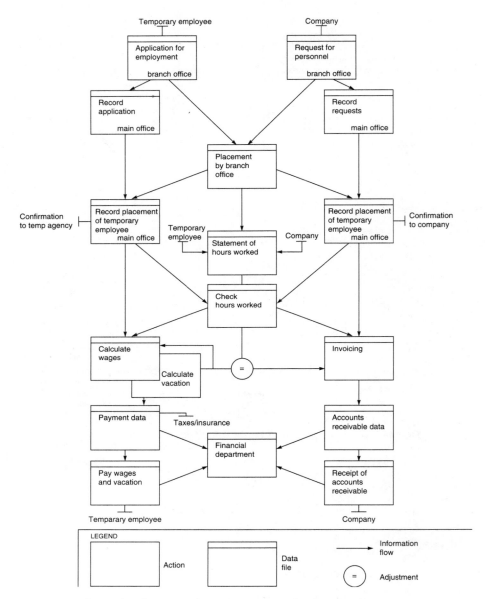

FIGURE II.B   Principles diagram of a temporary employment agency

APPENDIX
III

Hierarchical
Overview Diagram

III.1　General

The hierarchical overview diagram gives insight into the structure and relationships of the entire administrative system. It shows the internal hierarchy of the administrative business processes. The hierarchical overview is also designated with names such as hierarchical diagram, decomposition diagram, or structure diagram.

III.2　Features

In the hierarchical overview, one tries to divide the administrative business processes such that at the lowest level of detail, processes can be distinguished that can manageably be described piece by piece and subsequently analyzed and evaluated.

　　In making a hierarchical overview, one works from the top to the bottom and from general to specific (top-down) so that as much detail as is desired and necessary is implemented. One starts by naming the business processes (primary processes) and subdividing them into business subprocesses, if possible. In principle, the following can be distinguished:

- ▲ Primary processes
- ▲ Supporting processes, which can be divided into two types if required
  - — Processes with a preparatory/cyclical character, such as estimates, budgets, inquiries, or reports
  - — Processes that directly support the primary process, such as human resources services, material services, financial services, etc.

The functional decomposition is done until the supporting administrative business processes can be identified in a significant manner.

It is recommended that the administrative business processes initially be distinguished logically; in other words, according to the actual content of the process (by reviewing what happens). As an example, we present an arbitrary hospital. A global hierarchy of the administrative business processes is presented in figure III.A. Production (1) and management (2) are distinguished as the most important functions. Each of the functions is divided into subfunctions/tasks. Human resources is divided further in figure III.B.

The hierarchical overview can at the same time serve as the structure of the documentation of the administrative organization. The hierarchical overview is also intended to be a technique used in developing computer systems.

The hierarchical overview is the basis for the description of the processes. The hierarchical overview is also called the table of contents. On the basis of the overview, one can quickly locate a specific subdivision without having to glance through all of the documentation. One should pay attention to the numbering of the processes: the individual squares are vertically num-

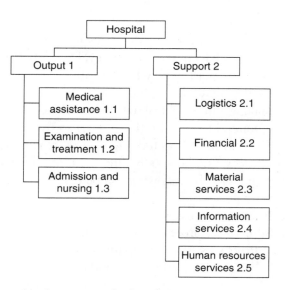

FIGURE III.A   Hierarchical overview of a hospital

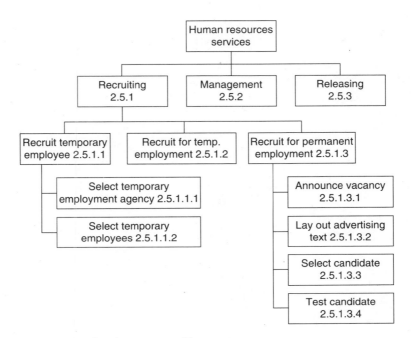

FIGURE III.B   Hierarchical overview of human resources processes

bered so that it remains possible to assign processes and deduce their hierarchy from the numbers.

Even though it is the intention that all the processes can only be reproduced with the help of the process diagrams or data flow diagrams (see section 5.5), depending on the factors that are to be reproduced for the study's objective, other diagramming techniques may also be admissible.

Global Overview of Processes and Divisions Diagram

IV.1 General

The global overview of processes and divisions diagram gives insight into the overall relationships of all the administrative business processes and divisions that are to be studied. The nature of the involvement of the departments (or staff members) in each of the processes is reflected while, if desired, the applied data collections are indicated.

IV.2 Features

The global overview, in addition to giving insight, is relevant for the analysis of the departments and the administrative business processes. The global overview can be further employed for analyses of

▲ The relationships between processes and departments
▲ The departments that are involved with a process
▲ The activities of each department
▲ The nature of the involvement of departments with a process

In view of the broad character of the global overview, in most cases, only the focus of a further analysis can be indicated. The global overview is then always used with other documentation techniques that go into more detail. Depending on the factors that are to be studied, form flow diagrams, form management diagrams, or detailed process diagrams, for example, will then be used.

The global overview is set up as a matrix in which the administrative business processes are presented vertically and the departments are presented horizontally. Symbols at the intersections of the rows and columns indicate relationships between departments and processes as well as the nature of the relationships.

A global overview of processes and departments is drawn up at the start of the documentation of the administrative organization. It can serve as the table of contents for all the process descriptions. All the processes and departments that are to be studied are listed (which is generally not all that simple in practice). Which departments are involved with which processes (and vice versa) is then indicated, for example by Xs, in the matrix without going into the nature of the relationship.

A global overview can be a good enabler for supervising the plan of the approach for documenting the administrative business processes of an organization. If all the requisite departments are reviewed, and no administrative business processes are forgotten, then the plan of approach is efficient (for example, which interviewer can, by means of holding interviews in a department, document which processes?).

IV.3 Rules

The following code indicates the nature of the involvement of a department with a business process. In the case of evaluating the existing functional divisions and internal control, the code can read as follows.

M = Manage
D = Dispose
S = Store
C = Control
E = Execute

This code provides the opportunity to evaluate the business process for internal control. In order to do this, functional combinations of a department must be known and an accurate task division employed. In addition, the various staff members within the departments should be indicated.

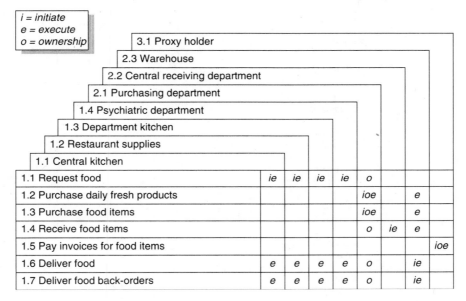

Hospital Administrative Organization Manual							
Section: 22. General Services				Page: 1			
Chapter: 4. Process descriptions				Version: 2			
Paragraph: 2. Adm. processes + department matrix				Author: J. de Wit			
Subpar.: 1. Food management				Modified: 06-10-1991			
				Date: 01-04-1992			

i = initiate
e = execute
o = ownership

3.1 Proxy holder
2.3 Warehouse
2.2 Central receiving department
2.1 Purchasing department
1.4 Psychiatric department
1.3 Department kitchen
1.2 Restaurant supplies
1.1 Central kitchen

1.1 Request food	ie	ie	ie	ie	o		
1.2 Purchase daily fresh products					ioe		e
1.3 Purchase food items					ioe		e
1.4 Receive food items					o	ie	e
1.5 Pay invoices for food items							ioe
1.6 Deliver food	e	e	e	e	o		ie
1.7 Deliver food back-orders	e	e	e	e	o		ie

FIGURE IV.A Global overview of processes and departments—general model

Figure IV.A provides a model for a purchasing process in a hospital. The processes in the example reproduce the administrative business process; the employed code is as follows:

I = Initiate
E = Execute
O = Own

In figure IV.B, the base model is expanded with a line and a column for presenting the files that are employed. Compared with the code of figure IV.A, the code for the nature of the involvement of a department with a process is given in much more detail. The code reads as follows:

Date:	03 - 13 - 1992	Document code:	
Project:	Adm. organization	Project phase:	Analysis
Project team:	Purchasing procedure	Subject area:	Purchasing processes
Documenter:	P. Jansen	Subject:	Complete overview of purchasing

#	Departments/functions	number	1.1 Receive mail	1.4 Record invoice	2.1 Receive items	2.3 Check items	6.4 Approve invoice purchase	6.5 Approve invoice finances	16.1 Process purchase invoice	12.2 Pay purchase invoice	18.4 Statistical processing	Applied files/documents
11	Applied files/documents		2	8; 21	11	109					81	
10	Warehouse	41			S,K,C M	S,M,C P						11; 109
9	Computer department	28							R	R		
8	Input/output control	24							C_4, C_5	C_5, C_6		
7	Purchase records	21			I	I	P,C_1		C_2, C_3	A,I	M	81
6	Invoice control	20	I	S,M,C		I	S	S	S,C_1			8; 21
5	Purchase department	18			I	I	P,C_2				I	
4	Financial accounting	8						C_2,I	I	C_1, C_2, C_4		
3	Receiving mail	7	K,S, Ma, M									2
2	Finance	6					P,C,A	I		C_3,D		

FIGURE IV.B Global overview of processes and departments—expanded model

S = Start of the process
K = Contact, external or with employees
A = Advice
D = Decision
P = Initial
 I = Information distribution
R = Automatic processing
C = Control
Ma = Mail or destroy
M = Manual processing on forms and/or in files

The example (figure IV.B) describes a few administrative business processes with regard to the processing of purchase invoices in an organization. The administrative business processes are recorded in the rows; the departments involved with the processes are recorded in the columns. By means of numbers, the documents, as well as the files that are used with the processes named in column 1, are recorded in column 11. At the bottom of columns 1 to 10, the files, documents, etc. that are updated in the involved department are noted.

Every M (manual processing on forms and/or files) in figure IV.B indicates the department/function and the process(es) that was (were) changed. The applied files/document number column (right hand top side of figure) and row (last row at the bottom of figure) indicates the document number that was changed (i.e., in figure IV.B, column 10 indicates that two processes, 2.1 (receive items) and 2.3 (check items), had one change each made by the warehouse. The applied files/document number row shows that two documents were changed by the warehouse.

For an example of an application, the reader is referred to section 4.8, in which the global overview plays a role with the analysis of the internal control, particularly the control of the technical functional divisions of an organization.

APPENDIX

V

Global Process Diagram

V.1 General

A global process diagram is intended to present the main concepts of an administrative process. The diagram is not appropriate for reproducing actions or data flows, but it can still be used as a table of contents for the description of the parts (subprocesses) that make up the administrative business process.

V.2 Features

The global process diagram reproduces the main pattern of the relationship between the various parts of an administrative business process. The global process diagram represents itself particularly well when the parts can be presented in a certain sequence. If a sequential order is entirely absent, then the relationships of the various parts can often be diagrammed better by using a hierarchical overview (see section 3.9.3) or a global overview (see section 3.9.4). In principle, positions/tasks for each organizational unit are presented without being described in detail (as on the level of detail of the activities or actions; see also figure 3.A).

The ways in which the administration of disbursements takes place in an arbitrary organization branch office are presented in figure V.A. Each section of the diagram represents a section of the operations within a department. For each section, a brief explanation is given. The sections are assigned three numbers that reflect the code of the department, the code of the administrative business process, and the sequence number, respectively. By means of the code, the underlying detailed descriptions for both the department as well as

Date:	4 - 10 - 1992	Document code:	
Project:	Adm. organization	Project phase:	Documenting
Project team:	Fin. processes	Subject area:	Cost accounts
Documenter:	J. de Wit	Subject:	Global process diagram

Processes

Branch offices — 1.1.1.

Main office — 2.1.1.

Cost accounts — 3.1.1.

Financial matters — 4.1.1.

Proxy holder — 5.1.1.

Division

A B

Explanation

– Receipt of purchase invoices in branch
– Authorization and coding

– Control invoice
– Record
– Produce payment order
– Control codes

– Control invoice and payment order

– Procuration
– Record in the register

– Divide into two separate processing streams:
 • further processing of payments and processing invoices totalling over $ 25,000 as well as invoices with periodical and rush payments
 • further processing of other invoices

Explanation of codes used

Department	x		
Process		x	
Process sequence for each department			x

Department:
1. Branch office
2. Main office
3. Cost accounts
4. Financial matters
5. Proxy holder
6. Input department
7. Computer department
8. Internal control

Process:
1. Cost accounts

FIGURE V.A Global process diagram of the disbursement administration

Date:	4 - 10 - 1992	Document code:	
Project:	Adm. organization	Project phase:	Documenting
Project team:	Fin. processes	Subject area:	Cost accounts
Documenter:	J. de Wit	Subject:	Global process diagram

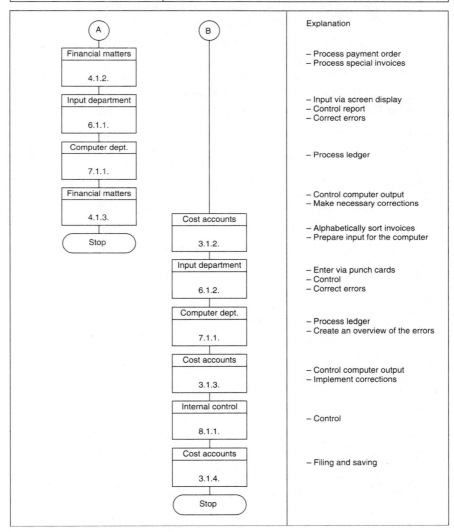

FIGURE V.A—Continued

code, the underlying detailed descriptions for both the department as well as the process can be sorted.

These detailed descriptions for each section will, depending on the objective of the documentation, be distinguished by a form flow, a form management, an instruction, or a detailed process diagram (see section 3.9.6. to 3.9.9). In view of the sorting of the operations for each department, the process diagram in this form can also be appropriate to serve as a table of contents for sets of instruction diagrams (see section 3.9.7).

Naturally, the number of factors that can be presented by the global process diagram is limited: the major concepts, the sequence, and the relationship of the actions as well as the involved departments and staff members can be represented.

Symbol	Definition
Department	Set of activities within a department
○	Page connector
⬭	Start, stop
△	Division
◇	Choice, decision

FIGURE V.B   Symbols for global process diagrams

V.3 Rules

The global process diagram belongs to the category of free diagrams. In general, no binding rules for the layout, technique, design, use of symbols, etc. are employed. To keep the diagrams clear and well-organized, we recommend using as few symbols as possible; detailed descriptions do not need to be presented this diagram. In practice, the symbols in figure V.B. seem to suffice. The sections (and the underlying descriptions) are also numbered freely. One should strive for a code that indicates the administrative business process, the sequence of the sections, and the department.

APPENDIX

VI Detailed Process Diagram

VI.1 General

A detailed process diagram provides insight into the sequence of activities/actions and the flow of documents in an administrative business process. The process diagram is particularly appropriate for obtaining an understanding of and analyzing the administrative business processes. The process diagram, as employed in the scope of this book, is also called a flowchart.

VI.2 Features

The detailed process diagram presents the sequence of the activities/actions of an administrative business process. For each activity/action, the documents or files that play a role are specified but the sequence of the activities/actions still determines the entries in the diagram. The department (or staff member) that performs the activity/action can also be indicated. Often, it will even be possible to draw the individual process diagrams within an administrative system in such a way that the diagrams reflect the activities/actions per department. However, as soon as this is not possible to do (for example, because of many contacts or document flows between departments), a global overview of the processes and departments will need to be constructed to get an understanding of all of the processes for each department.

To get an overview of all of the individual detailed process diagrams, drawing a global process can be a good activity. Each symbol or section of the global process diagram should then correspond to a detailed process diagram.

In the most often applied form (such as the process diagram, which is used in particular for the design of computer systems), a limited number of factors can be presented. The sequence of the activities/actions and the associated data sources can be presented well in process diagrams. Other factors that play a role in the involved administrative business process should be documented separately. These factors include quantities, financial significance, frequency, time elements, etc.

By means of an example, figure VI.A presents the administrative organization for purchasing food in a hospital. In the figure, one can clearly recognize that the flow of the activities determines the way in which the diagram is drawn. The department or staff member is specified for each activity and can also be mentioned several times in the diagram.

One of the advantages of the detailed process diagram is that the degree of detail with which the administrative business process is described does not influence the schematics. The desire to present as many factors as possible in the process diagrams often results in the presentation of a lot of text next to the diagram. Sometimes a detailed process diagram is adopted in which the diagram is presented on the left page while the text is presented on the right page. The text corresponds to the activities and indicates as much as possible the activities that cannot be presented in the diagram. On the left, next to the activities, the department or staff member involved with the activity as well as the sequence number is presented for each activity.

In practice, it appears that a combination of text and schematics often gives good results. The text enables those who are not accustomed to working with process diagrams to have fewer problems with understanding the diagram. Certainly, as soon as the text is redundant (other words are used to describe what can actually be understood from the diagram), reading the diagrams becomes much easier.

As a result of the addition of text, the number of pages required for drawing the process diagrams will often increase. This makes it necessary to set up a good table of contents (for example, by drafting a global process diagram; see section 3.9.5), but only larger. By the addition of text to the diagrams, the number of factors that are presented becomes large. The detailed process diagrams in this form are also a good basis for a description of the administrative organization. In the *Administrative Organization Manual* (see chapter 7), one can also see that the detailed process diagrams are combined on the left pages of the manual with the instruction diagrams (see appendix VII) on the right pages. As background information, an overview of the tasks for each department, a set of forms, an organizational structure diagram, and an overview of the use of different codes are made (see chapter 7).

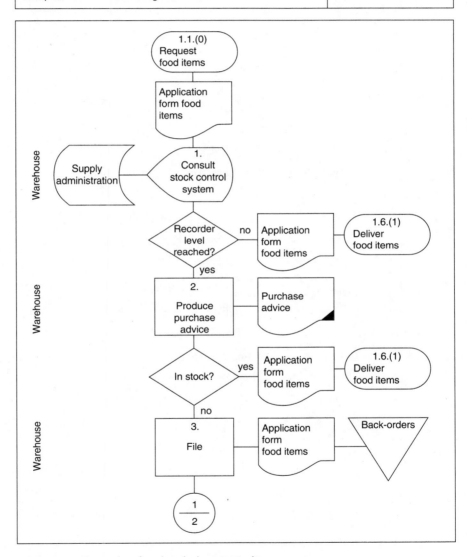

Hospital Administrative Organization Manual

Section:	22.	*General Services*	Page:	*1*
Chapter:	4.	*Process descriptions*	Version:	*2*
Paragraph:	4.	*Detailed process diagrams*	Author:	
Subpar.:		*1.3 Purchasing food items*	Modified:	*06-10-1991*
			Date:	*01-04-1992*

FIGURE VI.A   Example of a detailed process diagram

Hospital Administrative Organization Manual	
Section: *22. General Services* Chapter: *4. Process descriptions* Paragraph: *4. Detailed process diagrams* Subpar.: *1.3 Purchasing food items*	Page: *2* Version: *2* Author: Modified: *06-10-1991* Date: *01-04-1992*

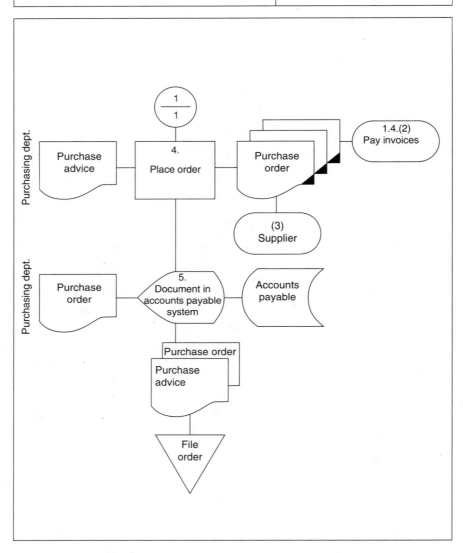

FIGURE VI.A—Continued

VI.3 Rules

An international standard for the symbols for drafting flowcharts, which we also call the detailed process diagrams, has been proposed by the ISO. The standard is ISO 1028, titled "Information processing. Flow-chart symbols." This standard notes that the concept of the flowchart also includes the so-called system flowcharts, program flowcharts, functional flowcharts, and configuration diagrams. The symbols are distinguished according to type, and as the activity/action, the information, the logical decision, or the connection between symbols or enablers requires, they are reproduced in drafting flowcharts (see figure VI.B).

As a general guideline, the diagrams should be drafted so that they can be read from left to right and from top to bottom. In drafting the diagram by hand, preferably standard templates should be used. Particularly handy are those templates in which the most often applied symbols are formed in different sizes so that—where possible—space can be saved. Documentation with automated enablers is, of course, preferred.

Input and output symbols should as much as possible be placed horizontally next to the activity to which they relate. The number of guidelines for drawing lines between symbols is large. The following rules should suffice:

- ▲ Only draw lines vertically or horizontally
- ▲ Draw short lines as much as possible; do not make it too difficult for the reader to follow the lines
- ▲ Limit the number of intersections and arrows as much as possible

Finally, a little bit about *connecting symbols (connectors)*. Connecting symbols are used to indicate that a flow line is interrupted (the out-connector) or that an interrupted flow line continues (in-connector). The out-connector and the in-connector are bound by an identical symbol. If the associated in- and out-connectors are placed on different pages, a code will also be used that refers to the page where the associated code is located (for example, XX.X; the first two positions indicate the page and the third indicates the sequence number of the in-connector on the page). A code of the out-connector can also be added to every in-connector for referencing purposes.

Symbol	Definition
1.	Beginning or endpoint of a series of activities that form a logical whole. References, if necessary, to the beginning or endpoint of a different administrative process.
2.	Activity/action.
3.	Interactive screen dialogue with which data from an automated system can be projected or processed. This symbol is considered to be an activity/action.
4.	Decision-making on the basis of the received information. Assigning names always includes a question.
5.	Form/data carrier and/or overview. A black corner indicates that the document is created at the specific spot.
6.	Computer file or direct access memory.
7.	Connector referencing the connector and page number of the diagram.
8.	Connector/file; the organization is coded in the lowest corner of the triangle.
9.	Connection line.
10.	Consult or compare.

FIGURE VI.B   Symbols for detailed process diagrams

APPENDIX VII Instruction Diagram

VII.1 General

Instruction diagrams, or instruction forms, exist to give the staff members in an organization an understanding of the administrative business processes that must be carried out and the administrative rules that must be followed. The instruction diagram is a unique tool for transferring knowledge: the highest requirements are placed on the documentation because each instruction must convey only one clear meaning.

VII.2 Features

In the places in this section where instruction is mentioned, a written instruction is meant. Naturally, in certain cases and depending on the knowledge level of the users, techniques such as instruction diagrams can be used. In particular, form flow diagrams, process diagrams, and form management diagrams are eligible for this. Combinations of these diagrams with text also occur in practice. Employing instruction diagrams with only text is preferred, however, because the instructions can be understood without having any knowledge of the applied diagramming technique.

As soon as the number of produced instruction diagrams is large, they should be entered into complete sets of diagrams. A global process diagram or a hierarchical overview of the instruction diagrams could prove to be useful.

Particularly by means of the codes of the individual diagrams, one should attempt to clearly indicate the relationship and sequence of the different administrative activities and to collect instructions for each department or staff member in a simple manner. This means that it is often necessary to divide the administrative business processes into pieces so that instruction diagrams can exist that can be grouped for each related set of actions and for each staff member (see chapter 7). The number of factors that can be reproduced is in general higher than that with other diagramming techniques. In addition to operations/activities (general and detailed), forms, and departments, factors such as time, frequency, and applied technique can be documented.

In practice, one often finds that the instruction diagrams are combined with detailed process diagrams in the *Administrative Organization Manual*. The detailed process diagrams are presented on the left pages of the manual while the associated instruction diagrams are presented on the right pages. The activity symbols of the process diagrams correspond to the "Activity" column in the instruction diagrams; the columns labeled "Description" and "Incidental action" serve to expand the process diagrams.

VII.3 Rules

Instruction diagrams are divided according to the requirements of the organization. Depending on the number of process diagrams and the number of departments, more attention will need to be paid, for example, to the header and the code of the instruction diagram; depending on the complexity of the diagrams, more or less space should be saved for explanations, etc.

An instruction diagram of processing rate variations is presented in figure VII.A. On the left page, the detailed process diagram that corresponds to the instruction diagram can be seen. Figure VII.A presents the department, the administrative business process, and the version that the instruction relates to in the header of the diagram. Each activity/operation is numbered, while in each case, the number of the next activity is indicated. The activities themselves are briefly described in a column so that it is possible to get an impression of the administrative business process quickly, without having to study the expanded column with explanations for each activity. In the column labeled "Incidental action," the activities are recorded that must be executed if the employed instruction cannot be followed. In general, the "Incidental action" column should be filled in as soon as there is talk about control actions (for example, actions that must be performed as a result of established errors, such

Commercial Company Administrative Organization Manual		
	Page:	*1*
Section: *5. Accounting*	Version:	*3*
Chapter: *4. Process description*	Author:	
Paragraph: *4. Detailed process diagrams*	Modified:	*07-31-1991*
Subpar.: *5.1.1.4. Processing differences in exchange rates*	Date:	*01-04-1992*

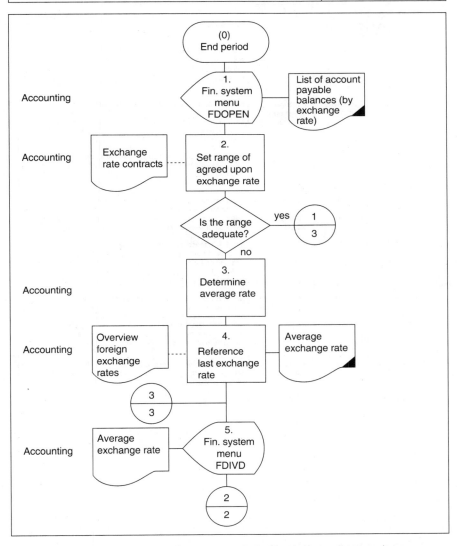

FIGURE VII.A   Detailed process diagram combined with an instruction diagram

Commercial Company Administrative Organization Manual		
Section: 5. Accounting Chapter: 5. Work instructions Paragraph: 2. Instruction diagrams Subpar.: 5.1.1.4. Processing differences in exchange rates	Page: 1 Version: 3 Author: Modified: 07-31-1991 Date: 01-04-1992	

Act. no.	Staff member/ department	Activity	Description	Incidental action
1.	Accounting	Fin. system menu FDOPEN	The menu item FDOPEN calls up the Accounting and Accounts Receivable list of balances, etc. Accounting determines the value of the payable account for each exchange rate.	
2.	Accounting	Set range of agreed upon exchange rate	Hedging contracts are closed with the banks: contracts are made regarding the exchange rate for a particular account for foreign exchange rates. For each exchange rate contract, Main Accounting determines to what extent the total accounts receivable sums fit within the exchange rate range. Two cases are possible. The range may be smaller or larger than the applicable exchange rate. In the first case, Accounting follows activity 4, in the second case, activity 9.	
3	Accounting	Determine average exchange rate (1)	For each exchange rate, one (1) or more contracts can be closed. In the case of one (1) contract, the exchange rate for the calculations is the one from the contract. In the case of several contracts, Main Accounting determines the average exchange rate as follows. The accounts payable balance, beginning with the first contract, is subtracted from the contract. The quantity that is determined for each contract is then subsequently multiplied by the agreed upon exchange rate which is valid for that contract.	
4	Accounting	Reference last exchange rate	Since the exchange rate contract does not cover all the exchange rate accounts payable, the remaining accounts payable balance are calculated with the daily exchange rate. Accordingly, the entire account for each exchange rate is divided by the amount of the respective exchange rate. This results in an average exchange rate.	
5	Accounting	Fin. system menu FDIVD	Accounting enters the exchange rate calculated by activity 4 or activity 9 with the help of the financial system menu item FDIVD.	

FIGURE VII.A—Continued

as initialing documents in the case of overstepping authority or consulting in particular situations). Columns at the beginning are reserved for the frequency with which the activities are carried out and the staff member who performs them. If necessary, a column can also be created for the codes of the applied information for each instruction. It is advisable to keep the text in the diagrams brief and to the point.

In comparison to other diagramming techniques, the use of text only would make the accuracy and thoroughness of the instruction diagram more difficult to control. Text simply gives the draftsman more freedom than using symbols. At any rate, to employ some kind of standard, one sees that in advance, a list is made of requirements:

- ▲ Names and codes of documents
- ▲ Names and codes of departments and staff members
- ▲ Terms and concepts
- ▲ Key words

A number of key words that are used for the various administrative/organizational activities/actions are listed here.

Processing Activities

approve	control	note
attach	correct	overwrite
authorize	decide	pay
calculate	dispose	print
add	enter	process
divide	establish	record
multiply	evaluate	see
square estimate	examine	sign
subtract	fill in	sort
code	initial	stamp
collect	join	type
compare	modify	weigh
consult	monitor	

Transporting Activities

carry	import (input)	send
distribute	pick up	supply
export (output)	receive	

Communicating Activities

announce	question	telephone
explain	report	tell

Documenting Activities

destroy	save	store
file		

APPENDIX
VIII

Form Management Diagram

VIII.1 General

Form management diagrams show the use and the route of the forms within an administrative organization. It often seems that it is necessary to diagram the route and the use of all sorts of forms. In addition to the forms, books, card trays, records, computer output, screen-display information, as well as all sorts of technical enablers, photos, sound recorders, light signals, and switchboards can be considered. In practice, the form management diagram has become known as the tic-tac-toe diagram.

VIII.2 Features

The form management diagram belongs to the category of bound diagrams. The layout as well as the symbols are generally firmly regulated. This lack of freedom and the degree to which the designer is required to control the completeness of the diagram make the form management diagram particularly appropriate as a means for analyzing the administrative business processes. This analysis can be focused on the efficient and effective use of the forms. The diagrams show what the flow of the documents past the departments is, which (copies of) documents are actually redundant, where data sets originate, as well as which of these data sets are significant and which are not.

The presentation of the actions for each form also makes it possible to analyze what the natures of these actions are, what the duplicates or lacking activities are, and how the activities are divided between the different departments and staff members.

279

In figure VIII.A, the characteristics of the form management diagram appear: a table form, in which the objects (documents) are represented in the columns and the activities are represented in the rows. The actions for each object are read from the intersection of an activity and an object. The actions are displayed in chronological order so that the diagram can be read row by row from top to bottom. The row is represented by means of a code or abbreviation in the department in which the action is executed. For each column, there is a little space under the name of the document to note the code number of the form. If one would like to use the form management diagram for studying the control of the technical functional divisions or for studying the division of tasks among departments or staff members, for example, then another, extra processing will need to be done: the actions must be sorted for each department/staff member in an independent overview. In practice, one also sees a variation of the form management diagram in which the actions are sorted according to department. To read the order of the actions, one should review the diagram according to the vertical lines.

The departmental variation in figure VIII.B has the drawback of being harder to read than the chronological diagram. Recording is also more difficult. The departmental diagrams seldom succeed in the first drafting step. Making changes is not easy. For these reasons in particular, we limit ourselves to discussing the chronological variation of the form management diagram.

With form management diagrams, it is possible to create a correct document a short time after an interview has been completed and to review the completeness of the documented processes. It is even quite possible to make the diagram during an interview when inventorying complicated processes or researching administrative business processes that the interviewee cannot seem to make clear. During the interview, the completeness of the documentation should be continuously reviewed, for example, by reviewing the columns of the diagram (are all the forms used; does every form have a final destination; for example, does it leave the organization or is it filed? are forms compared with each other? which object is used for other projects? etc.) or by analyzing the rules for the actions (are the actions necessary? are the forms filed? does a department do more to the form than receive or forward it? where do the data come from?).

If one wants to make the diagram during the interview, it is advisable to have a picture of the forms that play a role in the involved process in advance; the documentation can be controlled as much as possible for completeness based on that picture. One should understand the concept of object broadly;

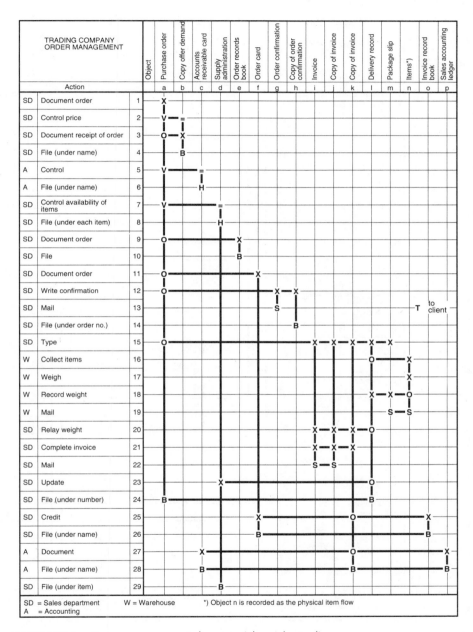

FIGURE VIII.A Form management diagram (chronological)

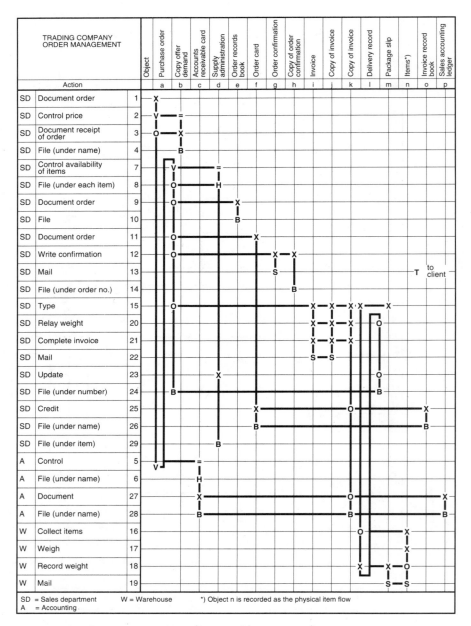

	TRADING COMPANY ORDER MANAGEMENT		Object	Purchase order	Copy offer demand	Accounts receivable card	Supply administration	Order records book	Order card	Order confirmation	Copy of order confirmation	Invoice	Copy of invoice	Copy of invoice	Delivery record	Package slip	Items*)	Invoice record book	Sales accounting ledger
	Action		a	b	c	d	e	f	g	h	i	j	k	l	m	n	o	p
SD	Document order	1	X															
SD	Control price	2	V	=														
SD	Document receipt of order	3	O	X														
SD	File (under name)	4		B														
SD	Control availability of items	7	V			=												
SD	File (under each item)	8	O			H												
SD	Document order	9	O				X											
SD	File	10					B											
SD	Document order	11	O					X										
SD	Write confirmation	12	O						X	X								
SD	Mail	13							S								T	to client
SD	File (under order no.)	14								B								
SD	Type	15	O								X	X	X	X		X		
SD	Relay weight	20									X	X	X		O			
SD	Complete invoice	21									X	X	X					
SD	Mail	22									S	S						
SD	Update	23				X								O				
SD	File (under number)	24	B												B			
SD	Credit	25					X					O					X	
SD	File (under name)	26					B										B	
SD	File (under item)	29				B												
A	Control	5	V		=													
A	File (under name)	6			H													
A	Document	27			X							O					X	
A	File (under name)	28			B							O					B	
W	Collect items	16											O		X			
W	Weigh	17													X			
W	Record weight	18											X		X	O		
W	Mail	19													S	S		

SD = Sales department   W = Warehouse   *) Object n is recorded as the physical item flow
A = Accounting

FIGURE VIII.B   Form management diagram (departmental)

the number of copies of each form must be known, and objects such as telephone reports, account tallies, and card trays must not be forgotten.

The form management diagram makes use of a small, simple set of symbols. Despite this, the technique does not score well if it is applied with the objective of transferring knowledge. The diagrams are particularly not easily readable experiences and as such are not particularly user-friendly. The quality of the form management diagram is much more related to the ability to use it for analyzing and evaluating administrative business processes.

As a result of the fact that the actions are presented in a chronological form, the diagrams can be easily rewritten in the form of work instructions (see section 3.8.7). This partly depends on the degree of detail with which the processes are described. The systematics are appropriate for several detail levels: on one line, one could record activities such as "invoice control" or "multiply number by price" (activity as well as action level; see figure 2.D).

The form management diagram is appropriate for presenting a number of factors: documents, actions, nature of actions, positions, and departments can be well represented in the diagram. Factors such as time elements, geographic location, frequency, technique, and the nature of the action are not or are barely represented.

VIII.3 Rules

VIII.3.1 General Rules

For the use of form management diagrams, a number of general rules should be followed.

- ▲ *Use a good, preprinted form.* The preprinted lines should not be too thick, because they should be distinguishable from the drawn lines. The use of forms on standard size paper is preferred by far. It may actually make sense to use a larger paper size to make the drawing easier and to later reduce it (by means of photocopying) down to standard paper size.
- ▲ *Number the objects and actions.* This makes modification easier. Number the objects used to correspond to an enclosed set of objects (for example, the form or the form inventory lists, on which the name, number, number of copies, objective, involved departments, etc. are specified).

▲ *Choose clear, single-sentence names for objects and actions.*
▲ *Do not repeat.* The objects that do not appear on a page when a procedure occupies many pages should not be repeated: the fewer objects mentioned per page, the easier the diagrams are to reference. Use references or connectors at the end of the page for each object so that the page that the objects reappear on are noted.
▲ *Make a table of contents of the entire administrative business process.* This can be accomplished by means of a global process overview (see section 3.9.5), for example, if the number of pages becomes too large.

VIII.3.2 Symbols and Symbol Use

All the standard symbols appear on a normal writing machine:

X	the object undergoes the described action
O	the object is used with an action aimed at another object
=	the object is used for control actions
V	the object is controlled
H	(halt) the object is temporarily filed or awaits further use
B	(file) the object is definitely filed
S	(close) the object is destroyed or leaves the process
T	(explanation) textual explanation for each line, at the right of the form
X-X	an action on several objects

Note that there is no so-called decision symbol.

The following guidelines apply in advance:

▲ An O is always used on a line in combination with an X: a new object (X) exists on the basis of another object (O)
▲ The symbols V and $=$ always appear on a line together (an object is controlled on the basis of another object)
▲ Each column of an object ends in an S, H, or B, or in a reference to another page

APPENDIX

IX **Form Circulation Diagram**

IX.1 General

The form circulation diagram (sometimes called form flow diagram) gives insight into the use and the route of forms in the administrative business process. In this regard, the form circulation diagram has the same objective as the form management diagram discussed in section 3.9.8. However, both diagrams look quite different. The form management diagram focuses on giving a detailed representation of the actions for each form in a chronological order; the form circulation diagram shows the form flow according to units or departments.

The concept of a form should also be broadly interpreted for the form management diagram: also card trays, records, books, computer output, or screen-display information can be represented in the diagrams.

IX.2 Features

The form circulation diagram belongs to the category of bound diagrams: with the use of the diagram, the layout and the symbols are in general predetermined (see section 3.8.1). The content of the diagram is such that the form flow is presented by means of symbols by which the forms are grouped in independent columns for each staff member or department. Actions are presented by means of a symbol with the form on which the action is focused (see figure IX.A).

The form circulation diagram is particularly appropriate to get an understanding of the administrative business processes quickly. This is also the

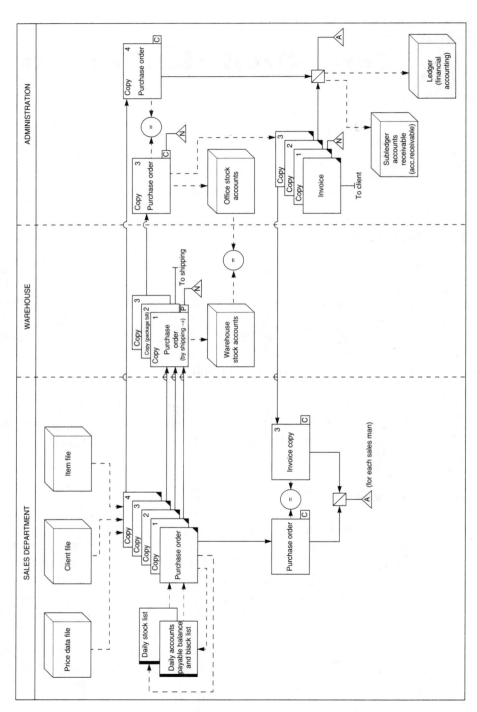

FIGURE IX.A Form circulation diagram: sales invoicing process

reason why this technique proved to be particulary appropriate (for example, with the actions of an accountant). In the section of the accounting file where the administrative organization of a company is described, a part of this description can be done very well in the form of the diagrams, while the diagrams also lend themselves well to redoing the descriptions of the main affairs of the administrative organization quickly. Many accounting offices also have chosen variations of the form circulation diagramming technique as the documentation standard for the control files.

Given the importance of these documentation techniques, it is good to review which factors can and cannot be well presented by the technique. The emphasis with these diagrams is in the form flow, a global presentation of the activities for each form, and the division of the form and the actions among the departments. This last factor can be particularly important when the division of the tasks and the functional divisions that exist in the company are analyzed.

As an example, a form circulation diagram is presented in figure IX.A. The diagram concerns a simple administrative business process of sales, delivery of goods, and invoicing in a company. Incoming sales orders are, after being checked with supply lists and credit overview by the sales department, copied onto an order form. Subsequently, the delivery of the goods by the warehouse and the invoicing by the administration location is done. Also, the stocking, accounts receivable, and ledger departments are updated.

A number of factors are not presented all that well by form circulation diagrams. It is true that an action can be presented for each form, but this is limited to mentioning connections with other actions, such as comparing, controlling, or initialing. The technique does not actually permit further definition of the detail of the actions (for example, the fact that an invoice is compared to an order form can be indicated, but not which parts of both forms are compared).

While the diagram should be read as much as possible from left to right and from top to bottom, the order of the activities is not always reflected in the diagram. Also, factors such as time, frequency, intensity, geographical location, and applied technique are generally not expressed by the diagram. In this form, the diagram of form flow is aimed at giving a detailed description of the routing of forms and of the main points of the actions, both of which are diagrammed for each department. The possibilities for controlling the completeness of the final diagram, as can be done to a certain extent with the form management diagram, are limited.

In practice, one sees a number of variations of form circulation diagrams that are intended to remove the drawbacks mentioned above. In order to present more information about the actions in the diagrams, often, a wide right column is reserved for describing the chronological order of the actions. This variation is quite applicable if the number of departments involved with the process is not so great that the width of the page has to be completely used for the columns. In the diagram, differences between the diagram and the text column are, for example, introduced by means of a circle with a number in it.

In figure IX.B, the sales-invoicing process is repeated and an explanation column is added. In both diagrams, the standard symbols for form circulation diagrams are replaced with those of the known flow chart techniques (see section 3.9.6). With the help of these symbols, the administrative business process is divided between the columns of the departments, presented in the process diagrams, in which the flow of the forms as well as the actions is indicated. This last variation was proven to be useful in practice, not only with the analysis of the processes but also as a means of informing others. Limiting the number of symbols used with this type of form circulation diagram is recommended. Based on experience, it seems that the number of symbols that are used with the detailed process diagrams (see section 3.9.6) are more than sufficient.

Figure IX.C is an example of this combination of form circulation diagram and detailed process diagram; it describes the same administrative business process presented in figure IX.A and IX.B. As a supplement to the process diagramming symbols discussed in section 3.9.6, a large arrow is recorded in the upper left corner to indicate where one should start to read the diagram. One can also see that in the lower right corner of a form, a small black corner indicates that the form was prepared in the involved department (this black corner also belongs to the standard symbols for the form circulation diagram). Just as in figure IX.B, a few references to explanations are recorded.

Just as in figures IX.A and IX.B, figure IX.C gives a good basis for further analysis of the described administrative business processes. Depending on the analysis objectives, a number of questions can be asked, such as the following:

▲ How can the sales administration keep up with the transactions in the accounts receivable and supplies balances as a result of sales that are, after 15 hours, reported to the administration and are not recorded on the accounts receivable or supplies list for the following day?

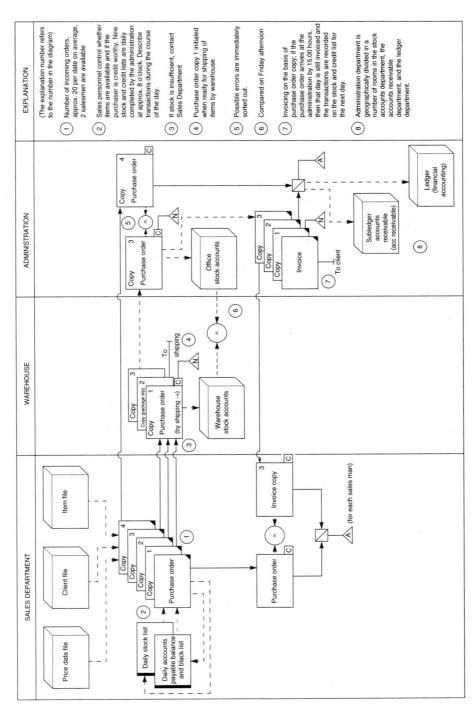

FIGURE IX.B Form circulation diagram: sales invoicing process (with explanation)

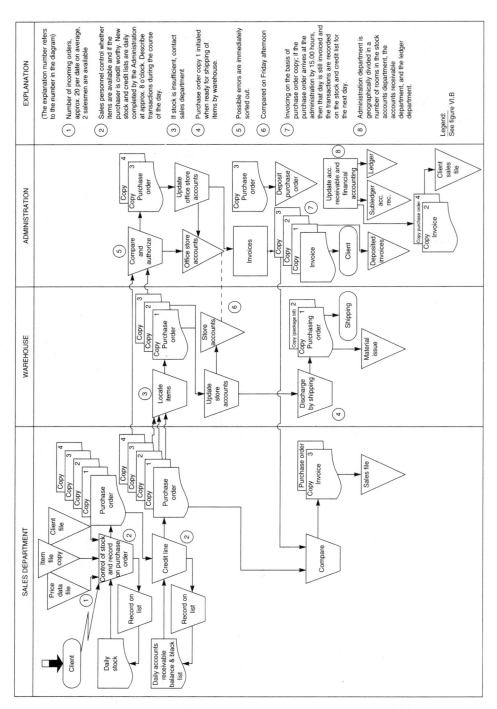

FIGURE IX.C Form circulation diagram in combination with a detailed process diagram: sales invoicing process

▲ Are enough technical control functional divisions introduced within the administration department?

▲ Is it possible to control the actions of the sales personnel (minimum and maximum costs, evaluate credit rating)?

▲ Which actions are being considered for computerization?

IX.3 Rules

The symbols that can be used for a normal type of form circulation diagram are presented in figure IX.D. It should be emphasized that the symbols have no similarity to those that are used for the detailed process diagrams. As such, one can update the symbols as desired. The presentation of automated enablers, computer processing, and computer files is not really possible with these symbols. It should be noted that there is no decision symbol. Depending on the situation in a company, a unique symbol list will also have to be used.

The diagram should be drafted from top to bottom and from left to right as much as possible. While this is not always possible, crossing and backtracking lines should be avoided.

The drafting of form circulation diagrams does not go very fast. Constructing a good diagram for a complex administrative business process usually requires a few attempts.

Symbol	Definition
	Form
2 / 1	Original form duplicated with 1 copy
→	Transferring documents is indicated by an unbroken line. If a form is transferred from one column to another, it is indicated again, bound by a line with an arrow.
‑ ‑ ‑ ►	A dotted line indicates processing: transferring information from one document to another, making entries, comparing data to each other, etc.
	A black corner on the right lower corner of a symbol indicates that the form involved originated in that department. Thus one can quickly determine where the different forms originated.
	A continuous line indicates that a form is sent to an external authority or to a department within the organization that is not important for the section of reviewing the organization.
	This means that the form is put aside. The filing method can be indicated by putting a letter inside the triangle (A = alphabetical, N = numerical sequence, D = date).
P	The initialing or signing of a form is indicated by a small square with a P on the right lower side of the symbol. This symbol is only presented at the location where the initialing or signing occurs; it is thus not repeated in a subsequent phase.

FIGURE IX.D Definitions of symbols associated with form circulation diagrams

Symbol	Definition
	Attaching two forms to each other is presented by a square with a diagonal line.
	Form A is attached to form B, after which the two are filed together.
	A system of associated cards (accounts payable cards, accounts receivable cards, stock accounts, etc.)
	Indication of a book or control page
	This means that the form is temporarily filed under the order of the date; in a later stage, the file is permanently filed according to numerical sequence.
	With the help of the form, a control action is performed. This is indicated by a small square with a C at the lower right. This symbol is only presented at the location where the controlling is done.
	Comparison: for example comparing a particular subledger with the corresponding ledger calculation

FIGURE IX.D—Continued

APPENDIX

X

Accounting System Diagram

X.1 General

The accounting system diagram is an appropriate document to get a detailed idea of the system of accounting processing in the company.

X.2 Features

The accounting system diagram gives insight into the accounting processes. In particular, it indicates in which account changes were made and what the changes were. For a more experienced reader, this diagram can serve as instructions for accounting. In addition, this diagram is important for reviewing the consequences of possible accounting changes in the company.

Having a good understanding of the accounting system of the company is usually necessary for completely understanding the content of the administrative business processes. As such, the accounting system diagram is an underestimated tool. It is surprising that in most cases, such diagrams do not comprise a section of the accounting files when the annual accounts are reviewed.

X.3 Rules

The diagram is drawn as a table in which the columns represent various calculations and the lines represent the various actions that lead to an entry. The methods of making entries to the calculations are represented by symbols for credits and debits that are connected by lines.

In practice, one generally sees two kinds of accounting system diagrams. The first type has columns that are split into debit and credit columns for each calculation. An X (or a different symbol) indicates which calculation is credited and which is debited, while a different symbol is used if the calculation, depending on the circumstances, is credited on one occasion and debited on another.

The second type of accounting system diagram does not have separate debit and credit columns, yet by means of symbols, it is indicated whether a debit or credit entry is involved. Obviously, the layout of the second diagram uses less space, but this makes reading it more difficult. Even though the set of applied symbols can be adapted as needed, the following three symbols are easy to use:

d = debit entry
c = credit entry
d/c = debit/credit (according to the circumstances, a debit or credit is added to the calculation)

Figures X.A and X.B give an idea of both types of accounting system diagrams. In figure X.A, an overview regarding questionable accounts receivable in a company is given in which an amount at the expense of the costs is

Ledger accounts / Entries	820 Sales		105 Accounts receivable		210 Calculated appreciation on questionable accounts receivable debits		220 Audited appreciation on questionable accounts receivable debits		180 Appreciation on questionable accounts receivable debits		250 Reserve for questionable accounts receivable debits		460 Losses on accounts receivable	
	D	C	D	C	D	C	D	C	D	C	D	C	D	C
– Closing sales record book	X	X												
– Monthly entry % of the turnover						X							X	
– Affirmed losses			X						X					
– End of year actual debit transfers							X			X				
– End of year entry					X			X				O	O	

Definition of applied symbols
x: entry according to column
o: according to circumstances, debit or credit entry

FIGURE X.A Accounting system diagram: individual debit and credit columns

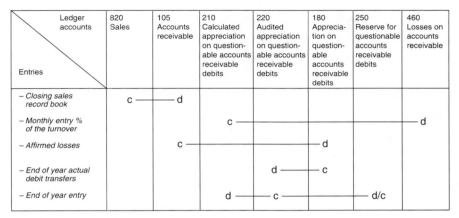

Entries \ Ledger accounts	820 Sales	105 Accounts receivable	210 Calculated appreciation on questionable accounts receivable debits	220 Audited appreciation on questionable accounts receivable debits	180 Appreciation on questionable accounts receivable debits	250 Reserve for questionable accounts receivable debits	460 Losses on accounts receivable
– Closing sales record book	c ——	d					
– Monthly entry % of the turnover			c ————————————————————————————————				d
– Affirmed losses		c —————————————————————			d		
– End of year actual debit transfers				d ——	c		
– End of year entry			d ——	c ————————————		d/c	

Definition of applied symbols
d   debit
c   credit
d/c debit- or credit entry
      depending on circumstances

FIGURE X.B   Accounting system diagram: combined debit and credit columns

entered monthly and the differences at the end of the year are compared to the actual accounts receivable debit found by using a saved invoice. (Note: the calculated 180 questionable accounts receivable debits are, during the course of the year, debited for verified losses.)

Figure X.B shows the same entries without using individual debit and credit columns.

The calculation numbers used are as follows:

▲ 820 sales
▲ 105 accounts receivable
▲ 210 calculated appreciation on questionable accounts receivable debits
▲ 220 audited appreciation on questionable accounts receivable debits
▲ 180 appreciation on questionable accounts receivable debits
▲ 250 reserve for questionable accounts receivable debits
▲ 460 losses on accounts receivable

APPENDIX XI

Guidelines for Designing Forms and Documents

The list below of guidelines for designing forms is also important for the analysis and evaluation of applied forms. The concept of forms should be broadly interpreted: charts, boards, computer output, chain forms, and even screen layouts can be included. The guidelines are classified according to the objective of the form, the layout, and the production (the format and the material).

XI.1 Objective and Content of the Form

No.	Point of Attention	Explanation
1.1.	Does the form have a function?	It should be determined whether the form is the most suitable information carrier for the case at hand. Can the data be documented in a different, better way? By introducing a form, is the efficiency of the administrative processing improved (for example, because other forms and operations can be dropped)?
1.2.	Does the content of the form relate to the function?	It is important to know what information is required to fulfill the function of the form. All the information that needs to be filled in must be available for the users. The form should have a brief and unambiguous name for the benefit of specifying the function.

No.	Point of Attention	Explanation
1.3.	Is the content of the form significant, clear, and complete?	All of the data (the previously printed data as well as the data that still needs to be recorded) is needed on the form. The text should be clear for the user of the form. Wherever possible, previously printed text should be used. The form should be designed as much as possible in uniformity with other forms that are in use.
1.4.	Are instructions needed for filling in the form?	Instructions for filling in the form should by preference be recorded on the form itself. The instructions are noted next to the appropriate section. Footnotes should be used as little as possible. A separate instruction for filling in the form, if necessary, must be referenced.
1.5.	Are the form requirements satisfied?	The source of the form should be clear to the user. The address, location, telephone, and reference can be indicated. Legal regulations (such as mentioning the name, place of business, room and commercial number, etc. on external forms) must be satisfied. On the form, the form or purchase number as well as the date of design should be noted.

XI.2 The Layout of the Form

No.	Point of Attention	Explanation
2.1.	Is uniformity taken into account?	Uniformity in the design of the forms in general improves the efficiency of working with the forms.
2.2.	Is the further processing of the form taken into account?	The possibility of mailing the form in window envelopes, further prepossessing with accounting machines, typewriters, copying equipment, etc. should be considered.
2.3.	Is the form readable?	The most important sections should be recorded in the upper right of the form. The layout of the sections of the form should agree as much as possible with the layout of the

document from which the data is taken. Documentation codes, such as department code, process number, subprocess number, sequence number, etc. should be shown in the upper right corner of the form (in a fixed location).

2.4. Is the form easy to fill in?

It is important that the sections that need to be filled in are displayed in a logical order (for the user). With so-called yes/no questions, it must be clear what the user should do; for example, checking or crossing out what is or is not applicable. There should be adequate space for filling in the data and answers that are expected to be lengthy.

2.5. Is space left over on the form in connection with storing, mailing, and processing?

It should be determined whether space is necessary for addressing or stamping the form (in some cases it is advisable to print the form with the layout of the stamp). Sometimes, some space should be left for binding or stapling forms, perforating or punching holes, gripping spaces for all sorts of equipment, etc.

2.6. With reprints, are new designs required?

If sections of a form that is regularly reprinted are often modified, then it is better not to record these on the form; let the user fill them in.

2.7. Do all the copies have a function? Is the function of each of the copies clear?

It is advisable that each of the copies of the form be marked with the reason for the copy.

XI.3 Producing the Form

No. *Point of Attention* *Explanation*

3.1. Is the format appropriate?

A normal format should be used as much as possible. The forms should not be too large or too small; in general, standard paper sizes are usually appropriate in connection with filling in, storing, applying, and consulting.

Guidelines for Holding Interviews

An interview is a form of conversation in which one or more researchers attempt to get information from an interviewee. During the study of the administrative business processes, the interview is especially important for reviewing the current state of affairs. By means of information obtained during interviews, the study will be supplemented with documentation and personal observation. A list of guidelines for holding interviews is presented below. A number of guidelines are recorded that are important for, during, and after the interview. For each interview, the points that are important will need to be specified.

XII.1 Preparing the Interview

No.	Point of Attention	Explanation
1.1.	Is the introduction to the interview well prepared?	It may be advisable to have a third individual introduce the interviewer to the interviewee (by preference, the manager of the interviewee). This is particularly true when the interviewer and the interviewee do not know each other and/or the objective of the study and the discussion is not known to the interviewee. The introduction can also be done in a meeting at the beginning of a project. The objectives and desired results of the project can be presented by the management of the organization in the meeting.

No.	Point of Attention	Explanation
1.2.	Which information can be studied in advance?	Studying possibly appropriate documents in advance results in the interviewer having a better understanding during the discussion with the interviewee and gives him the opportunity to evaluate the consistency of the interviewee's answers.
1.3.	What information should be obtained from the interview?	The interviewer should determine in advance what information he wants to have at his disposal at the end of the interview. It is important to know how accurate and how detailed the information must be. At the same time, the interviewer should also determine how other supplementary information can be obtained.
1.4.	Which staff members should be interviewed?	The interviewer should try to determine the organizational position, the character, and the idiosyncrasies of the interviewee in advance so that the level of the discussion can be assessed and the questions that can be interpreted as being plausible or awkward can be determined.
1.5.	Which location is the most appropriate?	In general, the interview should be held in a quiet room where the chance of interruption will be minimal. If the nature of the interview is considered to be important, the interview should be closed and the interviewee should not be visible to his coworkers or supervisor. The interviewee will feel most comfortable in his own surroundings; needed documents should be on hand there. Sometimes, a discussion in the office of the interviewee can give clues about the interviewee (the number of interruptions, the number of telephone contacts, etc.).
1.6.	How long should the interview last?	Depending on the estimate of the time needed for the discussion, another appointment can be made if necessary. In general, an interview about the administrative organization subject should not last longer than two hours.

No.	*Point of Attention*	*Explanation*
1.7.	What is the appropriate time to hold the interview?	The interview should be held at a good time for the interviewee. The chance for interruption should be minimal, and she should have enough of an opportunity to prepare for the interview.
1.8.	How many interviewers should there be?	The advantages of working with two interviewers are

▲ The interviewers can divide the tasks so that one asks the questions and the other observes or takes notes.

▲ The interviewers can supplement each other.

▲ The discussion is in general less awkward.

The disadvantages are

▲ The interviewee may feel less comfortable.

▲ The interview costs more man-hours.

Interviews in which several staff members are interviewed at the same time seem to be less successful because none of the interviewees can completely do justice to the questions.

XII.2 Holding the Interview

No.	*Point of Attention*	*Explanation*
2.1.	Has the interviewer sufficiently introduced himself to the interviewee?	The interviewer should start the discussion by telling the interviewee something about his background, education, and experience.
2.2.	Does the interviewee know enough about the study and the objectives of the interview?	The interviewer should briefly explain the objective of the discussion. Among other things, she should indicate the phase of the study and why the interview is desired. In a number of cases, it may be advisable to discuss the career, education, and experience of the interviewee.

No.	Point of Attention	Explanation
2.3.	Is the interviewee sufficiently clear about the nature of the interview?	In interviews in which confidential matters may be discussed, it is necessary for the interviewer to emphasize the confidentiality of the discussion. It can also, for example, be agreed upon that the interviewer will only make use of the information that appears in the interview report that is approved by the interviewee.
2.4.	At most, how long should the interview last (see also guideline 1.6)?	The length of the interview should be agreed upon at the beginning of the interview. If the length is insufficient, then another appointment should be made.
2.5.	Is the procedure during the interview clear; did the interviewee consent to have notes taken during the interview?	It may be advisable to explain the interviewing process, particularly to those staff members who have only been interviewed a few times. The interviewer should explain who takes the initiative, whether many short specific questions will be asked, that sometimes a short pause is required to make a few notes, etc.
2.6.	Are the rules taken into consideration?	Everything that could bother the interviewee should be avoided, such as smoking without permission, sitting down unasked, having the interviewee face the light, etc.
2.7.	Are all the desired documents supplied?	During the discussion, the interviewer should indicate which documents he would like to have at his disposal; it is a good idea to maintain a list of all the pieces so that they can be gathered after the interview.
2.8.	Does the interview remain neutral?	The interviewer should not discuss what has been said with the interviewee; she should not give a positive or negative opinion about what she hears. She should only collect information and postpone analyzing the information until after the interview. The interviewer should not influence the interviewee by telling him what other staff members have said about a subject. No advice should be given during the interview phase.

No.	Point of Attention	Explanation
2.9.	Is enough control and review incorporated?	The interviewer should control the consistency of the answers during the conversation and review the accuracy of the information obtained by summarizing or reviewing the answers. The interviewer should determine by means of the summary whether she understood everything, and the interviewee should determine whether his words came across well.
2.10.	Does the interviewee get a chance to explain herself?	The interviewer should take a discreet position; he should listen and show understanding and appreciation for the interviewee. The interviewee may want to say something that is outside the scope of the discussion subject. This may be indicated by going off on a tangent, hesitating, being mistaken, making a slip of the tongue, unexpectedly changing the subject, being inconsistent, or being silent. The interviewer should allow the interviewee to stray from what was asked.
2.11.	Are tangents sufficiently recognized?	As soon as the interviewee goes off on a tangent, important information can be revealed to the interviewer. The interviewer should, after some time, bring the conversation around to the original subject; it may be that the question was not well understood or that the interviewee is not coming to the point.
2.12.	Is a correct summary done?	The interviewer should at the end of the interview summarize the main points to make sure that the essence of the answers is understood.
2.13.	Does the interviewee feel that the topics have been exhausted?	The interviewee is asked if he would like to make a few supplementary remarks that could be important in the scope of the study. As much as possible, the interviewee indicates which questions he missed.

No.	Point of Attention	Explanation
2.14.	Are opportunities given to stay and talk?	The interviewer should give sufficient attention to the questions that the interviewee asks so that the discussion is actually complete. It often seems that the interviewees open up about all sorts of subjects when they are in an informal atmosphere. This information can sometimes be important for the study. An interviewee's request for continuing the discussion must not be rejected.
2.15.	Are suggestions given for further research?	The interviewer should indicate in the analysis report which staff members should be questioned in case further research is needed, which observations should be made, and which documents should be studied.
2.16.	Are clear agreements made about further progress?	The interviewer should indicate how the results are processed. She should also indicate what the next steps are (subsequent interviews with other staff members, follow-up interviews with those already interviewed, expected date of completion of the phase of the study, etc.). The interviewer should leave her telephone number and address behind.

XII.3 Closing the Interview

No.	Point of Attention	Explanation
3.1.	Are all the agreements kept?	The interviewer should promptly keep all the agreements made at the end of the discussion (such as follow-up interviews, sending the report, reliability information, sending back documents that were temporarily loaned, etc.).
3.2.	Is the interview complete and did it go into enough detail?	Whether the interview satisfied all the expectations is indicated by the analysis of the collected information. If necessary, extra information that is needed is collected in a follow-up interview or via other available sources.

No.	Point of Attention	Explanation
3.3	Are there opportunities to control the information?	During the analysis of the information, the information is compared to the results of other interviews or the results of documentation. Possible differences should be carefully checked with a follow-up interview with one or more staff members, if needed.
3.4	Was the progress of the interview satisfactory?	Finally, after the interview, the interviewer should examine for himself whether the interview went as desired and whether the interviewing technique was satisfactory.

Index

Index